SOUR GRAPES

Studies in the subversion of rationality

This book is published as part of the joint publishing agreement established in 1977 between the Fondation de la Maison des sciences de l'homme and the Press Syndicate of the University of Cambridge. Titles published under this arrangement may appear in any European language or, in the case of volumes of collected essays, in several languages.

New books will appear either as individual titles or in one of the series which the Maison des sciences de l'homme and the Cambridge University Press have jointly agreed to publish. All books published jointly by the Maison des sciences de l'homme and the Cambridge University Press will be distributed by the Press throughout the world.

Cet ouvrage est publié dans le cadre de l'accord de co-édition passé en 1977 entre la Fondation de la Maison des sciences de l'homme et le Press Syndicate of the University of Cambridge. Toutes les langues européennes sont admises pour les titres couverts par cet accord, et les ouvrages collectifs peuvent paraître en plusieurs langues.

Les ouvrages paraissent soit isolément, soit dans l'une des séries que la Maison des sciences de l'homme et Cambridge University Press ont convenu de publier ensemble. La distribution dans le monde entier des titres ainsi publiés conjointement par les deux établissements est assurée par Cambridge University Press.

SOUR GRAPES

Studies in the subversion of rationality

JON ELSTER

Associate Professor, Department of History
University of Oslo

CAMBRIDGE
UNIVERSITY PRESS

EDITIONS DE LA MAISON DES SCIENCES DE
L'HOMME

Paris

Published by the Press Syndicate of the University of Cambridge
The Pitt Building, Trumpington Street, Cambridge CB2 1RP
40 West 20th Street, New York, NY 10011-4211, USA
10 Stamford Road, Oakleigh, Melbourne 3166, Australia
and Editions de la Maison des Sciences de l'Homme
54 Boulevard Raspail, 75270 Paris Cedex 06

© Maison des Sciences de l'Homme and Cambridge University Press 1983

First published 1983
First paperback edition 1985
Reprinted 1987 (twice), 1991, 1993

Printed in the United States of America

Library of Congress catalogue card number: 82-22034

British Library cataloguing in publication data

Elster, Jon
Sour grapes.
1. Rationalism
I. Title
153.4'3   BF441

ISBN 0-521-25230-X hardback
ISBN 0-521-31368-6 paperback
ISBN 2-7351-0031-6 (France only)

CONTENTS

PREFACE AND ACKNOWLEDGEMENTS

An action is the outcome of a choice within constraints. The choice, according to the orthodox view, embodies an element of freedom, the constraints one of necessity. In non-standard cases, however, these equations do not hold. The title of an earlier book on rational and irrational behaviour, *Ulysses and the Sirens*, is a reminder that men sometimes are free to choose their own constraints. *Sour Grapes* conversely reflects the idea that the preferences underlying a choice may be shaped by the constraints. Considered together, these two non-standard phenomena are sufficiently important to suggest that the orthodox theory is due for fundamental revision.

The present book, then, supplements my earlier work. To some extent it also corrects what I now see as an overly enthusiastic application of the idea that men can choose their own character. The chapter on states that are essentially by-products suggests that there are limits to what may be achieved by character planning. There is hubris in the view that one can be the master of one's soul – just as there is an intellectual fallacy in the view that everything that comes about by action can also be brought about by action.

The book is also an attempt to spell out some strands in the complex notions of rationality, intentionality and optimality. Some of the issues raised in this connection are more fully discussed in my *Explaining Technical Change*. This holds in particular for the analysis of functional explanation.

My first acknowledgement is to G. A. Cohen, who has commented extensively and intensively on successive drafts of Chs. II, III and IV. Without his ability to force me out of a congenital intellectual laziness, the level of argument would have been much lower. Next, I want to thank the members of a Working Group on Rationality, set up under the auspices of the Maison des Sciences de l'Homme, for helpful discussion and constant inspiration. In particular my gratitude goes to Brian Barry, Donald Davidson, Dagfinn Føllesdal, Robert Goodin, Serge Kolm, Amélie Rorty, Amos Tversky and Bernard Williams. Finally I should mention what will be obvious to any reader – my immense intellectual debt to the outstanding work by Paul Veyne, *Le Pain et le Cirque*. In addition I want to make the following acknowledgements with regard to individual chapters. My ideas about collective rationality in Ch. I have been shaped in numerous discussions with Aanund Hylland, Rune Slagstad and the other participants in the project 'Democracy and Social Planning' set up by the Norwegian Research Council for the Humanities. An earlier, much briefer and somewhat confused version of Ch. II first appeared in *Social Sciences Information*, 1981. I am grateful to Elina Almasy for her editorial help, and to Wolf Lepenies for his useful comments. A slightly different version of Ch. III appeared in A. Sen and B. Williams (eds.), *Utilitarianism and Beyond* (Cambridge University Press, 1982). I received valuable comments on drafts of that version from the editors of the volume; also from Herman van Gunsteren, Martin Hollis, John Roemer and Arthur Stinchcombe. Ch. IV appeared – also in a somewhat different form – in M. Hollis and S. Lukes (eds.), *Rationality and Relativism* (Blackwell, Oxford, 1982). I am grateful to Martin Hollis for his editorial suggestions.

The University of Oslo, The Norwegian Research Council for the Humanities, the Maison des Sciences de l'Homme and All Souls College, Oxford, have also contributed materially to the writing of the book.

I

RATIONALITY

I.1 INTRODUCTION

The present work is largely about irrationality. Yet the discussion will hardly make sense without a prior analysis of the notion of rationality. This is embarrassingly rich. There is a bewildering multitude of entities that are said to be rational or irrational: beliefs, preferences, choices or decisions, actions, behavioural patterns, persons, even collectivities and institutions. Also, the connotations of the term 'rational' range from the formal notions of efficiency and consistency to the substantive notions of autonomy or self-determination. And in the background of the notion lurks the formidable pair of 'Verstand' vs. 'Vernunft', be it in the Kantian or in the Hegelian senses.

I begin with the focus on rationality as a formal feature of individual actions (I.2). This will provide what, following a similar terminology in Rawls,[1] I shall call the thin theory of rationality. It is thin in that it leaves unexamined the beliefs and the desires that form the reasons for the action whose rationality we are assessing, with the exception that they are stipulated not to be logically inconsistent. Consistency, in fact, is what rationality in the thin sense is all about: consistency within the belief system; consistency within the system of desires; and consistency between beliefs and desires on the one hand and the action for which they are reasons on the other hand.

The broad theory of individual rationality goes beyond these formal requirements (I.3). Rationality here involves more than acting consistently on consistent beliefs and desires: we also require that the beliefs and desires be rational in a more substantive sense. It is not too

---

[1] Rawls (1971), pp. 396ff., invokes 'the thin theory of the good to explain the rational preference for primary goods', while acknowledging that a fuller theory is needed to account for 'the moral worth of persons'.

difficult to spell out what this means in the case of beliefs. Substantively rational beliefs are those which are grounded in the available evidence: they are closely linked to the notion of *judgment*. It is more difficult to define a corresponding notion of a substantively rational desire. One way of approaching the problem is by arguing that *autonomy* is for desires what judgment is for belief, and this is how I shall in the main proceed.

The notion of rationality can also be extended in a different direction, from the individual to the collective case. Once again I shall begin with the more formal considerations (I.4). At this level, rationality may either be attached to collective decision-making (as in social choice theory) or to the aggregate outcome of individual decisions. In both cases the individual desires and preferences are taken as *given*, and rationality defined mainly as a relation between preferences and the social outcome. A broader theory of collective rationality (I.5) will also have to look at the capacity of the social system or the collective decision mechanism to bring the individual preferences into line with the broad notion of individual rationality. A collectively rational arrangement in this sense is one which fosters autonomous wants, or is able to filter out non-autonomous ones.

In this chapter I am concerned with rationality, in later chapters with irrationality. One way of looking at the relation between these two notions is the following. Rationality tells the agent what to do; if he behaves otherwise, he is irrational. I shall argue against this view. There are many cases in which rationality – be it thin or broad – can do no more than exclude certain alternatives, while not providing any guide to the choice between the remaining. If we want to *explain* behaviour in such cases, causal considerations must be invoked in addition to the assumption of rationality. In fact, I argue below that if we require rationality in the broad sense, this will be the rule rather than the exception.

I.2   INDIVIDUAL RATIONALITY: THE THIN THEORY

Along the lines suggested by Donald Davidson,[2] rational action is action that stands in a certain relation to the agent's beliefs and desires (which I collectively refer to as his *reasons*). We must require, first, that

---

[2] See in particular the essays collected in Davidson (1980).

the reasons are reasons for the action; secondly, that the reasons do in fact cause the action for which they are reasons; and thirdly, that the reasons cause the action 'in the right way'. Implicit in these requirements is also a consistency requirement for the desires and beliefs themselves. In what follows, the focus will mainly be on consistency, but first I have a few words to say about the three clauses that went into the definition of rational action.

The first clause can be taken in two ways. One might either say that the reasons are reasons for the action when, given the beliefs of the agent, the action in question is *the best* way to realize his desire. Or, more weakly, that the reasons are reasons for the action if it is *a* way of realizing the desire (given the beliefs). This distinction is related to, yet different from, the problem raised in the last paragraph of I.1 above. It is different because the question of unicity (is there *one* rational course of action?) must be distinguished from the question of optimality (is the rational course the *best?*) There might well be several alternatives that are equally and maximally good. I shall discuss these issues below. Here I only want to note how extremely thin is the theory of rationality we are dealing with here. If an agent has a compulsive desire to kill another person, and believes that the best way (or a way) of killing that person is to stick a pin through a doll representing him, then he acts rationally if he sticks a pin through the doll. Yet we might well want to question the substantive rationality of that desire and that belief.

The second clause of the definition is needed to exclude what we may call 'coincidences of the first class', in which a person has reasons for acting in the way he does, but is caused to do so by something other than these reasons. One might do by accident what one also has reasons for doing. Also, compulsive behaviour might occasionally be quite adequate to the occasion.

The third clause is needed to exclude 'coincidences of the second class', when the reasons do in fact cause the action for which they are reasons, but do so 'in the wrong way'. That reasons can cause an action 'in the wrong way' can be seen from the cases in which reasons cause an action for which they are not reasons. Davidson, for instance, argues that weakness of will can be explained along these lines.[3] The present case, however, is more complex, since the action which is caused by the reasons in the wrong way is the very action for which they are reasons.

[3] Davidson (1980), Ch. 2.

To see how this is possible, we invoke Davidson's notion of non-standard causal chains. An example from the external world is this: 'A man may try to kill someone by shooting at him. Suppose the killer misses his victim by a mile, but the shot stampedes a herd of wild pigs that trample the intended victim to death.'[4] We do not then want to say that the man killed the victim intentionally, since the causal chain is of the wrong kind. Correspondingly for the case of mental causality that concerns us here:

> A climber might want to rid himself of the weight and danger of holding another man on a rope, and he might know that by loosening his hold on the rope, he could rid himself of the weight and the danger. This belief and want might so unnerve him as to cause him to loosen his hold, and yet it might be the case that he never *chose* to loosen his hold, nor did he do so intentionally.[5]

Beliefs and desires can hardly be reasons for action unless they are consistent. They must not involve logical, conceptual or pragmatic contradictions. I shall first discuss consistency criteria for beliefs, and then at somewhat greater length for desires.

To evaluate the consistency of beliefs is not difficult, at least on the more superficial level at which we can assume that the beliefs have already been identified. At a deeper level we must accept Davidson's argument that identifying the beliefs of a person and assessing their consistency cannot be separated from each other. The process of belief imputation must be guided by the assumption that they are by and large consistent.[6] But once we have established the base line or background of general consistency, one may raise the question of local inconsistency of beliefs. The following holds only with this proviso.

We may look on beliefs either as subjective probability assessments, or as somehow *sui generis*. On the first reading, consistency simply means conformity to the laws of probability, so that the point probabilities of exclusive and exhaustive events add up to 1, the probability of the combination of any two of them is 0, etc. Similarly, the probabilities of compound events must have the right kind of relation to the probabilities of the elementary events, so that, say, a conjunction of independent events has a probability equal to the product of the component events.

For beliefs taken *sui generis* the obvious consistency criterion would seem to be that a set of beliefs are consistent if there is some possible world in which they are all true, i.e. if it is not possible to derive a

[4] *Ibid.* p. 78.　　　　[5] *Ibid.* p. 79.　　　　[6] *Ibid.* Ch. 12 and *passim*.

contradiction from them. Jaakko Hintikka has shown, however, that this is insufficient.[7] His criterion is that the beliefs are consistent if there exists a possible world in which they are all true *and believed*. The need for the last clause arises in cases of higher-order beliefs, i.e. beliefs about beliefs. Thus Niels Bohr at one time is said to have had a horseshoe over his door. Upon being asked whether he really believed that horseshoes bring luck, he answered, 'No, but I am told that they bring luck even to those who do not believe in them.'[8] Rigging the story a bit, this comes out as follows:

(1) Niels Bohr believes 'The horseshoe will not bring me luck.'
(2) Niels Bohr believes 'Horseshoes bring luck to those who do not believe they will bring them luck.'

Here there is no contradiction between the beliefs within quotation marks in (1) and (2), but we get an inconsistency if to these two beliefs we add (1) itself. So if we admit – as I think we should – that on intuitive grounds we would want to call the belief system inconsistent, we need the complex criterion to get a result in line with intuition.

To define consistency criteria for desires, we must first look more closely into the nature of the action in question. Roughly speaking, an action may be seen either as *doing something* or as *bringing about something*. When I take an apple from the fruit bowl, I am not setting up a causal process in the external world: I just do it (at will). By contrast, when I break the window by throwing an ash-tray at it, I bring about a change in the world by setting up a causal process that soon becomes independent of my will. (True, under other descriptions these characterizations may be reversed, but I am now concerned with the description under which the action is performed intentionally.) The explanations of these two actions are not quite assimilable to each other, although they both fall under the general scheme of rational action. I want an apple, and I take it: nothing more needs to be said. I may add, at the risk of some pedantry, that I believe there is an apple there; also, if I want a stronger form of explanation, that an apple is at the time what I want most, compared to the other options I believe to be available. In short, I *prefer* the apple. There is no need to go beyond this and add, falsely, that I take the apple *in order to* bring about a certain sensation in my taste organs, or to maximize a certain sensation. This would be true only in non-standard cases. I should add,

[7] Hintikka (1961). For some applications, see Elster (1978a), pp. 81ff.
[8] The story is told in Segrè (1980), p. 171.

however, that taste sensations may yet have explanatory force, at one remove: they are involved in the emergence and reinforcement of the preferences. They may be invoked in explaining my desire, not in describing it (see also II.10 below).

In the ash-tray case, however, we must invoke more than mere preferences to explain the action, assuming it is not a mere *acte gratuit* as in Gide's *Les Caves du Vatican*. To understand the action we must postulate a *plan*, and specify a future state of affairs for the sake of which it was undertaken. The goal – breaking the window – could have been achieved by many means. One explanation of my action is simply that I believed throwing the ash-tray was one way of achieving the goal; a more ambitious explanation that I believed it to be the best way. If someone asks, 'Why did he throw the ash-tray?', this might be because he wants to know whether it was an expressive act of anger, or had the instrumental purpose of breaking the window; or to inquire into the reasons for breaking the window; or to understand why the ash-tray rather than some other object was chosen. Focussing on the last question brings out the distinction between preferences and plans. Choosing the ash-tray over the coffee mug is a different kind of action from that of choosing the apple over the orange. And I shall now go on to argue that quite different consistency criteria come into play for actions guided by preferences and by plans respectively.

The consistency criteria for preferences involve, minimally, *transitivity*: if I prefer a to b and b to c, I should prefer a to c. More complex consistency criteria are required when preferences are defined for options with a more complex internal structure. I shall consider two such complications, stemming from *probability* and *time* respectively.

Preferences may be defined over *lotteries*, i.e. over probability combinations of options, some of which may themselves be lotteries. This can be important practically, and is also crucial for the construction of a utility function that allows comparison of intensity of preferences.[9] It is usual then to assume the *dominance principle*: if one prefers a to b and $p > q$, then one should rationally prefer the option of getting a with probability p and b with probability $(1-p)$ to that of getting a with probability q and b with probability $(1-q)$. Also, one usually assumes the *reduction principle* that if a compound lottery – a lottery having lotteries among the options – is reduced to simple

---

[9] For details about the construction, see Luce and Raiffa (1957), Ch. 2.

lotteries in the obvious way, the preferences should remain the same. Both assumptions have been challenged.[10]

Preferences may also be defined over whole *sequences* of options, bringing time into the picture in an essential way. In particular, we may define the notion of *time preferences* as an expression of the relative importance that at one point of time one accords to various later times or periods. Time preferences typically involve *discounting* the future, i.e. attaching less weight to future consumption or utility than to present. Such preferences are subject to two kinds of irrationality, that we may call respectively *incontinence* (or more neutrally *impatience*) and *inconsistency*. Incontinence involves discounting the future over and above what can be justified by mortality statistics and similar considerations. On the thin theory of rationality, we are not entitled to say that incontinence is irrational, unless the agent, at the time of acting incontinently, also believes that all things considered it would be best to wait. We would then be dealing with a case of weakness of will, briefly mentioned earlier. We might, on the other hand, espouse a broad theory of rationality that would enable us to characterize incontinence as irrational even when no such conflict is present.[11] By contrast, inconsistent time preferences are irrational even on the thin theory.[12] Consistency of time preferences is defined by requiring that a plan made at time t_1 for the allocation of consumption between times t_2 and t_3 should still remain in vigour when t_2 arrives, assuming that there has been no personality change or changes in the feasible set. With inconsistent time preferences one is never able to stick to past plans. It can be shown that consistent time preferences must be exponential, so that the future is discounted at a constant rate. George Ainslie has argued for the pervasiveness of non-exponential time preferences in human life, and shown that it is possible for an agent to exploit strategically this feature in order to overcome his incontinence.[13] Briefly

---

[10] See for example Dreyfus and Dreyfus (1978) or Kahneman and Tversky (1979).

[11] On the issue of the irrationality of time preferences, see Maital and Maital (1978). They defend time preferences as rational because utility-maximizing, i.e. as rational in the thin sense of the term. See also the demonstration by Koopmans (1960) and by Koopmans, Diamond and Williamson (1964) that discounting the future is logically implied by a set of reasonable (although not compelling) assumptions about the shape of the utility function.

[12] Strotz (1955–6); see also Elster (1979), Ch. II.5 I take this occasion to point to a serious mathematical error in my earlier treatment of inconsistent time preferences. In particular, the argument in Elster (1979), pp. 73ff., concerning the 'allocation of consistent planning' is largely incorrect. I am grateful to Aanund Hylland for spotting this mistake. It is corrected in the forthcoming Italian edition.

[13] Ainslie (1982).

the idea is that by grouping together several future choices the chances are increased that in each of them one will take the option with a later and greater reward. On the other hand this solution to the problem of impulsiveness may be as bad as the original difficulty, since the habit of grouping choices together may lead to rigid and compulsive behaviour.

In addition to incontinence and temporal inconsistency, time also introduces the danger of *inconstancy*, or irrational preference change (including change of time preferences[14]). Not all preference change, of course, is irrational; indeed at times it may be irrational not to change one's preferences in the face of learning. I shall postpone the discussion of this issue, however, since here we clearly appeal to the broad notion of rationality. True, in I.4 below I shall give an example of endogenous preference change that could perhaps be said to be irrational on purely formal criteria, but in general we must invoke substantive considerations of autonomy.

In the theory of rational choice preferences are often required to be *complete* as well as consistent, meaning that for any pair of options one should be able to express a preference for one of them or, failing this, indifference. From the point of view adopted here, there are no strong arguments for this condition. In fact, one could argue that it is irrational to commit oneself to a preference for one of the options if one knows very little about either. At the very least it would be irrational to put much trust in such preferences.[15] For the purposes of model building, however, it is clear that a full ordering of the available options is a much more powerful notion than a partial ordering. But if one is guided by reality rather than by convenience, there seems to be a choice between postulating partial or incomplete preference orderings, and postulating complete preferences subject to endogenous change as the agent learns more about the alternatives. Postulating preferences that are both complete and stable seems too remote from the real world.

In addition to consistency and completeness, it is often assumed that preferences have the property of *continuity*. Very broadly speaking, this means that if one prefers *a* over *b*, and *a* undergoes a very small change

[14] See Meyer (1977) and Samuelson (1976) for this idea.

[15] Cyert and de Groot (1975), pp. 230ff. A related but importantly different argument is offered by Tocqueville (1969, p. 582): in a democracy people 'are afraid of themselves, dreading that their taste having changed, they will come to regret not being able to drop what once had formed the object of their lust'. Whence the tendency of the Americans to eschew durable consumer goods. Whereas Cyert and de Groot argue that a rational person should anticipate that his tastes will change because of new experience, Tocqueville suggests that the Americans – rationally or not – act on the assumption that their taste will change irrationally in the future.

(as small as you please), then the preferences should not be reversed.[16] This requirement is violated in the case of so-called non-Archimedean preferences, an important special case of which is the lexicographic preference structure involving a hierarchy of values. If I am starving and am offered the choice between an option involving one loaf and listening to a Bach record and another involving one loaf and listening to Beethoven, then my love for Bach may make me prefer the first option. If, however, from the first option is subtracted even a very small crumb of bread, as small as you please, then I switch to the second because at starvation level calories are incomparably more important than music. There is nothing irrational in this preference switch, and so continuity cannot be part of rationality.[17] For model-building purposes, however, the condition is very important, since preferences that are transitive, complete and continuous can be represented through a real-valued *utility function*.

At this point two observations suggest themselves. First, to maximize utility is not to engage in the carrying out of a plan, choosing the best means to realize an independently defined end. In the modern theory of utility, it is essentially a short-hand for preferences, and implies nothing about more or less pleasurable mental states that could be seen as the goal of the behaviour. Now there are good reasons for thinking that this ordinal conception of welfare carries things too far, for surely we know from introspection that pleasure, happiness and satisfaction are meaningful notions, if only we could get a conceptual handle on them, which may prove difficult. My point here is that even if one should succeed in defining a cardinal measure of utility, it would be a mistake to believe that action could then always be explained in terms of utility maximization in the same sense as, say, investment may be explained in terms of profit maximization. The latter operation is (in the standard models[18]) conceived of as a plan undertaken consciously and *ex ante*, whereas the conscious and deliberate attempt to maximize utility tends to be self-defeating. It is a truism, and an important one, that happiness tends to elude those who actively strive for it. Much of Ch. II is devoted to a further analysis of this idea. Here I only want to

---

[16] For a more precise statement, see Rader (1972), pp. 147ff.

[17] For a strong argument to this effect, see Georgescu-Roegen (1954). The rhetoric of Marcuse (1964) can be understood within this framework: if the preferences can be mapped into the real line, we are indeed dealing with 'one-dimensional man'. Similarly Borch (1968, p. 22) observes that the postulate of continuous preferences amounts to saying that 'everything has a price'.

[18] For a discussion of non-standard models, see Elster (1982a), Ch. 6.

stress that even if actions may sometimes be explained as *attempts* to maximize utility in this *ex ante* sense, we would not be justified in thinking that the attempt would succeed; rather the contrary.[19] On the other hand, as I observed earlier, when the utility-maximizing consequences of behaviour *can* be invoked to explain it, they do so by providing a causal explanation of the preferences. Pleasurable inner states enter importantly into the explanation of behaviour, but not as the conscious goal of behaviour.

Secondly, we may usefully contrast *rational man* with *economic man*. The first involves – in the thin sense which we are discussing now – nothing but consistent preferences and (to anticipate) consistent plans. The second is a much better-endowed creature, with preferences that are not only consistent, but also complete, continuous and *selfish*. To be sure, economists have constructed a large variety of models involving non-selfish preferences,[20] but their reflex is nevertheless to attempt to derive all apparently non-selfish behaviour from selfish preferences.[21] This may perhaps be a good research strategy: when setting out to explain a given piece of behaviour, assume first that it is selfish; if not, then at least rational; if not, then at least intentional. But there can be no way of justifying the substantive assumption that all forms of altruism, solidarity and sacrifice really are ultra-subtle forms of self-interest, except by the trivializing gambit of arguing that people have concern for others because they want to avoid being distressed by their distress. And even this gambit, as Allan Gibbard has pointed out, is open to the objection that rational distress-minimizers could often use more efficient means than helping others.[22]

---

[19] As emphasized in van Parijs (1981) and Elster (1982a), one should distinguish between explanation in terms of intended and in terms of actual consequences of behaviour, although there is of course no general presumption that the intended consequences will fail to materialize – except for the class of cases that form the subject of Ch. II below.

[20] See the useful survey and discussion in Kolm (1981a).

[21] See in particular the important synthesis of biological and game-theoretic considerations in Axelrod and Hamilton (1981). They use a model of sequential Prisoner's Dilemmas to show (i) that genuinely altruistic motivation can arise out of natural selection by purely selfish criteria and (ii) that some cases of apparently altruistic motivation can be explained by assuming no more than selfish rationality. In other words, if people behave altruistically, it is either because they have been programmed to feel concern for others or because they have calculated that it pays to fake concern for others. The first explanation, while in a sense reductionist, allows rational resistance to the economic reductionism embodied in the second. Yet there probably are cases that are resistant also to biological reductionism, unless one postulates that fitness-reducing altruism can be explained by the fact that 'it is not worth burdening the germ plasm with the information necessary to realize such an adjustment' (Williams 1966, p. 206).

[22] Gibbard 1986.

I now turn to plans and their consistency criteria. To ask for such criteria is to presuppose that an action can be intentional and yet not be rational. I do indeed claim that there are such actions, and much of Ch. II deals with an important subclass of them. Before I go on to discuss the consistency criteria for plans, let me distinguish this claim from a different one, that a person could act intentionally and yet be on the whole irrational. Once again we must agree with Davidson that global rationality is a precondition for imputing intentions to a person, be they irrational. We must be able to make sense of a person on the whole, if we are to be able to say that some of his plans do not make sense.

A rational plan must fulfil two criteria. First, the end state in terms of which it is defined must be a logically coherent one. If it is true, as claimed by Sartre, that we all fundamentally want to be simultaneously *en-soi* and *pour-soi*, resting in ourselves like a thing and yet at a distance from ourselves that allows us to enjoy this, then we are indeed striving for an end that is logically or conceptually incoherent. Acting on this desire will be as self-defeating as the attempt to turn around, very swiftly, to catch one's own shadow. Similarly, the desire for a unilateral recognition – to be recognized by another whom you do not yourself recognize – is a desire to bring about a state that could not possibly obtain, since a condition for recognition is that it is reciprocal.[23] So, on this first criterion, a necessary condition for the consistency of a plan is that there should be a possible world in which it is realized.

As in the case of beliefs, however, we need a second criterion: there must be a possible world in which the plan is realized deliberately, i.e. in which one finds both the plan and its fulfilment. Take the plan to behave spontaneously. There is nothing incoherent in the end state which defines that plan, since people often do behave spontaneously. Yet trying to be spontaneous is a self-defeating plan, since the very act of trying will interfere with the goal. There is a possible world in which I behave spontaneously, but none in which I plan to do so and succeed. Plans that violate the first of these criteria are logically or conceptually contradictory; those that violate the second but not the first are pragmatically contradictory. In Ch. II below I am concerned almost exclusively with the latter kind of contradictory plans.

I conclude this section with some remarks on the ambiguity in the notion of rational behaviour, related to the distinction between an

---

[23] See also Elster (1976; 1978a, pp. 70ff.) for a further analysis of the sense in which unilateral recognition is an incoherent idea.

action being *a* way or *the best* way to realize my desire. I shall be concerned, that is, with the unicity and the optimality of rational behaviour. I shall do so by assuming that the agent wants to maximize some objective, i.e. realize some plan in the best way, and ask how he might be thwarted in his goal. Very similar arguments could be carried through with preferences instead of plans, but this I shall leave to the reader.

What distinguishes the various forms of maximizing behaviour is, first, the nature of the environment and, secondly, the extent to which it is known to the agent. The first divides into a passive or parametric environment, and a strategic one; the second into certainty, risk and uncertainty. Of the resulting subvarieties, decision under certainty in a parametric environment is the standard problem of optimization. Even in this simple case, we immediately see that there may be neither unicity nor optimality. There may well be several options that are equally and maximally good, according to the chosen objective.[24] Moreover, the feasible set may be 'badly behaved' so that there is no option that is optimal. A trivial example is the task of finding the smallest real number strictly larger than zero; a more substantive one the non-existence of optimal strategies in economic planning.[25]

In the case of parametric decisions under risk, the maximand becomes the expected value of the objective function, or some modification thereof that takes account of risk aversion and irreversibility. The case of parametric decisions under uncertainty is more controversial, since many deny that there is such a thing as genuine uncertainty or ignorance, i.e. cases in which we are unable to attach any numerical probabilities to the possible outcomes of action. I cannot here argue for my view that there are such cases, and that they are in fact very important.[26] Assuming, then, that these cases exist, we know that rationally one can take account only of the best and the worst consequences attached to each course of action.[27] Since there are many ways of doing this, e.g. by choosing the action with the best

---

[24] Cp. Ullmann-Margalit and Morgenbesser (1977) for a discussion of this issue. General equilibrium theory very explicitly recognizes the possibility of the producer and the consumer having several options that are equally and maximally good from the point of view, respectively, of profit-maximization and preference satisfaction. Yet, contrary to the normal canons of science, the theory would resist attempts to make these choices uniquely determined, since this might destroy the continuity properties on which depends the proof that an equilibrium exists.

[25] Heal (1973), Ch. 13.

[26] See Elster (1982a), Appendix 1, for a further discussion.

[27] Arrow and Hurwicz (1972).

worst-consequence or the one with the best best-consequence, it follows that neither unicity nor optimality will obtain. The fact that we have no reason for choosing between 'maximum' and 'maximax' does not imply that they are both optimal, as in the first case envisaged in the last paragraph. To assimilate the two cases would be to confuse indifference and incomparability.

If the environment is a strategic one, we are in the realm of game theory. Broadly speaking, game theory may be seen as a tool – indeed, as *the* tool – for the simultaneous handling of three sets of interdependencies that pervade social life. (1) The reward of each depends on the reward of all, through envy, altruism etc. (2) The reward of each depends on the action of all, through general social causality. (3) The action of each depends on the action of all, by strategic reasoning. The last is the specific contribution of game theory. I might add, lest someone should think that I embrace game theory as the solution to all problems, that I do not think it capable of handling the following. (4) The desires of each depend on the action of all. This refers to the fact that individual preferences and plans are social in their origin, which differs from the idea that they may be social in their scope, i.e. that the welfare of others may be part of the goal of the individual. Ch. III is largely devoted to a discussion of preference formation.

The interdependency of choices turns crucially on the notion of an *equilibrium point*, i.e. a set of strategies that are optimal against each other. One may then define the *solution* to a game as an equilibrium point towards which all the agents will tacitly converge. Some games have no equilibrium point, such as the following. 'Each player writes down a number. The one who has written down the largest number gets a sum from each of the other corresponding to the difference between the numbers they have written down.' Hyperinflation can work like this. Others have more than one equilibrium point, none of which has the salience that would single it out as the solution. One example is this: 'I want to go to the cinema, you want to go to a restaurant, but we would both rather be together than separate.' Knowing this *and only this* about each other, we will not be able to converge rationally to the one or the other place.[28] True, the italicized clause will in this case rarely be fulfilled, and so one can act on

---

[28] Cp. Luce and Raiffa (1957), pp. 90ff., 115ff., for a further discussion of this game, known as 'The battle of the sexes'.

expectations about what the other will do, derived from insight into how his or her mind works. In other cases, however, one may know nothing more about the other than the bare fact that he is rational, and is aware that the rationality is mutual, and then there may be no set of expectations that can be rationally defended. Here optimality breaks down: there is no course of action than which none better.

In other game-theoretic interactions unicity breaks down, with some quite intriguing consequences. Quite generally, whenever the solution to a game consists of mixed strategies, i.e. for each agent a choice between his available actions according to some (optimal) probability distribution, the individual will neither gain nor lose by deviating from the solution behaviour, provided that the others stick to it. In particular, the individual will not lose by choosing his 'maximin' strategy, i.e. the alternative that makes him as well off as possible, assuming that the others choose so as to make him as badly off as possible. It might therefore be tempting to choose this strategy, knowing that if the others stick to the solution nothing will be lost, and if they do not the damage will at least be contained. Yet knowing that the others are as rational as oneself, the idea that they might do the same could hold one back – hoping that they will be held back similarly. Clearly, the situation is highly unstable. The requirement that none shall gain from defecting ensures the uniqueness of the solution, but individual behaviour is less stably tied to it than when one actually would lose from defecting.[29]

I have mentioned three cases where optimality breaks down: badly-behaved opportunity sets, decision-making under uncertainty and games without a solution. These provide *the special argument for satisficing*, reserving the general argument for the next section. When the course of action 'than which none better' is not defined, one will have to go for something that is *good enough* or satisfactory, rather than optimal. In the case of planning, this might involve substituting an 'agreeable plan' for the optimal plan.[30] In the case of strategic interaction, it might involve maximin behaviour – substituting in fact caution for optimality. Observe, however, that in games that have no

[29] This difficulty is strongly emphasized by Harsanyi (1977).
[30] Hammond and Mirrlees (1973). Strictly speaking, the notion of an agreeable plan is not an instance of satisficing, since it is in a wide class of.cases uniquely determined. Although the notion of an aspiration level enters into the definition of an agreeable plan, it turns out to be independent of any particular aspiration level. Yet the underlying rationale is quite similar to that behind the notion of satisficing.

equilibrium point the maximin strategy may not be defined. If hyperinflation is conceived as a game in which the reward goes to the group that is able to negotiate higher wage increases than the others, with no holds barred, there is no demand that will ensure a 'satisfactory' outcome for a given group, or limit the damage that the others can do to it. In such perverse interaction structures reason is of little avail – or rather it tells us to change the situation when it is not possible to choose rationally within it.

I.3   INDIVIDUAL RATIONALITY: THE BROAD THEORY

I now want to inquire into the more substantive connotations of rationality. Nothing has been said up to now that would prevent us from speaking of suicide, homicide or genocide as rational behaviour. Nor have I given any reason for excluding from the domain of the rational the rain dance of the Hopi, consulting the horoscope before investing in the stock market, or going back to the house rather than crossing a black cat in the street. Logically speaking, it is possible that the whole world is engaged in a conspiracy to thwart my efforts to get redress, and in the thin sense it may be quite rational for me to act on this assumption. But clearly this sense is too thin. We need a broader theory of rationality that goes beyond the exclusively formal considerations of the preceding section, and that allows a scrutiny of the substantive nature of the desires and beliefs involved in action. We want to be able to say that acting rationally means acting consistently on beliefs and desires that are not only consistent, but also rational.

On the other hand we do not want to dilute the notion of rationality so that it comes to encompass all the good properties that we might want our beliefs and desires to have. I suggest that *between the thin theory of the rational and the full theory of the true and the good there is room and need for a broad theory of the rational.* To say that truth is necessary for rational beliefs clearly is to require too much; to say that consistency is sufficient, to demand too little. Similarly, although more controversially, for rational desires: the requirement of consistency is too weak, that of ethical goodness too strong.

My suggestion is that we should evaluate the broad rationality of beliefs and desires by looking at the way in which they are shaped. A belief may be consistent and even true, a desire consistent and even conformable to morals – and yet we may hesitate to call them rational if they have been shaped by irrelevant causal factors, by a blind psychic causality operating 'behind the back' of the person. The stress here should be on 'irrelevant' and 'blind', not on causality as such. I am not arguing that beliefs and desires are made irrational by virtue of having a causal origin. All desires and beliefs have a (sufficient) causal origin, but some of them have the wrong sort of causal history and hence are irrational. Since it is so hard to say exactly what would qualify as the right sort of history, I shall have relatively little to say about this (crucial) problem. I shall have more to say, here and later, about all the wrong sorts. Towards the end of this section I offer a brief typology of the ways in which beliefs and desires can be distorted and perverted. Some of these are further explored in Ch. III and Ch. IV below.

Consider first beliefs and belief formation. Clearly, a belief may be true and not rational; rational, and not true. The (substantive) rationality of beliefs concerns the relation between the belief and the available evidence, not the relation between the belief and the world. Moreover, as argued in more detail in Ch. IV, the assertion that the belief is rational must not be founded on a *comparison* between the evidence and the belief, but on an investigation into the actual causal story, since a person may by a non-rational route arrive at a belief that also happens to be grounded in the evidence. Furthermore, it is not enough to say that the belief is rational if it is caused by the evidence which makes it rational to believe in it, since in a given case it might be caused by the evidence in the wrong way, e.g. by the mechanism of compensating errors. All this closely parallels the discussion in I.2 about the relation between an action and the beliefs and desires which provide the reasons for it.

The positive characterization of rational beliefs can be made in terms of the notion of *judgment*, defined as the capacity to synthetize vast and diffuse information that more or less clearly bears on the problem at hand, in such a way that no element or set of elements is given undue importance. Clearly this is not a very helpful definition, but there is little doubt about the reality of the phenomenon. We all know persons who have this quality and others who lack it. In some walks of life it is indispensable to have it, and those who lack it are soon eliminated. Extreme cases are the competitive market, in which firms managed by people without judgment soon go bankrupt; and warfare, in which leaders and soldiers without judgment are at high risk. To some extent it is also true of politicians, in whom judgment and common sense – in addition to sheer stamina and a certain trained lack of sensitivity – are much more important than intelligence as conventionally defined. Within the sciences one may make a rough distinction between those which require logic above all, and those which mainly require the less formal exercise of judgment.[31]

It will not do for long, however, to talk glibly about 'the available evidence', for in doing so one begs the crucial question of how much evidence one should rationally make available to oneself before arriving at one's belief. This question admits to different answers according to the further use, if any, to which the belief is to be put. For the pure scientist, the question of further use does not arise, since the formulation of a true belief is the ultimate goal of his behaviour. The chances of arriving at a true belief increasing with the amount of evidence, it might appear that the search for truth is self-defeating, since a scientist committed to it would have to go on collecting evidence forever, always postponing the formation of a belief. The predicament is analogous to that of a society bent on the goal of consumption, which might appear to compel it to go on saving and investing forever, always postponing the enjoyment of the fruits for the sake of which the investment was undertaken. The answer is the same in both cases: since the original problem allows of no answer, the rational response is to restate it as one of finding 'satisfactory' levels of, respectively, evidence and investment.[32]

At first glance it would appear to be easier to determine the optimal amount of evidence in the practical context of a business decision. Here the limits on evidence arise before we get into the paradoxes of truth-maximizing, since collecting information involves costs for the firm and therefore should be undertaken only to the extent that it is (expected to be) profitable. To acquire no information about the environment is irrational; to go on collecting information for a very long time equally so; and hence there must be some optimal amount of information that the firm should acquire. But once again this begs the

---

[31] For some general remarks on the role of judgment in science, see the concluding chapter of Newton-Smith (1981).

[32] It is not easy to state the criteria that guide satisficing with respect to evidence for scientific theories. Perhaps the most important consideration is the degree of originality and novelty of the belief. If an idea has revolutionary potential, it would be rational to advance it even if backed only by a moderate amount of evidence, since the chances then are that the scientific community as a whole will explore it more fully than any single scientist could do in a lifetime. Yet this is not how science works, for the ability to produce revolutionary ideas seems to be highly correlated with the almost compulsive drive not to leave any objection unexplored and unanswered.

question, since 'the choice of a profit maximizing information structure itself requires information, and it is not apparent how the aspiring profit maximizer acquires this information or what guarantees that he does not pay an excessive price for it.'[33] The demand for an optimal amount of evidence immediately leads to an infinite regress.

This is *the general argument for satisficing*. It applies not only to business decisions, but to all other practical matters where there is a conflict between the need to invest time or money getting information and the need to spend time or money using the information one has got.[34] This means that when we leave the thin theory of rationality, the link between rationality and optimality is completely broken. Rational behaviour can be characterized as optimizing only – or at most – with respect to *given* beliefs about the world, but the principles of rationality governing belief acquisition cannot be spelled out in terms of optimization. At least this holds in the *ex ante* sense, that one cannot know in advance how much information it is optimal to obtain. One might conjecture that it does not hold in the *ex post* sense, at least not in the cases where decision-makers that (by fault of their own) happen to make unwise decisions are eliminated by competition, so that only those with an optimal information structure remain. Yet it turns out that this attractive idea, when developed in more detail, is less powerful than it might appear, unless one makes very restrictive assumptions about the environment. In any realistic model of, say, competition between firms, the environment facing a given firm will change so rapidly that no single information structure will remain optimal for the time it takes before competitors are eliminated. We are, in fact, dealing with adaptation to a moving target.[35]

To prevent misunderstanding, I ought to add that the relation between being right and being rational is somewhat more complex than I have suggested. The history of science shows that it may be rational to be wrong, yet not irrational to be right. In a letter to Mersenne, Descartes raised the question whether 'a stone thrown from a sling, the bullet from a musket or the arrow from an arbalist have

---

[33] Winter (1964–5), p. 262.

[34] 'At some point a decision must be taken on intuitive grounds. It is like going in a big forest to pick mushrooms. One may explore the possibilities in a certain limited region, but at some point one must stop the exploration and start picking because further explorations as to the possibilities of finding more and better mushrooms by walking a little further would defeat the purpose of the ride. One must decide to stop on an intuitive basis, i.e. without actually investigating whether further exploration would have yielded better results' (Johansen 1977, p. 144).   [35] For details, see Elster (1982a), Ch. 6.

greater speed and force in the midst of their flight than in the beginning', suggesting that this is indeed the 'vulgar belief' but adding that he had reasons for thinking differently.[36] Clearly, in 1630 the vulgar belief was rational. In the case of a man or a carriage, nobody would contest that the greatest speed is achieved some time after the beginning of the movement, and there was every reason to conceive of the movement of a projectile in the same way. It took the genius of Descartes to reconceptualize movement as a state rather than as a process.[37] One should not say, however, that the belief at which Descartes arrived by his astounding mental leap was irrational, since his theory, as it were, enabled one to perceive the evidence that supported it. The vulgar theory was rational in view of the facts known to it, that of Descartes by virtue of the novel facts it enabled him to establish. I am making the banal point that the relation between belief and observation is a two-way one, rather than the one-directional inductive process suggested by such phrases as 'the most rational belief given the available evidence'. This allows insight to be part of judgment, but does not require it.

It follows from what I said in the preceding section about uncertainty that in some cases the rational course is to form no belief whatsoever with respect to which of the possible outcomes will be realized. Let me recall here the distinction between the two notions of belief, as *sui generis* or as subjective probability judgments. If belief in the former sense is understood as a modal operator, it immediately follows that there is no rational need to form a belief on every issue, since the law of the excluded middle holds only for propositions, not for propositional attitudes. If 'N' stands for any modal operator analogous to necessity (belief, knowledge, obligation etc.) then 'p or not–p' and 'Np or not–Np' will both be true, but 'Np or $N(\text{not–}p)$' may be false. Yet the logical possibility of agnosticism is not always clearly perceived, since atheism seems a much more attractive alternative to faith. Alexander Zinoviev has offered a hallucinatory description of the Soviet Union as a society based on the systematic confusion between internal and external negation, i.e. between '$N(\text{not–}p)$' and 'not–NP'.[38]

---

[36] To Mersenne, 30 January 1630, in Descartes (1897–1910), vol. i, pp. 113–14.

[37] For the argument that this insight was due to Descartes rather than to Galileo, see Koyré (1966).

[38] Zinoviev (1979); See also Elster (1980a) for an exposition and interpretation of this logico-dialectical world view. The distinction between the two senses of negation is also explored in II.2 below.

This makes for a compulsive tendency to apply the law of the excluded middle to beliefs and the other modal operators, notably to obligation, as when he reports that after the death of Stalin there was a very brief period during which it was not obligatory to quote him, before the gap was closed by making it obligatory not to do so.[39]

Everybody will agree that it is a modal fallacy to apply the law of the excluded middle in such cases, yet the substantive importance of this might be doubted. If, namely, belief is understood as subjective probability judgment, with the modal interpretation corresponding to the case of subjective certainty, it might well be argued that one always can and always should form some judgment as to the probability of a given proposition being true, even if there is no presumption for this to be one of the extreme cases of 0 and 100 per cent. If, on the other hand, one accepts the idea that there is such a thing as genuine ignorance and uncertainty, then the attempt to form a judgment of probability may be quite irrational. The fact that one can define operational procedures whereby such probabilities can always be elicited from a person, by placing him in a sequence of hypothetical choice situations, is in my view neither here nor there, for all depends on whether he has any reason to have confidence in the probabilities thus brought out. Again I cannot develop here my arguments for this view.[40]

I now turn to the substantive rationality of desires, a vastly more intricate notion. I shall refer to this as *autonomy*, being for desires what judgment is for belief. The difficulty in characterizing autonomy is twofold. First, it appears insuperably hard to say what it means for a desire to have been formed 'in the right way', i.e. not distorted by irrelevant causal processes. Secondly, it might seem pointless to distinguish autonomy of desires from their ethical goodness; contrary, in any case, to the influential Kantian tradition. I believe the second objection can be answered by pointing to some instances in which we might clearly want to distinguish heteronomous desires from unethical ones. Yet without a good answer to the first, this leaves us with precision in the second decimal while ignoring the first, for how can we distinguish the autonomous from the ethical unless we know what autonomy means?

---

[39] Zinoviev (1978), p. 58. See also Zinoviev (1979), p. 582, where the essence of oppression is found in the fact that even the attempt to do away with it can only be carried out in an oppressive way, as in the injunction 'Don't be so obedient' further discussed in II.4 below.

[40] See also Elster (1979, Ch. III.4; 1982a, Appendix 1).

I can offer no satisfactory definition of autonomy. Beyond the rather obscure analogy with judgment, one might envisage an ostensive definition. Just as there are persons well known for their judgment, there are persons that apparently are in control over the processes whereby their desires are formed, or at least are not in the grip of processes with which they do not identify themselves. Yet the identity and even the existence of such persons is much more controversial than in the case of judgment, that allows for some operational evaluation in terms of differential survival. On the one hand it might appear that our way of identifying such individuals is so closely linked to our ethical views as to make it impossible to draw the distinction between autonomy and goodness. On the other hand one might fear that when the list of non-autonomous processes of desire formation is extended, as it has been in the past and surely will be in the future, it will come to gobble up all our desires, leaving nothing for autonomy.

Given my metaphorical characterization of irrationality in terms of 'blind' causality, it might appear tempting to suggest the following definition: autonomous desires are desires that have been deliberately chosen, acquired or modified – either by an act of will or by a process of character planning. This, for instance, is the ideal of self-determination underlying the Stoic, the Buddhist and the Spinozistic philosophies. In Chs. II and III below I discuss at some length the nature and the limits of self-management in this sense. Here I only want to argue that as a definition of autonomy the idea gives us both too little and too much. The definition is too weak because a desire stemming from intentional character planning can be no more autonomous than the intention from which it stemmed,[41] and so we at once get into a regress. There is no reason, moreover, to believe that second-order desires are always immune to irrelevant causal influences. If they were, the regress would be cut short, but as shown in the important work of George Ainslie, second-order desires may take on a compulsive character and become as heteronomous as the impulsive first-order desires they were supposed to protect us from.[42] The very activity of character planning may bring about a rigidity of character which is incompatible with the

---

[41] This will have to be qualified, since the desire might come to acquire an autonomous character even if originally it stemmed from a non-autonomous second-order desire – a possibility that in no way undermines my argument.

[42] Ainslie (1984) argues for this way of understanding the relation between impulsive and compulsive behaviour. Both modes of behaviour may be considered species of weakness of will, if that notion is simply understood as acting against what, all things considered, one thinks is

'tolerance of ambiguity' often said to be characteristic of ego-strength or autonomy. The definition would also be too strong, in excluding unplanned first-order desires from being rational or autonomous. From the plausible proposition that the *capacity* for second-order evaluation is a condition for personhood, we should not conclude that the actual exercise of this capacity is a condition for autonomy.[43] Through sheer moral luck[44] people may achieve autonomy without striving for it.

As a preliminary step to an understanding of autonomy, including the question of whether it is at all possible, we may survey some of the non-autonomous ways of the self. The present book as a whole, and Ch. III in particular, is largely devoted to such preliminary studies, to provide a background on which the broad notion of rationality might stand out. Yet even without knowing what autonomy means, it is possible to argue that it differs from ethical goodness. I shall give some arguments to show that the grounds on which we criticize desires as non-autonomous differ from those invoked when we dismiss them as unethical – leaving open the possibility that the unethical desires might also turn out to be non-autonomous.

Desires or preferences can be objectionable because of their origin (non-autonomous desires) or because of their content (unethical desires). The most prominent example of non-autonomous preferences discussed in the present work is that of 'sour grapes', i.e. adaptation of preferences to what is seen as possible. Other important varieties are conformism, i.e. the adaptation of one's preferences to those of other people, and sheer inertia. Also we should include the converse phenomena of counteradaptive preferences ('the grass is always greener on the other side of the fence'), anti-conformism and the obsession with novelty. Examples of unethical preferences are inherently more controversial. On most accounts these would include spiteful and sadistic preferences, and arguably also the desire for positional goods, i.e. goods such that it is logically impossible for more than a few to have them.[45] The desire for an income twice the average would be an example. The widespread desire for positional goods can

best (Davidson 1980, Ch. 2; Rorty 1980a, b). If the will is seen as invested in the ego, these two threats are represented by the id and the superego respectively, as argued by Ainslie (forthcoming). The importance of Ainslie's work lies in the extrication of these important notions from the obscure context in which they are usually embedded.

[43] See Frankfurt (1971), Dennett (1976) and C. Taylor (1976) for the view that the capacity for higher-order desires is constitutive of personhood.

[44] For this disturbing concept, see Williams (1981), Ch. 2, and Nagel (1979), Ch. 3.

[45] For the notion of positional goods see Hirsch (1976).

lead to less welfare for everybody, so that such preferences fail to pass the Kantian generalization test.[46] Also they are closely linked to spite, since one way of getting more than others is to take care that they get less – indeed this will often be a cheaper and more efficient method than trying to excel.[47]

To see how the lack of autonomy may be distinguished from the lack of moral worth, let me use *conformity* as a technical term for a desire caused by a drive to be like other people, and *conformism* for a desire to be like other people, with anti-conformity and anti-conformism similarly defined. (I return shortly to the distinction between drives and desires.) Conformity implies that other people's behaviour enters into the causation of my desires, conformism that they enter irreducibly into the description of the object of my desires.[48] Conformity may bring about conformism, but it may also lead to anti-conformism, as in Theodore Zeldin's comment that among the French peasantry 'prestige is to a great extent obtained from conformity with traditions (so that the son of a non-conformist might be expected to be one too)'.[49] Clearly, conformity may bring about desires that are ethically acceptable, yet lacking in autonomy. Conversely, I cannot see how to rule out the possibility of someone autonomously having anti-conformist preferences, even though I would welcome a proof to the effect that autonomy is incompatible not only with anti-conformity, but also with anti-conformism.

Yet I do not have to decide the latter issue, since the first case suffices to bring home the reality of the distinction. The meek conformist who acts morally because he is at all times supported by an environment that inculcates in him the right desires, can hardly claim autonomy. Autonomous moral action, indeed, implies the capacity to act morally even in non-moral environments. By this I do not mean that in such cases one should invariably follow the course that would have been best if adopted by all. By assumption this would not be conformist

---

[46] Haavelmo (1970) offers a model in which everybody suffers a loss of welfare by trying to keep up with the neighbours.

[47] We need to distinguish between taking the achievement of others as a parameter and one's own as the control variable, and manipulating the achievements of others so that they fall short of one's own. The first way of realizing positional goods clearly is less ethically objectionable than the second, but it could still be argued that it is less pure than the (non-comparative) desire to reach a certain standard of excellence. The desire for a positional good logically implies disappointment at the achievement of others, and psychologically the road from disappointment to envy and from envy to spite may be short.

[48] For this distinction, see Cohen (1978), p. 103. [49] Zeldin (1973), p. 134.

behaviour, yet it might be non-autonomous in some other way. Practical morality is largely about 'second-best' choices,[50] meaning that when others act non-morally, one may have to deviate not only from what they do, but from the behaviour to be adopted in the ideal situation of universally moral behaviour. To act blindly on some ethical rule that is not context-sensitive in this way would not be a sign of autonomy. Such behaviour is frequently found in rigid persons who need to have rules and shun the exercise of ethical judgment.[51] Although they may appear to be paradigms of morality and autonomy, they are in fact lacking in both.

In the present work, autonomy will have to be understood as a mere residual, as what is left after we have eliminated the desires that have been shaped by one of the mechanisms on the short list for irrational preference-formation. Similarly, the quality of judgment for beliefs is also to be understood as the absence of distortions and illusions. This provides some necessary conditions for rationality in the broad sense which, while far less satisfactory than a full characterization, can at least be seen as a first step to that goal. A broad typology of the distorting mechanisms can be constructed if we observe that, like the mental states they generate, such mechanisms can be either cognitive or affective in character. The end states can be cognitive or affective, i.e. described as beliefs or as desires. Similarly, their lack of rationality may be due either to faulty cognitive processes or to undue influence from some affective drive. This gives a total of four cases, which I shall shortly describe through some examples. First, however, there is a need to defend the distinction between desires and what I have called drives. Drives shape desires (and beliefs), but are not themselves desires, because they are not conscious and known to the person who has them. (It is misleading, therefore, to say with von Weizsäcker that a person who is obsessed with novelty has a 'preference for change'.[52]) Nor can drives be assimilated to meta-desires which, although they also shape

---

[50] According to the economic theory of the second-best 'it is not true that a situation in which more, but not all, of the optimum conditions are fulfilled is necessarily, or is even likely to be, superior to a situation in which fewer are fulfilled. It follows, therefore, that in a situation in which there exist many constraints which prevent the fulfilment of the Paretian optimum conditions, the removal of any one constraint may effect welfare or efficiency either by raising it, by lowering it, or by leaving it unchanged' (Lipsey and Lancaster 1956–7, p. 12). The ethical analogy is pursued in note 83 below.

[51] Ainslie (1980) cites William James to the effect that 'the highest ethical life consists . . . in the breaking of rules which have grown too narrow for the actual case'.

[52] Von Weizsäcker (1971), p. 356.

the first-order desires, do so in a largely different way, as argued in Ch. III below. Drives must be conceived of as non-conscious psychic forces that are geared to the search for short-term pleasure, as opposed to the conscious desires that may forgo short-term pleasure to achieve some longer-term gain.[53] The metaphor of 'forces' serves usefully to underline our ignorance of the substantive character of drives, that in the present state of the arts must be inferred from behaviour rather than studied directly.

Given this distinction, we may look at some cases in which the broad rationality of beliefs and desires is distorted by drives or cognitive defects. I shall not survey the four categories, only explain them by examples that, while important, are not exhaustive of their classes.

Adaptive preference formation is the adjustment of wants to possibilities – not the deliberate adaptation favoured by character planners, but a causal process occurring non-consciously. Behind this adaptation there is the drive to reduce the tension or frustration that one feels in having wants that one cannot possibly satisfy.

Preference change by framing occurs when the relative attractiveness of options changes when the choice situation is reframed in a way that rationally should make no difference. In a recent study Amos Tversky and Daniel Kahneman found this effect to be pervasive in choice situations, and in many ways similar to optical illusions. They quote an example from L. J. Savage of 'a customer who is willing to add £X to the total cost a new car to acquire a fancy car radio, but realizes that he would not be willing to pay £X for the radio after purchasing the car at its regular price', and add that 'many readers will recognize the temporary devaluation of money which facilitates extra spending . . . in the context of a large expenditure such as buying a house or a car'. Also, when allocating time or money, we appear to use internal book-keeping procedures that sometimes acquire a power of their own and make us reverse a decision if an expense is transferred from one account to another. If we go to pick up a theatre ticket costing £5 and on our way lose a five pound note, this will not stop us from going, but if we have bought the ticket and then lose it, we might not want to buy another one.[54] In such cases no drive is involved, only rigid cognitive processing.

---

[53] See Elster (1979), Ch. I.3, for the argument that the ability to wait and to use indirect strategies (one step backward, two steps forward) requires consciousness and thus cannot be imputed to the unconscious.

[54] Tversky and Kahneman (1981); see also Tversky (1982).

Wishful thinking is the shaping of beliefs by wants, making us think that the world in fact is how we want it to be. A desire, say, for promotion may bring about a belief that promotion is imminent. Like adaptive preference formation, this is a 'hot' rather than a 'cold' process, but unlike that phenomenon the end result is a belief rather than a desire. Since the causes are so similar we might expect the phenomena sometimes to be substitutes for each other, and this is indeed what we shall find in Ch. III and Ch. IV below.

Inferential error is the cold way to irrational beliefs. The varieties of such errors have recently been surveyed by Richard Nisbett and Lee Ross, who conclude that the 'intuitive scientist' – i.e. each of us in our everyday life – is prone to a depressingly large number of unfounded judgments and inferences stemming from defects in the cognitive apparatus. Such mistakes are like framing shifts in preference with respect to the causal mechanism, and like wishful thinking with respect to the effect. A typical example could be that 'an individual judged *very* likely to be a Republican but rather *unlikely* to be a lawyer, would be judged *moderately* likely to be a Republican lawyer',[55] as if the probabilities were additive rather than multiplicative. Here the belief is not even rational in the thin sense. In many other cases, however, what is affected is judgment rather than consistency.

I.4 COLLECTIVE RATIONALITY: THE THIN THEORY

The very notion of 'collective rationality' might appear to be suspect, or, if not, trivial. It would be suspect if it involved an appeal to the collectivity over and above the individuals who make it up, an appeal that would justify the 'people' (i.e. the individual persons) having to sacrifice their interest for the sake of the 'people' (i.e. the mythical collective entity). On the other hand the notion would be quite trivial if it simply involved the collectivity in its decision-making capacity, or – alternatively – referred distributively to the rationality of the individuals who make it up.

To show that there is indeed room for a non-suspect and non-trivial theory of collective rationality, I shall first draw attention to a feature sometimes found in individually irrational behaviour. This is the phenomenon of *improving oneself to death*, or ruining oneself by a series of

---

[55] Nisbett and Ross (1980), p. 146.

stepwise improvements. It is difficult not to conclude that such behaviour is irrational. If, therefore, we can find analogues at the collective level, this might persuade us to speak of collective irrationality and, correlatively, of collective rationality.

I shall give two examples of such behaviour at the level of the individual. The first is that of intransitive preferences, i.e. preferring a to b, b to c and c to a. What, someone might ask, is so bad about this? Well, we might try to answer him, the fact that a person has such preferences shows that he doesn't know his own mind. But, the objector might persist, what's so bad about *that?* We might then come up with the ingenious answer suggested by Howard Raiffa,[56] that a person with such preferences might be led to bleed himself to death through a series of voluntary choices. For since he prefers a to b, he must be willing to pay some amount of money, perhaps very small, to exchange b for a;[57] likewise, to pay some money to exchange a for c; and a further amount to exchange c for b. By the end of this process he is left with b as in the beginning, but short of some money. By repetition of this process the individual could in fact improve himself to economic ruin.[58] A second example is adapted from C. C. von Weizsäcker.[59] Imagine a person who regularly (although non-consciously) adjusts his preferences so as to prefer more strongly the commodity of which he currently has less. Assume, moreover, that he is exposed to the following sequence of two-commodity bundles: $(1/2, 3/2)$, $(3/4, 1/2)$, $(1/4, 3/4)$, $(3/8, 1/4)$ ... Then, if at a given time he is consuming bundle n in the sequence and for the next period is offered the choice between bundle n and bundle $n + 1$, he will always choose the latter, since it offers more of the commodity of which he currently has less. But since the sequence converges to zero, these stepwise improvements pave the road to ruin.

A collective analogue is the following. One hundred peasants all own land adjacent to a river. On each plot there are some trees and some land for cultivation. As the peasant families get larger, they decide to cut down the trees to get more land for cultivation. When the trees are cut, the roots lose their grip on the subsoil and land is lost to the river through erosion – not only the land on which the trees used to grow, but

---

[56] Raiffa (1968), p. 78.
[57] Assuming continuity of preferences: there is no trade-off if money is lexicographically preferred to all the options over which the cyclical preferences are defined.
[58] Assuming that the sums of money given up do not add up to a smaller sum than the initial endowment of the individual.
[59] Von Weizsäcker (1971).

also some of the land previously used for cultivation. A necessary condition, however, for erosion to occur on any individual plot is that the trees are cut down on all adjacent plots. No single family, that is, can harm itself by cutting down the trees on its own land, provided that the neighbours do not follow suit. Thus if all families cut down their trees in order to get more land, they will all get less – an interpersonal analogy to the intertemporal irrationality discussed above.[60] The actions are individually rational in the thin sense, given the belief that no other families will undertake similar actions, and they may even be so if it is foreseen that others will in fact behave similarly.

To bring this out more clearly, I shall complete (and in one case change) the story in three different ways, corresponding to three different relations between belief and behaviour. In *the first version* I assume that trees being cut down on all adjacent plots is a necessary *and sufficient* condition for erosion on the individual plot. I assume, moreover, that if erosion occurs, any trees left on the plot will be lost to the river; finally I stipulate that the trees can provide wood for some useful purpose. It is then clear that each family will have an incentive to cut its trees, whatever (it believes that) the other families will do, for if the neighbours do not all cut their trees, the family can do so and get more land for cultivation, and if they do, it should cut its losses and at least get the wood. In this case the belief regarding the behaviour of others is irrelevant. If the peasant began thinking about it, he would realize that they will indeed cut their trees, but he has no need to arrive at any belief concerning them before making his own decision. As a game – it is, in fact, a Prisoner's Dilemma[61] – the situation is trivial, since the solution is made up of dominant strategies.

In *the second version* I assume that erosion will occur on the individual plot if and only if the trees are cut down on the adjacent plots *and* on the plot itself. Then if (it is believed that) the neighbours will cut down their trees, the family has an incentive not to do so and avoid the erosion. If, however, (it is believed that) some of the neighbours will not cut down their trees, the family has an incentive to do so in order to acquire more land for cultivation. This game – referred to as 'Chicken'[62]

---

[60] As argued by Derek Parfit (1973 and unpublished work) the analogy from intrapersonal (intertemporal) to interpersonal relations is in many respects close and compelling. One of the uses to which the analogy may be put is to make us accept the notion of collective irrationality and, correlatively, that of collective rationality.

[61] For surveys see Rapoport and Chammah (1965) or M. Taylor (1976).

[62] For a survey see Taylor and Ward (1982).

– is not only not trivial, but rather perverse, since it is in the interest of everybody to behave differently from their neighbours. On the one hand the belief of the individual concerning the behaviour of others is crucial for his own decision, but on the other hand there is no rational way he can form an expectation about what they will do. We are dealing with a game without a solution.

In *the third version* I change the original story and assume that the peasants have experienced erosion and want to stop it by planting new trees. For erosion to be stopped on any given plot, it is necessary and sufficient that trees be planted on that plot and on all adjacent plots; if the neighbours do not follow suit, any trees that are planted will be lost to the river. The non-trivial solution to this game – an Assurance Game[63] – is that all families plant trees, since when all do this no one has an incentive to do otherwise and it is better for all when all do it than when no one does it. On the other hand they will do so only if they believe that the others will do so too, since there are penalties associated with going it alone. In this case the formation of a belief concerning the behaviour of others is crucial (unlike the first version), and (unlike the second version) one can arrive at the belief knowing only that others are as rational and well-informed as oneself.

The first version provides a case in which individually rational actions lead to collectively disastrous results, whether the individual beliefs are rational or not. The second version is undetermined: collective disaster may or may not ensue, depending on the (necessarily non-rational) beliefs that the agents entertain about each other. In the third version the disaster will be avoided if the agents have the information (about one another's preferences, rationality and information) that make the belief in cooperation a rational one.

Given this background, we may define two notions of collective rationality. The *economic notion of collective rationality* implies that people, by individually rational actions, bring about an outcome that is good for all, or at least not bad for all. Failure of such collective rationality may occur in one of the three ways just described: by isolation, by perverse interaction structures, and by lack of information. Elsewhere I have referred to such failures as 'social contradictions'.[64] The *political notion of collective rationality* implies that people by concerted action are able to overcome these contradictions. For example, a central theorem

[63] For surveys see Sen (1967, 1974).   [64] Elster (1978a), Ch. 5.

of welfare economics says that in the absence of externalities the market system is collectively rational in the economic sense.[65] Since, however, externalities are in fact all-pervasive, the State appears as a collectively rational political solution.[66] To be sure, we may require much more of a political system than collective rationality in the sense of avoiding outcomes that are worse for all than some other, attainable, outcome, but this would at least appear a minimal demand to make on such a system.

In the preceding discussion I have made two vast simplifications, by assuming that there are just two options for each agent and that the agents are identically placed and motivated. In the general case, of course, social interaction involves agents with different opportunities and preferences, confronting a large number of alternatives. It is clear that these complications increase the scope for collective irrationality in the economic sense, and the need for rational political institutions to overcome it.

Social choice theory is a useful tool for stating the problem of how to arrive at socially optimal outcomes on the basis of given individual preferences. In very broad outline, the structure of the theory is as follows.[67] (1) We begin with a *given* set of agents, so that the issue of the normative justification of boundaries does not arise. (2) We assume that the agents confront a *given* set of alternatives, so that for instance the issue of agenda manipulation does not arise. (3) The agents are supposed to be endowed with preferences that are also *given*, and assumed to be independent of the set of alternatives. The last clause means that we can ignore the problem of adaptive preferences and similar problems. (4) In the standard version – and the only operational version so far – preferences are assumed to be purely ordinal, so that it is not possible to express intensity of preferences or to compare them across individuals. (5) The preferences are, finally, assumed to be rational in the thin sense.

Given the above, we want to arrive at a social preference ordering of the alternatives, satisfying the following criteria. (6) The ordering

---

[65] This holds, however, only in the weak sense that there exists a Pareto-optimal market equilibrium from which the agents have no incentive to deviate once it is (somehow) attained. But there is in general no certainty that out-of-equilibrium trading will bring about this optimum, yet this property is what we would really require of a collectively rational system. Weintraub (1979) offers a good introduction to this set of problems.

[66] Baumol (1965) remains a good statement of this view.

[67] For more precise statements the reader should consult Arrow (1963), Sen (1970) or Kelly (1978).

should be complete and transitive. (7) It should be collectively rational, in the sense of never having one option socially preferred to another which is individually preferred by all. (8) The social preference ordering should in some sense respect the individual preferences. The last idea covers a variety of notions, such as *anonymity* (all individuals should count equally), *non-dictatorship* (*a fortiori* no single individual should dictate the social choice), *liberalism* (all individuals should have a private domain within which they are dictators) and *strategy-proofness* (it should not pay to express false preferences). (9) The social choice between two given options should depend only on how the individuals rank these two options, and thus not be sensitive to changes in how they rank other options. This is the condition of *independence of irrelevant alternatives*, violated, for instance, if individual preferences vary with the set of alternatives.

The substance of the theory is given in a series of impossibility and uniqueness theorems, stating that a given subset of these conditions either are incapable of simultaneous satisfaction or uniquely describe a specific method for aggregating preferences. Social choice theory raises a large number of problems – some of them difficulties discovered by the theory, others that are rather objections to it. To some extent the difficulties also point to objections, since the various impossibility theorems of the theory also provide reasons for thinking that something must be wrong with the whole framework. I shall not discuss all the impossibility theorems, since some of them do not appear to go to the heart of the matter. Arrow's theorem, in particular, stems from the purely ordinal way in which the preferences are expressed. With more information about the preferences this paradox need not arise.[68] More fundamental, it appears to me, is the fact that the expressed preferences – be they ordinal or cardinal – are a very fragile foundation for a theory of the common good, for the two reasons I shall now indicate. (The further problem that the individual preferences are only required to be rational in the thin sense I postpone to the next section.)

In actual fact, preferences are never 'given' in the sense of being directly observable. If they are to serve as inputs to the social choice process, they must be *expressed* by the individuals. The expression of preferences is an action, which presumably is guided by these very

---

[68] For the role of information about preferences, see d'Aspremont and Gevers (1977) and Sen (1979).

same preferences.[69] It is then far from obvious that the individually rational action is to express these preferences as they are. Some ways of aggregating preferences are such that it may pay the individual to express false preferences, i.e. such that the outcome will be better according to his real preferences if he does not express them truthfully. The condition of strategy-proofness for social choice mechanisms was designed to exclude this possibility. It turns out, however, that the systems in which honesty always pays are strongly unattractive in other respects.[70] We then have to face the possibility that even if we require that the social preferences be collectively rational (or Pareto-optimal, in the language of the theory) with respect to the expressed preferences, they might not be so with respect to the real preferences. Strategy-proofness and collective rationality stand and fall together; and since it appears that the first has to fall, then so must the second. It becomes very difficult indeed to defend the idea that the outcome of the social choice mechanism somehow represents the common good if there is a chance that everybody might prefer some other outcome.

Amos Tversky has pointed to another reason why choices – or expressed preferences – cannot be assumed to represent real preferences in all cases.[71] When a person makes a choice, he may later be held responsible for it, by himself or by other persons. In particular, he may come to regret risky decisions that *ex ante* were perfectly rational, if *ex post* they turn out to go wrong. Anticipating this regret, the person may choose a bet with a smaller expected value if the uncertainty is thereby reduced or eliminated. The expressed preferences then, in Serge Kolm's phrase, become possibility-dependent.[72] This, of course, violates the condition of the independence

---

[69] Presumably, but not obviously, since the agent might have several preference structures and rely on higher-order preferences to determine which of the first-order preferences to express, as suggested by Sen (1976).

[70] Pattanaik (1978) offers a survey of the known results. Basically they say that the only strategy-proof mechanisms for social choice are the dictatorial one (the dictator has no incentive to misrepresent his preferences) and the randomizing one of letting the probability that a given option will be chosen equal the proportion of voters who have it as their first choice.

[71] Tversky (1981).

[72] If for convenience we speak of utility functions instead of preferences, the notion of possibility-dependence can be understood in two ways. First, the utility function (defined with single options as arguments) may vary systematically with the feasible set. Secondly, that set may itself be an argument of the utility function, together with the actual option chosen within it. Mathematically the two interpretations are equivalent, but substantively they differ. The first suggests that the presence of irrelevant alternatives can make a difference for the utility derived from a given alternative, whereas the second implies that there is utility attached to

of irrelevant alternatives – not with respect to the real preferences, but with respect to the preferences people choose to express, which are the only ones to which we have access. In Ch. III it is argued at some length that in an important class of cases the real preferences may also depend on the feasible set – yet another reason for being sceptical about the normative power of social choice theory.

I.5 COLLECTIVE RATIONALITY: THE BROAD THEORY

The thin theory of collective rationality rests upon the thin theory of individual rationality, in that the individual preferences that serve as inputs to the social choice are only required to have the formal consistency properties spelled out in I.2. I now want to consider the objection that politics thus conceived might be a case of 'Garbage in, garbage out', if individual preferences lack substantive rationality.

Within social choice theory and related approaches,[73] collective rationality is seen as a question of coordinating or aggregating individual preferences, of preventing the individuals from tripping over one another's feet or from dumping their junk into one another's backyards. The substantive rationality of the agents is never made into an issue, nor is the morality of their preferences. No doubt there are strong reasons for not doing so. Social choice theory rests on the assumption of the citizen's sovereignty, much as welfare economics rests on that of the consumer's sovereignty. The state is only the state of the citizens. They may well have preferences that a moral philosopher might regard as selfish, spiteful, destructive, conformist or ephemeral, but it would be unwarranted censorship on his part if he tried to limit their expression. Nobody, the argument goes, knows better than the individuals what is good for them, and what is good for them is expressed in their preferences. The only task of the State, therefore, is to create a mechanism that allows the individuals to express their preferences over the whole range of social arrangements, and not only

these alternatives themselves. In Tversky (1981) it is suggested that this utility could be negative, because people shy away from responsibility. In other cases it might be positive, because people value freedom (III.3).

[73] Among the latter one may cite the 'public choice' theorists (stemming from Buchanan and Tullock 1962) who make unanimity a condition for political decisions. They argue for unanimity on the libertarian grounds that anything short of it will violate the rights of the minority, unlike the consensus theorists (see below) who believe that unanimity will emerge by rational discussion.

over the set of options that are within his private sphere of action. This mechanism may work more or less well. The problems mentioned towards the end of the last section might conceivably thwart the attempt to realize collective rationality. Yet no other arrangement for taking social decisions can be justified. In particular one would never be justified in not taking account of preferences of specific persons, or not taking account of preferences of a specific kind.

In many contexts these arguments are indeed telling, but I do not believe them to be fully conclusive. They rest on two implicit assumptions: that the only alternative to the aggregation of preferences is the censoring of preferences, and that censoring of preferences always is objectionable. Both assumptions can be challenged, the first on the ground that the political system could be geared to the task of changing preferences rather than aggregating them, and the second on the ground that self-censoring might not be objectionable in the same way as paternalist censoring would be. Before I elaborate, let me give notice that I shall not in the following pay much attention to the difference between morality and rationality in the broad sense. No doubt consistency would require me to treat separately the ability of political systems to foster or otherwise favour broadly rational preferences and the corresponding ability with respect to ethical preferences, but I am not able to breathe life into this distinction.

I shall not say much about self-censorship as a way of filtering or 'laundering' preferences.[74] In principle, the individual or the collectivity might decide that in the future certain kinds of preferences are not to count as inputs to the social choice process, but there are several objections to putting this into practice. For one thing, it would often be needlessly complicated. If one wanted, for instance, to exclude sadistic preferences, it would be much simpler to exclude the top-ranked alternative of the sadist from the feasible set. Similarly, one might want to exclude 'nosey' or interfering preferences, but again this could be done more simply by withdrawing certain choices from the social choice process and leaving them instead in the hands of the individuals concerned.[75] There may be some cases in which one might want to filter the preferences themselves – where the choice is a properly political one and the top-ranked alternative not in itself objectionable – but these

---

[74] For a fuller discussion, see Goodin 1986.
[75] As suggested by Sen (1976) – see also note 69 above.

probably are neither numerous nor very important.[76] In any case the proposal flounders on the general difficulty of knowing when an individual or a community should be allowed to precommit itself in such a way that a later change of mind is made impossible.[77]

Much more important – in theory and for practice – is the idea that the central concern of politics should be the *transformation of preferences* rather than their aggregation. On this view the core of the political process is the public and rational discussion about the common good, not the isolated act of voting according to private preferences. The goal of politics should be unanimous and rational consensus, not an optimal compromise between irreducibly opposed interests. The forum is not to be contaminated by the principles that regulate the market, nor should communication be confused with bargaining. From these contrasts it is easy to identify the writers I have in mind. They include Rousseau and Hegel, Hannah Arendt and Jürgen Habermas – writers that differ strongly in many respects, yet agree on the need for purging the private, selfish or idiosyncratic preferences in open and public debate. In the following I shall first reconstruct a theory of collective rationality in the broad sense from the writings of these and other authors, and then sketch some objections to it. The latter are not mainly to be understood as arguments against the theory understood in an ideal sense, that of Rawls's 'full compliance theory'.[78] Rather I intend to point to some practical obstacles that are likely to arise in the process of getting from here to there. Some of the objections, however, may go somewhat deeper. Yet I should state explicitly that the theory is one with which I largely identify myself, and that my playing the Devil's Advocate is intended as a step towards fortifying it rather than demolishing it.

There would appear to be two main premises underlying the theory, at least in the versions by which I am mainly inspired.[79] The first is that there are certain arguments that simply cannot be stated publicly in a political setting. In political discussion it is pragmatically impossible to assert that a given solution be chosen simply because it favours oneself or the group to which one belongs. By the very act of engaging in public

---

[76] If, for instance, someone prefers a state in which he earns little and everybody else very little over one in which everybody has moderately large incomes, then we might suspect but not know for sure that his preferences were due to spite. But the suspicion would harden into certainty if we observed that he also preferred the first state to one in which everybody earned very little, for then we could hardly impute his preference to a desire for the ascetic life.

[77] See Schelling (1980, 1982) for discussions of this issue.

[78] See Rawls (1971), pp. 245ff., for this notion.

[79] Habermas (1982) is a very useful statement of the 'ethics of discourse'.

debate – by choosing to argue rather than to bargain – one has ruled out the possibility of such claims. Workers or women, for instance, cannot claim advantages simply by virtue of their status. They must argue that the status entitles them to advantages because of certain ethically relevant features that, if found in other groups as well, would entitle the members of the latter to similar benefits. To argue on grounds of entitlement, rather than simply negotiating from strength, logically implies the readiness to accept the claims of others that are similarly placed in the relevant respects.[80]

Now this argument shows only that in political debate one has to pay some lip-service to the common good. A second premise states that over time one will in fact come to be swayed by considerations about the common good. One cannot indefinitely praise the common good 'du bout des lèvres', for – as argued by Pascal in the context of the wager – one will end up having the preferences which initially one was faking. This, unlike the first, is a psychological rather than a conceptual premise. To explain why going through the motions should bring about the real thing, one might argue that people tend to bring what they mean into line with what they say, in order to reduce dissonance, but this is a dangerous argument to employ in the present context. Dissonance reduction does not tend to bring about autonomous preferences, as explained at some length in Ch. III below. Rather one would have to invoke the power of reason to break down prejudice and selfishness. By speaking in the voice of reason, one also exposes oneself to reason.

To sum up, then, the conceptual impossibility of expressing selfish arguments in public debate, and the psychological difficulty of expressing other-regarding preferences without coming to acquire them, jointly bring it about that public discussions lead to realization of the common good. The *volonté générale*, then, will not simply be the Pareto-optimal realization of given (or expressed) preferences,[81] but the emergence of preferences that are themselves shaped by concern for the common good. By rational discussion, for instance, one would be able to take account of the interests of future generations, whereas the Pareto-optimal realization of given preferences might well include a total disregard for later generations. Also, and crucially, one would

---

[80] Midgaard (1980) proposes a set of rules that are intended to be conceptually constitutive of any rational discussion.

[81] As suggested by Runciman and Sen (1965).

now be able to avoid the problem of strategy-proofness. By one stroke one would achieve more rational preferences and a guarantee that they would in fact be expressed.

I now want to sketch some objections – seven altogether – to the theory just set out. The *first objection* involves a reconsideration of the issue of paternalism. Would it not, in fact, be unwarranted interference to impose on the citizens the obligation to participate in political discussion? (It has even been argued that this could be a form of repression, as in a slogan from the German student movement: 'Diskussion ist Repression.' There certainly are contexts in which this is an appropriate slogan, but I shall nevertheless disregard it here.) Many would attempt to answer this objection by arguing that there is a link between the right to vote and the obligation to participate in discussion. To acquire the right to vote, one has to perform certain civic duties that go beyond pushing the voting button on the television set.

There appear to be two different ideas underlying this argument when it is put forward in debates about democratic institutions. First, only those should have the right to vote who are sufficiently *concerned* about politics to be willing to devote some of their resources – *time* in particular – to it. Secondly, one should try to favour *informed* preferences as inputs to the voting process. The first argument favours participation and discussion as a sign of interest, but does not give it an instrumental value in itself. It would do just as well, for the purpose of this argument, to demand that people should pay for the right to vote. The second argument favours discussion as a means to improvement: it will not only select the right people, but actually make them more qualified.

These arguments might have some validity in a near-ideal world, in which the concern for politics was evenly distributed across all relevant dimensions, but in the context of contemporary politics they seem to miss the point. The people who survive a high threshold for participation are disproportionately found in a privileged part of the population. At best this could lead to paternalism, at worst the high ideals of participation could create a self-elected activist elite who spend time on politics because they want power and not because they are concerned about the issues. As in other cases, discussed below, the best may be the enemy of the good. I am not saying that it is impossible to modify the ideal in a way that allows both for rational discussion and for low-profile participation, only that any institutional design must respect that there is a trade-off between the two.

My *second objection* is that even assuming unlimited time for discussion, unanimous and rational agreement would not necessarily ensue. Could there not be legitimate and unresolvable differences of opinion over the nature of the common good? Could there not even be a plurality of ultimate values?

I shall not discuss this question, since it is in any case preempted by my *third objection*. Since there are in fact always time constraints on discussions – often the stronger the more important the issues – unanimity will rarely be achieved. And for any constellation of preferences short of unanimity, one would need a social choice mechanism to aggregate them. One can discuss only for so long, and then one has to make a decision, even if strong differences of opinion should remain. This objection, then, goes to show that the transformation of preferences can never do more than supplement the aggregation of preferences, never replace it completely.

This much would no doubt be granted by most proponents of the theory. True, they would say, even if what Habermas calls 'the ideal speech situation' can never be fully realized, it will nevertheless improve the outcome of the political process if one goes some way towards it. The *fourth objection* questions the validity of this reply. In some cases a little discussion is a dangerous thing, worse in fact than no discussion at all, viz. if it makes some but not all persons align themselves on the common good. The following story well illustrates the problem:

Once upon a time two boys found a cake. One of them said, 'Splendid! I will eat the cake.' The other one said, 'No, that is not fair! We found the cake together, and we should share and share alike, half for you and half for me.' The first boy said, 'No, I should have the whole cake!' Along came an adult who said, 'Gentlemen, you shouldn't fight about this: you should *compromise*. Give him three quarters of the cake.'[82]

What creates the difficulty here is that the first boy's preferences are allowed to count twice in the social choice mechanism suggested by the adult: once in his expression of them and then again in the other boy's internalized ethic of sharing. And one can argue that the outcome is socially inferior to what would have emerged had they both stuck to their selfish preferences. When Adam Smith wrote that he had never

---

[82] Smullyan (1980), p. 56.

known much good done by those who affected to trade for the public good, he may only have had in mind the harm that can be done by *unilateral* attempts to act ethically and rationally. The categorical imperative itself may be badly served by people acting unilaterally on it.[83] Also, an inferior outcome may result if discussion brings about partial adherence to rationality in all participants, rather than full adherence in some and none in others, as in the case of the two boys. Serge Kolm has argued that economies with moderately altruistic agents tend to work less well than economies where either everybody is egoist or everybody is strongly altruist.[84] What is involved in all these cases is the problem of the second-best, referred to in I.3 above. The point is not that there may be no obligation to act morally in situations where nobody else does so,[85] but that the moral obligation in such cases may be quite different from what it would be on the assumption of universally moral behaviour.

A *fifth objection* is to question the implicit assumption that the body politic as a whole is better or wiser than the sum of its parts. Could it not rather be the case that people are made more, not less, selfish, or irrational by interacting politically? The cognitive analogy suggests that the broad rationality of beliefs may be positively as well as negatively affected by interaction. On the one hand there is what Irving Janis has called 'group-think', i.e. mutually reinforcing bias.[86] On the other hand there certainly is some truth in the idea that many can think better than one, since they can pool their opinions and supplement each other in various ways.[87] Similarly the broad rationality of desires and preferences could be enhanced as well as undermined by interaction. Neither of the following statements is true as a general view of the human condition, but each of them may have applications in specific instances:

[83] Pursuing note 50 above, let us assume that it ought to be the case that everybody acts in a certain way, but that as a matter of fact one knows that many people will not act in that way. Although I then have an unconditional obligation to act in that way, my conditional obligation – given the circumstances, including the fact that other people may misbehave – may be different. Unilateral disarmament could provide a dramatic instance in which action according to the categorical imperative would be unethical, by creating a power vacuum where other nations might rush in.

[84] Kolm (1981a, b).

[85] This is the point emphasized in Lyons (1965): if the grass will be harmed in any case by people other than myself walking on it, my obligation not to walk on it is suspended.

[86] Janis (1972).

[87] Lehrer (1978) has proposed a formal algorithm for such opinion pooling. Hogarth (1977) has a survey of similar methods.

In every human group there is less reason to guide and check impulses, less capacity for self-transcendence, less ability to comprehend the needs of others, and therefore more unrestrained egoism than the individuals who compose the group reveal in their personal relationship.[88]

American faith was not at all based on a semireligious faith in human nature, but on the contrary, on the possibility of checking human nature in its singularity, by virtue of human bonds and mutual promises. The hope for man in his singularity lay in the fact that not man but men inhabit the earth and form a world between them. It is human worldliness that will save men from the pitfalls of human nature.[89]

The first passage reminds one of the aristocratic disdain of the *mass,* which transforms individually decent people – to use a characteristically condescending phrase – into an unthinking horde. While rejecting this as a general argument, one should not go to the extreme represented by the second passage. The Greeks were well aware that they might be tempted by demagogues, and in fact took extensive precautions against this tendency.[90] The American town extolled by Hannah Arendt surely was not always the incarnation of collective freedom, since on occasion it could also serve as a springboard for witch hunts. The mere decision to engage in rational discussion does not ensure that the transactions will in fact be conducted rationally, since much depends on the exact structure and framework of the interaction. The random errors of private and selfish preferences may to some extent cancel each other, and thus be less to be feared than the massive and coordinated errors that arise through group-think. On the other hand it would be excessively stupid to rely on mutually compensating private vices to bring about public benefits in the typical case. I am not arguing against the need for public discussion, only for the need to take the question of institutional and constitutional design very seriously.

A *sixth objection* is that unanimity, were it to be realized, might easily be due to conformity rather than to rational agreement. I would in fact tend to have more confidence in the outcome of a democratic decision if there was a minority that voted against it than if it was unanimous. I am not here referring to people expressing the majority preference against their real one, since I am assuming a secret ballot to prevent this. I have in mind that people may change their real preferences, as a result of seeing which way the majority goes. Social psychology has amply shown the strength of such bandwagon effects.[91] It will not do to

---

[88] Reinhold Niebuhr, quoted after Goodin (forthcoming).   [89] Arendt (1973), p. 174.
[90] Finley (1973); see also the comments in Elster (1979), Ch. II.8.
[91] Asch (1956) is a classic study of this mechanism.

argue that the majority to which the conformist adapts his view is likely
to pass the test of rationality and autonomy even if his adherence to it
does not, since the majority could well be made up of conformists each
of whom would have broken out had there been a minority he could
have espoused.

   To bring the point home, consider the parallel case discussed in III.3
below. We are tempted to say that a man is free if he can get or do
whatever he wants to get or do. But then we are immediately faced with
the objection that perhaps he only wants what he can get, by some such
mechanism as 'sour grapes'. We may then add that other things being
equal the person is freer the more things he wants to do which he is not
free to do, because this shows that his wants in general are not shaped
by his feasible set. There is clearly an air of paradox over the statement
that a man's freedom is greater the more things he wants to do while not
being free to do them, but on reflection the paradox embodies a valid
argument. Similarly it is possible to dissolve the air of paradox attached
to the view that a collective decision is more trustworthy if it is less than
unanimous.

   My *seventh objection* amounts to a denial of the view that the need to
couch one's argument in terms of the common good will purge the
desires of all selfish elements. There are in general many different ways
of realizing the common good, if by that phrase we now simply mean
some arrangement that is Pareto-superior to uncoordinated individual
decisions. Each such arrangement will, in addition to promoting the
general interest, bring an extra premium to some specific group, which
will then have a strong interest in that particular arrangement.[92] The
group in this case may come to prefer the arrangement because of that
premium, although it will argue for it in terms of the common good.
Often the arrangement will be justified by a causal theory – an account,
say, of how the economy works – that shows it to be not only *a* way, but
the way to promote the general interest. The economic theories
underlying the early Reagan administration may well have been
shaped in this way. I am not imputing insincerity to the proponents of
such theories, but there may well be an element of wishful thinking.
Since social scientists disagree so strongly among themselves as to how
the world works, what could be more human than to pick on a theory
that uniquely justifies the arrangement from which one stands to

---

[92] For an interesting discussion of such predicaments, see Schotter (1981), pp. 26ff., 43ff.

profit? Politics frequently involves controversies over means, not only or even mainly about ends. The opposition between private interest and general interest in any case is too simplistic, since the private benefit may causally determine the way in which one conceives of the common good.

These objections have been concerned to bring out two main ideas. First, one cannot assume that one will get closer to the good society by acting as if one had already arrived. If, as suggested by Habermas, free and rational discussion will only be possible in a society where political and economic domination have been abolished, it is by no means obvious that abolition can be brought about by rational argumentation. Perhaps irony, eloquence and propaganda will be needed – assuming that the use of force to end domination would be self-defeating. Secondly, even in the good society the process of rational discussion could be fragile, and vulnerable to individual or collective self-deception. To make it stable there would be a need for structures – political institutions – that could easily reintroduce an element of domination. Accepting that politics should, if at all possible, embody the broad notion of collective rationality, we must yet investigate the extent to which it is possible.

II

STATES THAT ARE ESSENTIALLY BY-PRODUCTS

II.1 INTRODUCTION

Some mental and social states appear to have the property that they can only come about as the by-product of actions undertaken for other ends. They can never, that is, be brought about intelligently or intentionally, because the very attempt to do so precludes the state one is trying to bring about. In I.2 above I cited spontaneity as an example of such 'inaccessible' states. I shall refer to them as 'states that are essentially by-products'. There are, of course, many states that arise as by-products of individual action, but here I focus on the subset of states that can *only* come about in this way. Since some of these states are useful or desirable, it is often tempting to try to bring them about – even though the attempt is certain to fail. This is the *moral fallacy of by-products*. Moreover, whenever we observe that some such state is in fact present, it is tempting to explain it as the result of action designed to bring it about – even though it is rather a sign that no such action was undertaken. This is the *intellectual fallacy of by-products*. The present chapter is an exploration of these fallacies.

I first discuss the core case of an individual trying to bring about in himself a state that cannot be commanded in this way (II.2). I then have to confront an important objection: even granting the impossibility of bringing about these states just on the will's saying so, could there not be technologies allowing us to bring them about by indirect means (II.3)? I next discuss the self-defeating attempts to bring about such states in other persons, either by commands (II.4) or by non-verbal behaviour designed to impress (II.5). I then try to meet the corresponding objection, that one might be able to bring about the intended effect by faking the non-instrumental behaviour that will elicit it (II.6). A case of particular interest is that of the artist, who is

43

constantly tempted by the twin traps of bravura and narcissism (II.7). Similarly, an irrational political system may have the property that whatever the government tries to do intentionally is thwarted, and that whatever results it can take credit for were unintended (II.8). Another striking political phenomenon is the widespread tendency to erect into goals for political action effects that can only be by-products, such as self-respect, class-consciousness etc. (II.9). Finally I draw some general conclusions from these case studies, insisting on the dangers of the search for *meaning* in all social phenomena (II.10).

I shall briefly indicate some of the works and traditions that I draw upon in this chapter. Within psychology one important point of departure has been Leslie Farber, and his notion of 'willing what cannot be willed'; another was the work of Gregory Bateson, Paul Watzlawick and their associates, with their pioneering study of paradoxical commands. Within philosophy Zen Buddhism is perhaps the mode of thought closest to what I am saying here. I know next to nothing about this school of thought, but then I am not sure there is very much to be known in a theoretical way. In fact, the belief that there is a *doctrine* to be *known* appears to be a sign that one has not yet understood anything. (The misunderstanding, however, may be indispensable for ultimate understanding, as suggested below.) Whatever I may have absorbed of Buddhism in general and of Zen in particular derives from D. T. Suzuki, Raymond Smullyan and Serge Kolm. With regard to the study of society more broadly conceived, the following pages are greatly indebted to the work of Alexander Zinoviev on Soviet Russia and that of Paul Veyne on Classical Antiquity. To the former I owe, among other things, my understanding of the distinction between external and internal negation, between the absence of willing and the willing of absence – and of the concomitant fallacy that one can will the absence of willing. To the latter I owe my insight into the self-defeating nature of attempts to impress by generosity or conspicuous consumption.

II.2   WILLING WHAT CANNOT BE WILLED

A paradigmatic case of this fallacy can be documented in some detail from Stendhal's diary, which he kept from 1801 (when he was eighteen) to 1817.[1] His constant obsession is with the idea of *becoming natural*. This

[1] The following draws upon Elster (1982b).

involves, at the very least, not to give an impression that one is trying to make an impression. 'Nothing is so agreeable as those sallies that do not appear to require any wit in their author, that make us laugh without feeling obliged to give our admiration.'[2] Accordingly he formed the project to 'say whatever comes into my head, to say it simply and without pretension; to avoid striving for an effect in conversation'.[3] He did not find this an easy task, but fortified himself with the following remark: 'I shall be certain to succeed if only I learn to show my indifference.'[4] This idea, however, is contradictory in terms, since the intentional element involved in the desire to appear indifferent is incompatible with the lack of intentionality that characterizes indifference. A related inconsistency is embodied in the following remark, that would lose its crispness in translation: 'Pour être aimable, je n'ai qu'à vouloir ne pas le paraître.'[5] Surely, this is willing what cannot be willed. A true statement would have involved external rather than internal negation: 'Pour être aimable, je n'ai qu'à ne pas vouloir le paraître.' Observe that Stendhal is not trying to make an impression on others by faking qualities that he does not have. He wants to impress himself on them by being or becoming a certain kind of person – a person who could not care less about making an impression. Ultimately he found that he could never become this kind of person, since his attempts to be natural tended to overshoot or undershoot the mark,[6] and so he turned instead to fiction as a way of enacting his desire by proxy.

Sleep is another paradigm for the states that are essentially by-products. The attempt to overcome insomnia by sheer will is, like the desire to become natural, a paradigm for the irrational plans (I.2) that form the topic of this chapter. The phenomenology of insomnia is complex, but the following stages seem to correspond to a common pattern. First, one tries to will an empty mind, to blot out all preoccupying thoughts. The attempt, of course, is contradictory and doomed to fail, since it requires a concentration of mind that is incompatible with the absence of concentration one is trying to bring about. Secondly, upon understanding that this is not going to work, one tries to induce a state of pseudo-resignation to insomnia. One acts, that is, as if one were persuaded that sleep is going to elude one, by taking up

---

[2] Stendhal (1981), p. 124.   [3] *Ibid.* p. 117.
[4] *Ibid.* p. 837.   [5] *Ibid.* p. 896.
[6] *Ibid.* p. 197: 'In my fear of gallopping too fast, I apply the briddle too hard, which is bad.'

a book, having a snack or a drink, etc. But at the back of one's mind there is always the idea that one can cheat insomnia by ignoring it, and that the cheerful indifference to sleep will make sleep come at last. But then, thirdly, one understands that this is not going to work either. Next, real resignation sets in, based on a real, not a sham, conviction that the night will be long and bleak. And then, finally and mercifully, sleep comes. For veteran insomniacs, who know the game inside out, the last stage never arrives. They know too well the benefits of resignation to be able to achieve it.

Insomnia can be helped or cured in a variety of ways. One therapeutic technique is of particular interest in the present context.[7] The therapist tells the insomniac that the next night he must note very carefully, every five minutes, all the symptoms of insomnia, such as dizziness, headaches, a dry throat. This, the therapist says, is essential if he is to be able to come up with some suggestions for overcoming the insomnia. The patient, naively and obediently, does as instructed, and promptly falls asleep. Sleep has come, but as a by-product – and in this context it is essentially a by-product, since the effect would have been spoiled had the therapist told the patient about the point of the instructions.

The two cases have in common the feature that the object of the desire is a privative state – the absence of a specific form of consciousness such as attention to the impression one is making, or the absence of consciousness in general. Moreover, they share the feature that the means chosen to bring about this state is singularly ill-conceived, since it tends to posit and entrench the very object whose absence is desired. If I desire the absence of a dog, my desire will not by itself make it present. If I desire the absence of some specific thought, or of thought in general, the desire by itself suffices to ensure the presence of the object. The idea is well-known from many contexts, ranging from the nursery to the philosophical treatise. A trick that rarely fails to puzzle children is to tell them that here is a magic carpet that will take them anywhere they want – on the sole condition that while using it they shall never think the word 'humph'. Sartre invokes the same idea in order to refute the psychoanalytic theory of repression: how can one repress a thought unless it is also represented and indeed present to consciousness?[8] More generally, Alexander Zinoviev, drawing on his

---

[7] I am grateful to Sissel Reichelt for information about this technique.
[8] Sartre (1943), pp. 88ff.

training in many-valued logic and in dialectics, has used the distinction between external and internal negation to throw light on some tragi-burlesque aspects of Soviet society.[9] For instance, the dissident opposition positively desires to be persecuted, since persecution – *qua* internal negation – is also a form of recognition.[10] A book that strongly castigates decadent Western painting is immediately sold out, since one can hardly criticize the pictures without reproducing them.[11] The government is in a fix, since it cannot ignore the dissidents without appearing to admit they are right, nor come down hard on them without drawing attention to their views.[12]

The general idea is that one cannot bring about by internal negation a state characterized as one of external negation, any more than it is possible to create darkness with a flashlight. An instructive application is given by comparing two poems by Emily Dickenson, one that fails and one that succeeds in understanding that it is inherently impossible to will an empty mind:

> The Soul selects her own Society –
> Then – shuts the Door –
> To her divine Majority –
> Present no more –
>
> Unmoved – she notes the Chariots – pausing
> At her low Gate –
> Unmoved – an Emperor be kneeling
> Upon her Mat
>
> I've known her – from an ample nation –
> Choose One –
> Then – close the Valves of her attention
> Like Stone – [13]

The poem is not an attractive one, with its overtones of self-pity, self-aggrandizement and bad faith. The second stanza in particular approaches the ridiculous, bringing to mind a couplet from *I Can't Get Started*:

> When J. P. Morgan bows, I just nod –
> *Green Pastures* wanted me to play God

[9] Having written his doctoral dissertation on the method of Marx's *Capital*, Zinoviev turned to many-valued logic (see also for instance Zinoviev 1963). His work confirms my argument (Elster 1978a, Chs. 4–5) that dialectical logic, if it is to make any sense at all, must be expressed in the language of formal logic. See also Elster (1980a) for an interpretation of Zinoviev's satirical work as an extension of his logical studies.

[10] Zinoviev (1979), p. 745.

[11] Zinoviev (1978), p. 134.

[12] *Ibid.* p. 230.   [13] Dickinson (1970), no. 303.

In the third stanza we encounter the fallacy of willing the mental absence of a repulsive object. The metaphor of the valves of attention is misleading, since attention – unlike valves – cannot be shut off at will. In a poem written some twenty years later, this insight is communicated as effortlessly as in breathing:

> To be forgot by thee
> Surpasses Memory
> Of other minds
> The Heart cannot forget
> Unless it contemplates
> What it declines
> I was regarded then
> Raised from oblivion
> A single time
> To be remembered what –
> Worthy to be forgot
> Is my renown[14]

A natural reading of the poem is as an expression of humility, but I believe it also contains the germ of a lesson in vengeance. To paraphrase another poem about the paradoxes that are involved in willing an absence, Emily Dickinson here seems to be saying, 'If thou wilt forget me, take heed of forgetting me.'[15] The state of forgetfulness is essentially a by-product.

The impossibility of willing a mental absence is also emphasized in Buddhism, especially in Zen. The Zen doctrine of 'no-mind' is largely negative, with the stress on the pitfalls that lie ahead for those who want to *achieve* or attain the state of unconsciousness. The 'awakening in the Unconscious . . . is never to be taken for an attainment or for an accomplishment as the result of such strivings'.[16] Or again:

Emptiness constantly falls within our reach; it is always with us, and conditions all our knowledge, all our deeds, and is our life itself. It is only when we attempt to pick it up and hold it forth as something before our eyes that it eludes us, frustrates all our efforts and vanishes like vapour.[17]

The text can be read in the light of another Zen saying, 'Not knowing that one knows is best.'[18] Emptiness and unconsciousness mean only the state of relating directly to the world, *without relating also to the relating*. I see no need for understanding this as a Humean philosophical doctrine, to the effect that there is no enduring self, although this

[14] *Ibid.* no. 1560.
[15] Cp. John Donne, *The Prohibition*: 'If thou hate me, take heed of hating me.'
[16] Suzuki (1969), p. 65.   [17] *Ibid.* p. 60.
[18] Lao Tzu, quoted after Capra (1976), p. 27.

interpretation is quite common. It makes better sense as moral psychology, as an argument that the good things in life are spoiled by self-consciousness about them. It is tempting to believe that the goal of Zen is to achieve the state of non-relation to self, but on further reflection it is clear that this state is essentially a by-product. Nevertheless the belief cannot be wholly false, since Zen masters do accept pupils and train them. In the next section I discuss the indirect strategies that may be available to bring about the 'goal-less goal' of Zen.

I have discussed the self-defeating attempt to will the absence of a mental object. This phenomenon should be distinguished from two others, closely related, yet clearly different. First, by willing the absence of some extra-mental object, one may keep it artificially alive. Generally speaking, to desire the physical absence of someone or something is also to lend it a mental presence, *qua* object of the negating attitude. By wanting the non-existence of the object, one confers existence on it. This in itself is not paradoxical, since the existence created differs in mode from the existence denied. We approach a paradox, however, when the object has no other existence than what it achieves *qua* being refuted existence. Paul Veyne suggests that the cult of the Roman Emperor did not rest on a substantial belief in his divinity.[19] The subjects no doubt found it comforting to think that their rulers were somehow superior, since – in Tocqueville's phrase – 'nothing comes more natural to man than to recognize the superior wisdom of his oppressor'.[20] Yet in real emergencies they always addressed themselves to the traditional divinities; they believed in the Emperor much as small children can believe in Santa Claus and yet ask their parents about the price of the Christmas gifts. But even though the cult of the Emperor had no believers, it had some fanatical non-believers – the Christians. The Emperor's divinity was taken seriously only by those who denied it. Similarly, who in the Eastern bloc today takes Marxism-Leninism seriously except the dissident opposition? A doctrine or an idea can survive only if it has some kind of existence in somebody's mind, be it an existence *qua* denied only. It is definitely dead only when no one bothers to argue against it. Zinoviev suggests that in the Soviet Union the standards of rationality and humanity do not even have the recognition created by an active denial.

[19] Veyne (1976), p. 561.   [20] Tocqueville (1969), p. 436.

Evil has become banalized, an external negation of the good rather than an internal negation.[21]

Secondly, one may depend in one's being on the need to eliminate some object or person, and then find that as the project approaches completion, one must draw back in order not to destroy oneself together with the object on which one has come to depend. This is perhaps the most lasting insight of Hegel's *Phenomenology of Mind*: 'Desire and the self-certainty obtained in its gratification, are conditioned by the object, for self-certainty comes from superseding this other: in order that this supersession can take place, there must be this other.'[22] Or in Donne's phrase, 'Thou wilt lose the style of conqueror, if I, thy conquest, perish by thy hate.'[23] Familiar examples are the fanatical anti-communist or the militant atheist whose lives would lose their meaning should their effort be crowned by victory. This brand of anti-believers often are ex-believers, as also suggested by Hegel.[24] In fact, the anti-believer may be the only one to keep the belief alive, and in the struggle against his own past may only be affirming his identity over time.

To sum up so far: the absence of consciousness of something cannot be brought about by an act of consciousness, since this privative state is essentially a by-product. Yet not all states that are essentially by-products are privative. There are also positively defined states that similarly elude the mind that reaches out for them. Here is a list offered by Leslie Farber:

I can will knowledge, but not wisdom; going to bed, but not sleeping; eating, but not hunger; meekness, but not humility; scrupulosity, but not virtue; self-assertion or bravado, but not courage; lust, but not love; commiseration, but not sympathy; congratulations, but not admiration; religion, but not faith; reading, but not understanding.[25]

The case of lust, surely, is badly chosen, since nothing is as disastrous for sexual desire as the desire to experience it. The insomnia case described above can be restated identically in terms of sexual impotence. Also we may pass over the case of sleep, already discussed.

---

[21] 'The most able careerist is the one with the least talent as a careerist. The best asset is a complete absence of any qualities which are in any way remarkable' (Zinoviev 1979, p. 398).

[22] Hegel (1977), p. 109.   [23] See note 15 above.

[24] Hegel (1977), pp. 55ff., is a general statement to the effect that the Spirit in its Odyssey constantly confronts its own past confrontations. For particularly instructive examples, see *ibid.* pp. 221ff. and 229ff. Similarly psychologists of religion appear to take it for granted that apostasy never takes the form of mere agnosticism (Pruyser 1974, p. 248).

[25] Farber (1976), p. 7.

The remaining cases are all important. Many of them are states that are instrumentally useful, yet cannot be chosen for their instrumental utility. This holds, notably, for courage:

It is commonplace that behaviour which is not motivated by instrumental considerations may yet be instrumental in securing both the general interest and the individual's own interest. The Prussian soldiers who regarded themselves as merely on leave from death did not set out to serve their own interests, but they were on the average less likely to suffer casualties than soldiers less self-abnegating.[26]

You can cheat death, like insomnia, by ignoring it – on the condition that cheating is not the ulterior motive. Recall here the final shots from *Being There* with Peter Sellers, a film that epitomizes the notion of states that are essentially by-products. It is indeed by being there, not by doing anything in particular, that the protagonist soars to the highest positions. His success in politics is not due to his being good at politics, but to his not caring about politics. In the final scene he literally walks on the water, choosing with somnambulistic confidence the one underwater ridge that will carry him safely through, as a soldier can find his way through a minefield by sheer insouciance where he would be lost by a more cautious approach. The irony is that he succeeds because his new friends wrongly believe him to be beyond the self-doubt that devours them, whereas in fact he has never come that far; he is *cis* where they believe him to be *trans*. They believe him to have realized the desired synthesis of *en-soi* and *pour-soi*, whereas in fact he is sheer wooden *en-soi*.

Belief, like courage, can be instrumentally useful, and yet be out of reach for instrumental rationality. It is part of the notion of a belief that to believe something implies the belief that one holds the belief for a reason, and not merely because of the utility of holding that belief.[27] Beliefs are justified by their ancestors, not by their descendants.[28] As further discussed in IV.4 below, it may often be the case that a necessary condition for achieving a little is the mistaken belief that one will accomplish much, but this could not serve as a *reason* for having

[26] Ryan (1978), p. 35.
[27] Williams (1973), Elster (1979), Ch. II.3, and Winters (1979) offer various arguments to show that it is not possible to believe at will, in various senses of that phrase.
[28] This slogan is not very precise, and lends itself to different understandings. In another context (Elster 1979, p. 4) I did in fact suggest the opposite slogan, 'Ideas should be judged by their descendants, not by their ancestors.' The point is that when adopting a belief one can do so only because one has *grounds* for doing so. These grounds may include the *observational* consequences of the belief, when they are in fact observed – but not the consequences that would follow from the mere fact of the belief being held (with the exception of self-fulfilling beliefs).

excessive self-confidence. Bootstrap-pulling works only when one looks the other way. It is of course possible to fake a belief, if what is useful is other people's belief that one has it rather than the belief itself, but I do not think one can fool oneself in the same way.

The distinction between scrupulosity and virtue corresponds to that between rule-bound ethics and rule-transcending ethics. Ainslie notes that 'Theologians have long known of the dangers of "scrupulosity", the attempt to govern oneself entirely by rules . . . Loevinger put conscientiousness ("the internalization of rules") high in her sequence of ego development, but below an "autonomous" state characterized by "toleration for ambiguity".'[29] As parents know, one first has to teach children the importance of distributive justice, and then how unimportant it is compared to generosity and compassion. The first task is easy because it only involves going by the book, the second incomparably more difficult since the states in question are essentially by-products. Nor can one non-autonomously decide to become autonomous. The attempt, for instance, not always to do what one's parents are doing typically takes the form of always not doing what they are doing.

Some of Farber's other instances suggest the notion of 'states that cannot without ridicule be invoked in the first person singular'. It is sometimes said that to invoke dignity is to forfeit it; the same holds essentially for such states as romantic irony, humility or innocence. This is a major theme in Stendhal's writings throughout his life. He notes 'how great is the silliness of Voltaire, when he has a person saying: I feel such and such. It is as great as possible.'[30] Similarly one invites disbelief by saying: I remember that I felt such and such. 'It is very difficult to describe from memory what was *natural* in your behaviour; it is easier to evoke what was *artificial* or *affected* since the effort needed to put on an act also engraves it in memory.'[31] To Stendhal's general aversion against exposing his own feelings[32] there is added the doctrine that the important emotions in his life have not left any traces to expose.[33]

---

[29] Ainslie (1980).
[30] Stendhal (1981), p. 124. See also Stendhal (1970), p. 66.
[31] Stendhal (1981), p. 267.
[32] Stendhal (1950), p. 96: 'I feel like an honest woman prostituting herself. At every moment I need to overcome the delicacy of the honest man who abhors talking about himself.'
[33] See for instance Stendhal (1949), Chs. 13 and 47.

II.3   TECHNOLOGIES FOR SELF-MANAGEMENT

By now the reader may be bursting with frustration, muttering to himself that *of course* it is possible to bring about in oneself the purported by-product states, by choosing some indirect method or technology. One cannot will sleep, but one can will taking a sleeping pill and hence sleep, at one remove. One may not be able to will religious belief by a single mental act, but one may do as suggested by Pascal, go through the motions of acting as if one believes, counting on the imitation to bring about the real thing. It is true that one cannot will love, but one can nevertheless put oneself in the way of love, i.e. place oneself in the kind of situation where one is liable to fall in love.[34] If one cannot will happiness, one may at least make onself ready for it.[35] And of course there is the general Aristotelian argument that one may become virtuous by acting as if one already were so.[36] The states argued above to be essentially by-products are, or so the objection would go, simply those that take a bit more time and effort to bring about.

Before trying to answer the objection, I shall make two conceptual points that allow a fuller characterization of the states that are essentially by-products. The first point acknowledges one sense in which the objection is clearly correct. It is sometimes possible to realize a state that is essentially a by-product by action designed to bring it about, viz. if it comes about by fluke or a non-standard causal chain (I.2). Since the point is of some general importance, I shall briefly consider a range of examples, including attempts to bring about by-product states in other persons as well as in oneself.

The other day my eight year old son was instructing me to laugh. Now it is certainly possible to bring about a state of being amused in another person, e.g. by telling him a joke, but one cannot do so by commanding him to be amused, since the recipient of the instruction

[34] 'How, then, is it possible to describe love with words like rationality, which imply choice and calculation? . . . One cannot choose to fall in love with the person a computer might designate as the perfect match, but one can choose to put oneself in a circumstance in which love might occur, and might happen with people likely to be compatible. A person wishing to have the sort of life which comes only with marriage to a person one loves and who loves one back must usually put himself or herself in the way of love, even if one cannot choose one's emotions freely' (Heimer and Stinchcombe 1980, p. 700).

[35] Davidson (1980, p. 70) writes: 'Moralists from Aristotle to Mill have pointed out that trying to be happy is unlikely to produce happiness, and Schlick was so convinced of this that he revised hedonism to read, not "Do what you can to be happy", but "Be ready for happiness".'

[36] *The Nicomachean Ethics* 1103. See also Burnyeat (1980) for exposition and comments.

cannot decide to be amused. (This must be related to the fact that one cannot tickle oneself to laugh.) So I found the instruction ridiculous and laughable; in fact I laughed at it, and thus he achieved the result he desired, but non-standardly. Similarly one might conceive a person commanding one to admire him, and one might in fact admire him for the colossal effrontery of saying this.

For another example, consider the highly paradoxical goal of Buddhist character planning, to will the absence of will. The novice who sets out to achieve this goal is in principle doomed to fail, and yet the failure may be turned into success if his activities can be so constrained that the very process of searching for the goal also brings it about. (This is not the only way of overcoming the paradox. Another technique is discussed later in this section.) Serge Kolm has strikingly illuminated this method by La Fontaine's fable of the labourer and his children.[37] The children (presumably) were too lazy to earn a living by working in the fields, as their father wanted them to, so he told them instead that there was treasure buried in the ground. Eager to get rich in a hurry, they overturned the soil in an unsuccessful search for the treasure, and in doing so made it so fertile that they did indeed get rich – as a non-standard effect of actions undertaken for this end. Similarly the Zen masters appear to take advantage of the naive attempt of the novice to achieve by striving an outcome that is essentially a by-product.

Psychotherapy offers an analogy. How are we to reconcile the facts – or rather impressions – that (i) there is a great deal of successful therapy, (ii) therapists believe that a good theory is essential for success and (iii) very little of the variance in therapeutic success is explained by the therapist's choice of one theory rather than another? Often the theory tells the therapist to bring about some intermediate state (analogous to the buried treasure) as an indispensable stepping stone to the final goal of mental health (corresponding to wealth in the fable). In psychoanalysis, for instance, it is argued that the intermediate state of insight or 'Bewusstwerden' is required for the final goal of 'Ichwerden' to be realized. My suggestion is that in therapy the final goal is not in fact realized instrumentally through the intermediate state, but as a by-product of the attempt to bring about that state. Moreover, there may be several, different intermediate states that, if

[37] Kolm (1979), p. 550.

pursued seriously, can lead to this outcome. Crudely put: the therapist must believe in some theory for the therapeutic activity to seem worth while, and it will not be successful unless he thinks it worth while. Therapist and patient are accomplices in a mutually beneficial *folie à deux*.

An even more striking example is provided by the process of growing up. The adolescent wants to be an adult right away; in fact, adolescence may be characterized as one prolonged attempt to skip adolescence. These attempts, while necessarily unsuccessful, are yet fertile and in fact indispensable for bringing about adulthood. Premature attempts are among the causal conditions for maturity. Here we observe as a regular, not only accidental, phenomenon that a state which is essentially a by-product is brought about by the effort to bring it about, since the general constraints on the process are such as to make the result of striving for the goal coincide with the realization of that goal. Other processes with different constraints do not show this happy tendency for premature attempts to bring about maturity. In backward nations, for instance, the attempt to skip stages in economic development usually brings disaster.[38]

The second conceptual point concerns the distinction between what is intended and what is foreseen. By saying that an outcome of an action is a by-product, I do not imply that it must be unanticipated. It may be foreseen and also highly desirable, and yet only a by-product of an action undertaken for some other end. This would seem to go against a commonly accepted view, that if an effect of an action is both anticipated and desired, it must also be intended.[39] In legal contexts the distinction may not be worth making, since an agent must be assumed to have equal responsibility for intended effects and anticipated desired effects. But in everyday moral life I believe it to be quite important. One may coherently (i) want to be admired, (ii) believe that as a result of some currently performed action one will be admired, (iii) perform the action for some different purpose than to elicit admiration and indeed (iv) know that it is impossible to be admired for actions performed for the sake of eliciting admiration. If asked *why* one performed the action, one can then truthfully answer that one did so in

---

[38] I am referring here to the contemporary underdeveloped countries. For nineteenth century European development there is a sense in which one may talk about the 'advantages of backwardness' (Veblen 1915), since by skipping stages a nation may be able to assimilate the results achieved by others without going through the travail of development.

[39] Kenny (1970), p. 156, must be understood in this way.

order to achieve some specific end, such as 'getting it right' or 'beating the opposition', not in order to be admired.

These remarks enable me to give a fuller characterization of the states that are essentially by-products: they are states that cannot be brought about intelligently and intentionally. They may, as explained in the preceding paragraph, be brought about knowingly and intelligently, if the agent knows that as a result of his action the effect will come about in a certain way. They may also come about intentionally and non-intelligently, if the agent achieves by fluke what he set out to bring about.

I now turn to the objection stated above. I shall suggest a series of replies, of roughly increasing force. First, even if a certain state can be achieved by indirect means, it may still be a fallacy to believe it can be achieved at will. Moreoever, it can hardly be denied that people often try to achieve by one stroke and at will what can at most be realized at one or more removes. Many of the moral and intellectual strictures of the present chapter apply to these overly eager attempts, independently of the existence of indirect technologies. One way of meeting the objection, therefore, would simply be to redefine the notion of essential by-products to include only the states that resist being brought about at will, in the sense in which one can raise one's hand at will. I believe, however, that this would imply an unwanted loss of generality, and that there are some states that are recalcitrant even to indirect technologies.

Before I go on to argue for this view, I want to suggest a second reply. Even assuming the technical feasibility of bringing about the states in question by indirect means, there may be a cost-benefit problem that stops us from doing so. Not everything that is technically possible is also economically rational. The state in question may be desirable, but not so desirable that one wants to set up a complex causal machinery to bring it about. Furthermore, planning by such methods might in itself have undesirable side effects on one's character. If I plan for courage by an ingenious scheme for self-improvement, I might lose some of the easy-going spontaneity that I also value. Again I refer to Ainslie's notion that the attempt to overcome impulsiveness may bring about compulsive and rigid behaviour – and I might well want to avoid this effect. To be sure, these answers do not remove the objection, since they show only that it may not be rational to strive for the states in question, not that they are inherently out of reach for intentional action. Yet they do establish a thesis similar to my original one. Some states are such that a rational man would never try to bring them about deliberately, because it would be impossible to do so directly and too costly to do it indirectly. Yet they may be highly desirable, and easily within reach if he abstains from trying to bring them about.

My third reply is the most ambitious; it is also the one I feel least confident about. I shall argue that there are states that resist the indirect as well as the direct attempts to bring them about. Consider again the notion of willing the absence of will. Serge Kolm has argued that this may succeed even if one does not have a master to lead one by the nose, viz. if one employs will to phase out the will, taking care that one never requires more will for the next step than what is left after the preceding step.[40] But, as he also recognizes, there may be a problem here if the process does not have the right convergence properties. It might converge to some finite and strictly positive amount of will, or the convergence time might exceed the duration of a human life. In an earlier work I made a similar argument about a possible defect in Pascal's argument for the wager: 'in the gradual process of a growing belief and a dwindling reason, might there not come a point where the first is not yet strong enough to support the religious behaviour and the second no longer strong enough to to so?'[41] Similarly, when planning for spontaneity, might there not come a point when one is too spontaneous to carry on with the plan, and yet not spontaneous enough for the plan to have been fulfilled? Or again, even if it is possible to build up courage by using and reinvesting what little one has got, the series of gradual increments of courage might add up to a smaller total than desired. The common difficulty underlying all these problems may be called *the hammock problem*, after the following experience. Gently rocking myself to sleep in a hammock, I found that just when sleep was coming, my body became so relaxed that I could no longer sustain the rhythmic motion that led me to sleep, and so I woke up and had to start all over again.

Closely related to the hammock problem is the *problem of the self-eraser*. In some cases the technology will not be efficacious unless it includes a sub-technology for erasing from memory any traces it may have left. The decision to believe, for instance, will hardly have any impact unless the person can bring himself to forget that his belief is the

---

[40] Kolm (1979), pp. 551–2.   [41] Elster (1979), p. 49, note 29.

result of a decision to believe. The hammock problem in this case may be stated as one of achieving a properly synchronized self-erasing process, so that the technology is not wiped out before it has done its work. Clearly, planning for forgetfulness poses this problem in an acute form, and one may also try to imagine the contortions one would have to go through when planning for innocence.

Are there any states that inherently – for conceptual and not only for empirical reasons – give rise to the hammock problem and the problem of the self-eraser? I do not know. It may well turn out that these difficulties always turn on the value of certain variable personality parameters, so that states that are out of reach for some persons would be accessible by incremental methods for others. And even for the former, it might be possible to affect the parameter value by a process of higher-order character planning, i.e. of planning designed to make planning possible. Here, however, the second reply given above might well be decisive. The upshot of this discussion is, I believe, that for all practical purposes we may at least talk of states that are essentially by-products *for a given person*. I do not exclude that a stronger conclusion might be derived, but I do not see how to do so.

By looking at another set of cases, however, we may be able to give a more definite answer to the objection. The states just described are those that can be reached, if at all, only by incremental change. Other states can hardly be reached in this way, but only by a dramatic conversion. Emily Dickinson in a letter wonders about a friend, 'Is'nt [*sic*] it wonderful that in so many years Sarah has changed so little – not that she has stood still, but that she has made so peaceful progress.'[42] And the implied suggestion surely is that the ascent of the mind normally is not so peaceful, but rather passes through valleys of 'doubt and despair'.[43] This is the Hegelian theory of progress through the negation of the negation;[44] of self-estrangement as a condition for serenity – though not, of course, as the consciously chosen instrument

---

[42] Quoted after Sewall (1974), p. 372.   [43] Hegel (1977), p. 49.

[44] The more interesting instances of the negation of the negation adduced by Hegel, Marx and Engels are, I believe, of the following pattern. A sequence *p-q-r* of developmental stages counts as a case of the negation of the negation if (i) the stages are pairwise incompatible, which excludes cases of cumulative, organic growth; (ii) the direct step from *p* to *r* is impossible, which excludes cases in which the intermediate step is directly chosen to lessen the strain and (iii) the step from *q* to *p* is impossible, which excludes most physical processes. Thus defined, the principle of the negation of the negation is not open to the objection of Acton (1967) that 'it can be made to fit almost anything by carefully choosing what is to count as the negating terms', although it remains far less than a general 'dialectic law'.

to achieve serenity.[45] To invoke Hegel is not to suggest that the issue is clouded in obscurity. Tocqueville, the most lucid of writers, offers an analysis of belief formation along exactly the same lines:

A great man has said that *ignorance lies at both ends of knowledge.* Perhaps it would have been truer to say that deep conviction lies at the two ends, with doubt in the middle. In fact, one can distinguish three distinct and often successive stages of human understanding. A man may hold a firm belief which he has adopted without plumbing it. He doubts when objections strike him. Often he succeeds in resolving these doubts, and then he again begins to believe. This time he does not grasp the truth by chance or in the dark, but sees it face to face and is guided forward by its light . . . One may count on it that the majority of mankind will always stop short in one of [the first two] conditions: they will either believe without knowing or will not know precisely what to believe. But only a few persevering people will ever attain to that deliberate and self-justified type of conviction born of knowledge and springing up in the very midst of doubt.[46]

This suggests that the second, mature form of belief is essentially a by-product of learning and experience. I find it impossible to envisage someone inducing doubt in himself as part of a technology for attaining reflective belief, for someone who was that sophisticated would not hold the naive and dogmatic belief in the first place. If the solution is at hand, the problem does not exist.

Similarly, despair is instrumentally efficacious only if genuine, and can hardly be genuine if consciously chosen or induced. The characteristic quality of despair – the quality by virtue of which it is character forming – is that it is an intensely unpleasant experience, to be avoided or escaped at any cost, not to be chosen as part of a rational life plan. True, someone might try to rig the situation in the hope that despair will arise, with emotional growth and enhanced maturity as the further outcome. Despair, when contemplated at a distance, is less deterring than when actually experienced. Indeed, the deliberate cultivation of emotional crises in certain contemporary sub-cultures appears to rest on this philosophy. I have no formal proof that it could not work. Could not a person decide, say, to go to Calcutta in order to induce in himself a state of despair at the plight of the poor, so as to be

[45] 'And so Spirit has retreated in itself and against itself; it must overcome itself as the true hostile obstacle to itself; the development which in Nature is a peaceful emergence, is in Spirit the hard and infinite struggle with itself' (Hegel 1970, vol. 12, p. 76). So far, so good. Hegel goes on, however, with the following disastrous piece of nonsense: 'What the Spirit wants, is to achieve its own Concept; but it hides this from itself, and takes pride and enjoyment in this alienation from itself.' The first passage states that spiritual – as distinct from organic – development passes through a succession of crises; the second adds that the latter are somehow consciously chosen, in a feat of cosmic self-deception.

[46] Tocqueville (1969), pp. 186–7.

able to understand emotionally and not only intellectually his duty to humanity? My strong intuition, however, is that a person who was sufficiently self-centred to think in this way would also be immune to the impact of the experience. To seek for this solution is to show that the problem is insoluble.

II.4   Commands

I have mainly looked at cases of a person trying to induce in himself a state that turns out to resist deliberate induction. I now turn to cases of one person trying to set up in another a state that is essentially a by-product. In this section I consider the simplest case, that of trying to bring about by a command states that can only arise spontaneously. In the next section I take up the more complex case of self-defeating attempts to influence others by non-verbal means, or by verbal means other than commands.

The impossibility of inducing certain states by command is often related to that of creating intentionally the same states in oneself. The famous injunction 'Be spontaneous!' is pragmatically inconsistent for the very same reason that makes it contradictory to try to be spontaneous (I.2).[47] The injunction does in fact tell the person to whom it is addressed that he should try to be spontaneous. Consider also a parent telling his child, 'Remember that you must not even think about this forbidden thing.' The instruction is inconsistent because it tells the child to do something that it cannot conceivably do successfully, viz. trying not to think of something. In the case of the magic carpet cited above, the child will soon see through the instruction to avoid thinking 'humph', but in the present case the child may have such respect and fear for the parent that it will do its uttermost to fulfil the obligation, building up enormous guilt in the process.

Other cases of contradictory commands are more complex, in that they cannot in the same way be reduced to instances of willing what cannot be willed. Consider another famous injunction, 'Don't be so obedient.' This differs from the command to be spontaneous in that the state to be induced – that of non-obedience – contains an essential

---

[47] The study of these pathological commands is at the core of what is variously referred to as 'double-bind theory', 'communication therapy' and 'the Palo Alto school of psychiatry'. The originator of the approach was Gregory Bateson (1956); a recent statement is Watzlawick (1978). As will be clear from the present discussion, their work is largely an independent rediscovery of Hegelian and Sartrian insights, fleshed out with rich clinical evidence.

reference to the person trying to set it up. The order does not instruct the recipient to set up a state which it is inherently impossible to realize in a deliberate manner. On the contrary, the recipient might have decided on his own not to obey the order emitted by the other – but he cannot coherently obey the order to disobey. If, following the order to disobey, he disobeys some later order issued by the other, he is not really following the injunction – but nor would he have been had he obeyed the later order.

These examples suggest the following conceptual machinery. First, observe that the command to do p implies that the recipient is to do p intentionally. It is less clear whether the command to do p also implies that the intention to do p be subordinated to the intention to fulfil the command, i.e. whether it counts as conforming to the command if one does p intentionally, but for one's own pleasure. Four cases are to be distinguished. (1) One does p in order to fulfil the command, but would not have done p in the absence of the command. (2) One does p because one wanted to do so in any case, but would also have done so in the absence of any such desire. (3) One does p because one wanted to do so in any case, and would not have done so had one not so desired. (4) One does p because one wants to, and the want is caused by the command, but one does not do p in order to conform with the command. The first case is one of standard causation of behaviour by command, the last one of non-standard causation. The third case is one of standard autonomous causation, the second one of causal over-determination. In the discussion below I shall refer to cases (1) and (2) as *following* the command, and to cases (3) and (4) as *fulfilling* the command.

Next, let us refer to commands and intentions as propositional attitudes, together with wishes, denials, beliefs etc. A propositional attitude towards p can be contradictory for several reasons. (i) The proposition p may itself be a contradictory one. 'I wished that I lived in a society in which everybody earned more than the average income (in that society)' is a contradictory attitude because it entertains a contradictory proposition. By contrast, 'I wish that he would not even think about that forbidden thing' or 'I wish that he were less obedient' are not in any way contradictory attitudes. (ii) There may be a pragmatic contradiction between the attitude and the proposition towards which it is directed. Here I shall only consider two cases. (a) The intentional attitude is incompatible with states that are essentially by-products. (b) The command attitude is incompatible with states that must emerge autonomously within the person, if we believe that the essence of a command is that it should be followed, not merely fulfilled. (iii) There may be a pragmatic contradiction between the proposition and some attitude presupposed by the propositional attitude. This explains why it is inconsistent to command spontaneity: the command presupposes in the recipient an intentional attitude that is incompatible with the state to be brought about. Type (iii) inconsistency, therefore, reduces to the more basic type (iia).

Love is sometimes taken as an example of a state that is essentially a by-product, as in the passage by Leslie Farber quoted earlier. In that case the injunction 'Love me!' might be inconsistent for reasons of type (iii) or (iia): one cannot ask a person to do something that it is impossible to do intentionally. One could also argue, however, that falling in love is not like falling asleep, in spite of the verbal similarity. In love there may come a moment of choice, a decision to align oneself on the other person, in the expectation of the attitude being reciprocated. It is the moment corresponding to Donne's exhortation, 'True and false fears let us refrain' – the decision that henceforward hesitation no longer makes sense, even if there should be grounds for hesitating. Assuming this, does the injunction 'Love me!' make better sense? The answer may turn upon the distinction between following a command and fulfilling it. According to Sartre, the lover wants – incoherently – that the command shall be fulfilled autonomously as well as followed heteronomously:

The lover cannot be satisfied with that superior form of freedom which is a free and voluntary engagement. Who would be content with a love given as pure loyalty to a sworn oath? Who would be satisfied with the words, 'I love you because I have freely engaged myself to love you and because I do not wish to go back on my word'? Thus the lover demands a pledge, yet is irritated by a pledge. He wants to be loved by a freedom, but demands that this freedom as freedom shall no longer be free.[48]

What about following a command to love, taken by itself? I believe that although one may follow a command out of love, the love itself cannot be set up by command. Hence the desire that the other should love one by following a command to do so is irrational. According to Paul Veyne this desire was characteristic of the bad emperors or tyrants in Rome:

Let us first make a distinction to which the Ancients were very sensitive, that between the princes whom one adores and those who solicit adoration; the latter are tyrants who want to be loved on command. In one of Seneca's tragedies, a courtier of the tyrant asks

[48] Sartre (1943), p. 434.

his master: 'Do you not fear that public opinion could turn against you?' The tyrant replies that the most savoury privilege of royalty is to force the people to support him, nay, to praise the actions of the prince. A really powerful man is recognized by the fact that he can command eulogies; when a king can only afford to behave well, he has lost possession of his crown.[49]

In military life the distinction between following an order and fulfilling it, with the further subdivisions indicated above, is crucial. The classics of black humour – *The Good Soldier Schweik, Catch 22* and *The Yawning Heights* – exploit the pathological potential of this aspect of military life. Here is Zinoviev on the Soviet army:

> The patriot . . . informed them that he had been sentenced to ten days for requesting to be sent to the front, but that he could see no logic in this, since fifty cadets were being despatched to the front without having the slightest desire to go. Deviationist observed that this merely demonstrated the iron logic of the social laws, since, according to these laws, Patriot's destiny was at the whim of his superiors and not under his own control, and by putting in a request for transfer to the front, he had offended against the social laws by evincing a wish to control his own fate by his own will.[50]

In fact, this attitude pervades the whole of Soviet life, not just the army. In the Soviet Union emigration is, ambiguously, a crime as well as a punishment. You may be ordered to leave the country, on the condition that you do not entertain the forbidden desire to do so – a desire that would have been punishable by emigration had this not been against the 'iron logic of the social laws':

> I was forced to leave of my own free will at the will of a free people, with only one difference – that in the end I myself wanted to leave and so for two years I was prevented from doing so since my voluntary desire to fulfil the wishes and the will of the people was self-will. And a free people cannot allow that. They even want to fulfil their own will as regards me despite my own will.[51]

Implicit in such commands to do *p*, then, is also a command not to want to do *p*. This is to demand subvariety (1) of following a command. That is in itself a perversion of the notion of a command, which usually is an injunction to do something even if one does not want to, without the additional and senseless injunction that one should not want to. The point of a command is that it can be backed by (standard) causal efficacy if necessary, not that it *must* operate through causal efficacy. To require actual efficacy in all cases is to make the exercise of power more, not less, difficult. In a society based on the systematic confusion between external and internal negation, there occurs a further degradation of the notion of a command when the obligation that one

[49] Veyne (1976), p. 569.   [50] Zinoviev (1979), p. 64.   [51] *Ibid.* p. 541.

should not want to fulfil it is raised to an obligation that one should want not to fulfil it. In Zinoviev's wildly distorted and disturbingly accurate vision of Soviet life, the rulers prefer the subjects complying against their will to their voluntary or even indifferent compliance. To be sure, they cannot order the subjects to have or not have certain desires, but they can at least select among the available injunctions those which the subjects resist fulfilling.

These phenomena have a family resemblance to Joseph Heller's *Catch 22*: the desire to fly combat missions would prove you insane and constitute grounds for exemption, provided you make a request – but a request for exemption shows that you are sane and therefore eligible to fly. The pathology is less striking here, since the expression of the desire for exemption is only a sufficient, not also a necessary, condition for service. Yet the logic is sufficiently twisted for many to have dismissed *Catch 22* as a wild exaggeration, that does not even make sense as an overblown image of a real tendency. It is then intriguing to read the following report: 'A one-legged man seeking a state mobility allowance had to struggle up four flights of stairs to the room where a tribunal was to decide his claim. When he got there the tribunal ruled that he could not have the allowance because he had managed to make it up the stairs.'[52]

The ancestor of the paradoxical injunctions discussed by the Palo Alto school is Diaghilev's 'Etonne-moi!' Is there, in fact, any way of fulfilling or following this command? How can one surprise a person who expects to be surprised? Raymond Smullyan has brought out the logical problems involved, in a variant of the well-known 'examination paradox':

On April 1 1925 I was sick in bed with grippe, or flu, or something. In the morning my brother Emile (ten years my senior) came into my bedroom and said, 'Well, Raymond, today is April Fool's day, and I will fool you as you have never been fooled before!' Late that night my mother asked me, 'Why don't you go to sleep?' I replied, 'I'm waiting for Emile to fool me'. My mother turned to Emile and said, 'Emile, will you please fool the child'. Emile then turned to me, and the following dialogue ensued:
Emile: So, you expected me to fool you, didn't you?
Raymond: Yes.
Emile: But I didn't, did I?
Raymond: No.
Emile: But you expected me to, didn't you?
Raymond: Yes.
Emile: So I fooled you, didn't I?[53]

[52] *Observer*, 17 February 1980.   [53] Smullyan (1978), p. 3.

Let us change the story a bit, and assume that the younger boy had asked his older brother to fool him. Let us assume, moreover, that the abstention from (first-order) fooling was not a deliberate one on the part of Emile. In that case the (second-order) fooling would have been a fulfilment of the order, although not a following of it. Similarly, if Diaghilev's interlocutor had simply walked away from him, the conceited maestro would no doubt have been stunned – but he might not have seen this as following his injunction. It is as if someone told another person 'Be autonomous!', and was told in reply 'Fuck you!' Here the fulfilment would have been of subvariety (4), since the command in fact would have been causally efficacious in bringing about the fulfilment, as in the case of my boy who got me laughing by ordering me to laugh.

Again Smullyan has a story – 'a quintessential Zen incident' – which illuminates another aspect of the problem:

The story is of a Zen master who was delivering a sermon to some Zen monks outside his hut. Suddenly he went inside, locked the door, set the hut on fire, and called out, 'Unless someone says the right thing, I'm not coming out'. Everybody then desperately tried to say the right thing and, of course, failed. Along came a latecomer who wanted to know what all the fuss was about. One of the monks excitedly explained, 'The master has locked himself inside and set fire to the hut and unless somebody says the right thing, he won't come out!' Upon which the latecomer said: 'Oh my God'. At this the master came out.[54]

And Smullyan goes on to spell out the lesson of the story, which turns out to be about the occasionally self-defeating character of instrumental rationality:

Obviously, what the master wanted was a response which was wholly spontaneous. Any response which was 'designed' to persuade the master to come out would have *ipso facto* failed. When the latecomer said, 'Oh my God!' he was not trying to say the right thing; he did not say it with any idea that it would bring the master out; he was simply alarmed! Had anyone else said 'Oh my God' for the *purpose* of getting the master out, the master would probably have sensed it and accordingly would not have come out.

Here the command 'Say the right thing' is – at the very opposite from the pathological military cases – a command that is to be fulfilled and not to be followed. This might appear to be totally incoherent. It is as if one said, 'Do as I want, but not because I tell you to.' Yet one can make sense of the command in terms of the subvariety (4) distinguished above. One may utter a command in the expectation that it will induce by non-standard causal means an action that in fact fulfils it. The story

[54] Smullyan (1980), p. 95.

is indeed quintessential Zen, illustrating as it does the indirect technique employed by the labourer of La Fontaine's fable.

It is puzzling and thought-provoking that certain paradoxical instructions appear both on the road to wisdom and as the agency of madness. On the double-bind theory a person can be driven into schizophrenia by trying to satisfy impossible and contradictory demands, one important class of which are the pragmatically contradictory commands. The practice of Zen employs similar means, but for the purpose of liberating the person from the obsession with instrumental rationality and the habit of relating everything to the self. The command to be spontaneous, when issued by a nagging spouse, will get you into a fix; when issued by a Zen master it could get you out of one.

II.5   TRYING TO IMPRESS

It is fairly obvious that one cannot in general elicit mental states in another person through commands. Overt behaviour is responsive to orders, but not the intentions behind it. To produce a mental state in another person one usually has recourse to non-verbal behaviour, or to verbal behaviour other than commands. Here I shall look at the self-defeating desire to make an impression on other people. The general axiom in this domain is that nothing is so unimpressive as behaviour designed to impress. 'Man merkt die Absicht und wird verstimmt.' But more needs to be said on the topic.

Taking my cue from Paul Veyne, the effort of the artist to 'épater la bourgeoisie' is an attempt to bring about in others a state that is essentially a by-product.[55] The (moderately enlightened) bourgeoisie not only are not shocked, but are positively flattered by attempts to shock them, since they know that they are honoured in the breach. They sense that someone who deliberately sets out to shock the bourgeoisie is as intimately tied to them as those who try to imitate their way of life, and will fail as surely as the latter, though for different reasons. A real threat to the bourgeoisie would not come from the *enfants terribles*, most of whom come from their ranks and will return to them, but from those who could not care less about how the bourgeoisie perceive their life-style.

[55] Veyne (1976), p. 99.

Other cases are a bit more complex. Take the following characterization of A. J. P. Taylor by Bernard Crick: 'Taylor is an admirable writer: not merely does he not pause to look over his shoulder at what fellow scholars may think; he actually enjoys shocking them.'[56] At one reading this is inconsistent. After first imputing non-conformism to his hero, Crick goes on to describe him as an anti-conformist. However, as argued in I.3 above, the anti-conformist is only the negative slave of fashion, who constantly has to monitor the choices of the majority so as to be out of phase with them. The anti-conformist no less than the conformist must keep looking over his shoulder. But perhaps Crick only meant to say that when Taylor finds himself having minority views, he enjoys it. Or again we may draw on a distinction made in II.3 above, and argue that one may anticipate and welcome the fact of being in a minority, yet not be guided in one's behaviour by an anti-conformist intention (or drive). In any case I believe that George Orwell – of whom Crick is also the biographer – would be a better example of someone who genuinely did not write to please, to shock or to distinguish himself. This, indeed, was perceived as shocking, as the antics of Taylor are perhaps not.

The example of 'épater le bourgeois' is used by Veyne to introduce what is perhaps the major theme of *Le Pain et le Cirque*, the idea that the civic giving or 'evergetism' in Classical Antiquity was impressive only because and to the extent that it was not designed to impress:

> There is something paradoxical about expressive rationality and the way it is adapted to its end: it will not produce its effect if it is too rational. A person who delights in himself and his own greatness has little thought for the impression he makes on others and will not calculate it precisely. And this the others know: they know that an authentic expression is one that disregards the onlookers and does not measure its effects. The self-important who indulge in excessive calculation do not see the spectators smiling behind their back. The spectator does not believe in a calculated expression, since real greatness delights in itself only. Only the expression that does not seek to produce an impression succeeds in making one.[57]

The reason why the subjects in Classical Antiquity were prepared to accept their rulers as divine, or at least quasi-divine (II.2), is that the latter behaved with the narcissistic disregard for the impression they made on others that is the true mark of the gods. True, the rulers often served the city by their gifts, such as bread, circus, baths, monuments or aqueducts. Yet it would be a vulgar and invalid interpretation to seek the motive behind the gifts in their utility. The absence of

---

[56] *Sunday Times*, 9 November 1980.   [57] Veyne (1976), p. 679.

instrumental rationality in the gifts is epitomized in the Trajan column, the details of which can be seen only through strong binoculars.[58] The magnificent carvings were not intended to be of use or even of aesthetic value to anyone, unlike the loftily placed Gothic capitals intended for the eye of God. The uncalculated waste made the subjects respect the donor. No doubt this respect had its useful side, perhaps in preventing popular unrest that might otherwise have emerged, but this was not a motive behind the giving. Similarly for the gifts that did have explicitly utilitarian effects, such as the aqueducts.[59] Their excessive grandeur of conception and execution testified to the non-utilitarian motives of the donor. If they also – for that very reason – induced a (useful) state of admiration in the subjects, this was only and essentially a by-product.

I should add that the acts of rulers and donors were not irrational, in the sense of a failure of rationality. The history of the Soviet Union shows that the lack of rationality in this sense does not impress the subjects. The Roman emperors were non-rational, in that their behaviour was expressive rather than instrumental. They wanted to contemplate themselves in their works, to communicate with posterity, but cared little about the impression they made on the populace. Such at any rate is the account proposed by Veyne. I have no competence to assess it, except to say that it rings true. In any case I believe that his account of wasteful behaviour is superior to the standard sociological explanations, to which I shall now turn.

Veyne rightly takes Thorstein Veblen to task for his vulgar theory of the leisure class.[60] Veblen insists so much on the leisured gentleman's need to impress that he is led to impute to him all kinds of complicated motives that, transparently, only represent a backward deduction from the observed consequence that the spectators of the leisured classes are in fact impressed. For instance, Veblen argues,

the whole of the life of the gentleman of leisure is not spent before the eyes of the spectators who are to be impressed with that spectacle of honorific leisure which in the ideal scheme makes up life. For some part of the time his life is perforce withdrawn from the public eye, and of this portion which is spent in private the gentleman of leisure should, for the sake of his good name, be able to give a convincing account. He should find some means of putting in evidence the leisure that is not spent in the sight of the spectators.[61]

Veblen seems to believe that all rich behave like the *nouveaux riches*, whose attempts to impress are notoriously unsuccessful because they

[58] *Ibid.* p. 676.
[60] Veyne (1976), pp. 97ff.

[59] *Ibid.* p. 641; cp. also Finley (1965), p. 179.
[61] Veblen (1970), p. 46.

try too hard. Though knowing little of the life-style of the leisured classes, I can hardly believe that they are concerned to impress those who have to work for a living. Rather they seem to have difficulties even in understanding that such people exist; let them eat cake. Be this as it may, Veblen's sociology of wealth completely misses the important point stressed by Veyne – the thoroughly narcissistic attitude of the wealthy. The attitude is both incompatible with the intention to impress, and a condition for the ability to impress – at least if we use the term 'ability' in a somewhat wider sense than the usual one.[62]

The modern version of *The Theory of the Leisure Class* is Pierre Bourdieu's *La Distinction*. It has strengths and weaknesses broadly comparable to Veblen's work, memorable for its welter of phenomeno-logical insights, while badly flawed in its theoretical structure.[63] Bourdieu, however, is more sophisticated than Veblen. He knows, for instance, that in many cases the lack of instrumental calculation is a condition for instrumentally defined success.[64] He is also extremely sensitive to the nuances that distinguish the rich from the *nouveaux riches*, or the upper from the petty bourgeoisie. In both cases the former impress, the latter fail by trying. The petty bourgeoisie are 'imprisoned, whatever they do, in the dilemma of anxious over-identification and a negative attitude whose very revolt is an admission of defeat'.[65] They do not have the 'assurance dans l'ignorance'[66] which enables one to walk safely through the cultural minefield. They show 'un air de tension dans la détente même',[67] while the opposite no doubt is true for the upper crust of the bourgeoisie.

But these insights and nuances are not consistently respected. *La Distinction*, in my view, is ambivalent and ambiguous to an extent that at times approaches sheer muddle. The basic flaw of the argument is that the cultural behaviour of the various classes is explained twice over: once as a result of the (conscious or non-conscious) strategies of distinction, and then again as the result of the adaptation to necessity. The first is a strange amalgam of intentional and functional

---

[62] In the standard usage the term 'ability' has an intentional component that, by assumption, is absent in these cases. Generally speaking, ability implies that trying implies succeeding: if I am able to do x, and want to do x, then I do x. If so, one cannot be able to do x in the cases in which a condition for doing x is that one does not try to do x. Current discussions of these problems (e.g. Kenny 1975 and Davidson 1980, Ch. 4) do not seem to me to capture the sense in which we *can* do the things that we cannot do if we try to do them.

[63] See Elster (1981) for a fuller discussion of Bourdieu's work.

[64] Bourdieu (1979), p. 94.   [65] *Ibid.* p. 105.

[66] *Ibid.* p. 71.   [67] *Ibid.* p. 419.

explanation, the second a straightforward causal account. Even setting aside their internal problems, it is hard to see how they could be compatible with each other. Next, both accounts do indeed have serious internal difficulties. I shall deal here only with the first, reserving the second for later discussion (III.2). Bourdieu is too aware of the fact that a conscious strategy of distinction can be self-defeating to fall into the trap that ensnared Veblen,[68] yet he is unable to give a plausible account of what it means to adopt a non-conscious strategy. In one context he argues that violations of grammar can serve to exclude would-be intellectuals from higher culture, and then adds:

Such strategies – which may be perfectly unconscious, and thereby even more effective – are the ultimate riposte to the hypercorrection strategies of pretentious outsiders, who are thrown into self-doubt about the rule and the right way to conform to it, paralysed by a reflexiveness which is the opposite of ease, and left without a leg to stand on.[69]

It may well be true that the proneness of intellectuals to play around with language acts as a deterrent to those who think that culture is a question of following rules, but to conclude from this to an *explanation* of that proneness in terms of the deterrent effect is unwarranted. At the very least one would have to suggest a causal mechanism whereby this behaviour was maintained by these unintended and beneficial consequences.[70] Similarly, although it is true that the way of life of the bourgeoisie is such that it is difficult for an outsider to pass for an insider, and equally true that this fact may be useful for the bourgeoisie, it takes an uncritical or hypersuspicious mind to conclude that this is *why* the bourgeoisie behave as they do. Max Scheler writes in *Ressentiment* – with Veblen's work one of the main ancestors of *La Distinction* – that envy arises when 'our factual inability to acquire a good is wrongly interpreted as a positive action against our desire'.[71] Bourdieu is engaged in a theoretical analogue of this operation. He is concerned, to the point of being obsessed, with the obstacles met by pretenders, impostors, imitators and upstarts. Instead, however, of

---

[68] He does not, however, consistently avoid this fallacy. Thus on p. 273 of Bourdieu (1979) he argues that the 'genuinely intentional strategies . . . merely ensure full efficacy, by intentional reduplication, for the automatic unconscious effects of the dialectic of the rare and the common, the new and the dated, which is inscribed in the objective differentiation of class conditions and dispositions'. I believe this to be a mere lapse, however, from the view that a strategy, for being unconscious, is 'thereby even more effective'.

[69] Bourdieu (1979), p. 285.

[70] Van Parijs (1981), pp. 159ff., attempts to provide a mechanism through which 'distinguishing behaviour' can be explained by its consequences, yet too sketchily to carry convincing power. See also my comments in Elster (1982c).

[71] Scheler (1972), p. 52.

tracing these difficulties to the inherent problem that one cannot choose intentionally the attitudes that are essentially by-products, he finds their explanation in the non-conscious strategies adopted by the classes whose way of life is being faked or imitated. This, in my view, is to fall into the intellectual fallacy mentioned in the first paragraph of this chapter, and further discussed in II.10 below.

II.6   FAKING

The axiom that behaviour designed to impress invariably fails to impress is obviously vulnerable to the objection that one can induce the relevant states in others by *faking* the non-instrumental behaviour in question. Clearly, this is often the case. One may frequently be able to bring off the coup by carefully prepared insouciance, studied indifference, finely calculated generosity or thoughtfully planned spontaneity. Many ploys of seduction turn upon such strategies, sometimes compounded by disarming frankness about what one is doing. In Hamsun's novel *Mysteries* the protagonist Nagel first dazzles poor Dagny by his strange talk and behaviour, and then clinches it by telling her that it was all meant to dazzle. Surely, an avowal of lack of spontaneity must be spontaneous! Valmont, in *Les Liaisons Dangéreuses*, successfully fakes his way into the affections of the Présidente de Tourvel – while the seduction of Cécile de Volanges does not require more than a bit of blackmail. For another example of successful faking, suggested by Ernest Gellner (in discussion), we may take the Maghrebian 'big man' who keeps a watch on who is approaching his house so that he can receive the visitor with the appropriate amount of uncalculated generosity.

Innumerable examples of this kind could be cited. Still there are many cases in which faking is very difficult, perhaps even impossible, and may also be self-defeating. I shall discuss these three replies to the objection in this order. The reader should also keep in mind the more general replies suggested in II.3 above.

Some states are very hard to fake successfully. The detached observer can almost always tell the difference between studied indifference and genuine indifference. We are – no doubt for good evolutionary reasons – so sensitive to the eye movements of other people that we can detect very small nuances in their attitudes. Someone who just lets his eye roam over a room, coming haphazardly to rest on some persons while sliding over others, can easily be distinguished from the intentional indifference of someone who by his darting side glances betrays that he knows very well that there is someone there whom he does not want to notice. True, the deception may succeed if the senses of the intended victim are too blunted to perceive it, perhaps because the spectacle of an indifferent lover is so painful that one is unable to see that the indifference is deliberate and therefore really a form of attention. (And, conversely, one may ·be so misled by passion that one believes that the eye which came to rest on oneself accidentally did so deliberately.) Yet even though passion may be blind to faking, this is not to say that it can be elicited by it.

For a literary example consider Lucien Leuwen's love for Mme de Chasteller – one of the most touching and affectionately comical love affairs in world literature. The two lovers enact Stendhal's private philosophy of love, that 'It is only by loving less that one can have courage in love',[72] and that 'the vulgar soul is capable of calculating correctly the chances of success', whereas the tender soul, 'even with all possible wit never has the ease to say the simplest and most assuredly successful things'.[73] Hence they are both incapable of reaching out to one another, since to tell the other about one's love would be a sign of its vulgar quality. It is the very qualities in Lucien that inspire the love of Mme de Chasteller for him that prevent him from seeing and taking advantage of the obvious signs of love. At one stage in their tender and comic ballet she deigns to answer a letter from Lucien, deceiving herself into thinking that the haughty and severe tone justifies her writing at all. Lucien, to be sure, takes the letter at face value and is unable to see that the fact of writing is infinitely more revealing than what she actually says. Stendhal comments in a wry aside:

'Ah! Mme de Chasteller replies!' Such would have been the reaction of a young man from Paris more vulgarly brought up than Leuwen. 'In the greatness of her soul she has finally made a decision. The rest is a matter of form, that will take one or two months depending on my dexterity and on her more or less exaggerated notions about what ought to be the defence of a woman of the highest virtue.'[74]

The two lovers go on like this for a while, almost succeeding in telling each other about their love, yet never quite. At one point Mme de Chasteller scolds him for his frequent visits, which could damage her reputation:

[72] Stendhal (1965), Fragment 47.
[73] Stendhal (1965), Ch. XXIV.   [74] Stendhal (1952), p. 960.

And so? said Leuwen, who could hardly breathe. Up to that point the attitude of Mme de Chasteller had been measured, reserved and cool, at least in the eyes of Leuwen. The most accomplished Don Juan might not have found the timbre of voice in which he pronounced that phrase – *and so?* There was no talent in Leuwen, it was the impulsion of nature, the natural. That simple word by Leuwen changed everything.[75]

In these passages Stendhal compares Lucien first unfavourably and then favourably to the professional seducer of Valmont's type, implying that Valmont would not have got anywhere with Mme de Chasteller. Not that Lucien gets very far either, at this stage, but the reasons for his failure are totally different. Loved because of his inability to fake, he is unable to muster the courage to exploit the love that he inspires. Needless to say, even Mme de Chasteller might have been taken in by someone sufficiently clever. In these matters, the success of the deception depends on the relative sophistication of perpetrator and victim. But the converse also holds: for every Don Juan there is a woman who can see through him. No deception can be unconditionally successful, and one cannot fool all of the people all the time.

Let me pursue this last observation. In the French presidential elections of 1981 François Mitterand campaigned under the slogan 'Force tranquille'. He successfully put himself across as a person of integrity and wisdom, removed from the 'politique politicienne'. Did he fake the appearance of uncalculating strength, or was it the real thing? Here are two comments by Richard Eder on his campaign:

Mr. Mitterand's crowds always wait; he is unfailingly late. On his way around France he lingers over a meal, stops to admire the view, breaks off for a long telephone chat with friends. With an equal measure of conviction and calculation, he flourishes the insistence that politics is not machinery and should never be well-oiled.[76]

Clearly his mournful visage, his slow speech, his air of taking thought, suggest a kind of authenticity, a refusal of gimmickry, that is employed to show up the more mechanical showmanship of Mr. Giscard d'Estaing. Is it a gimmick itself?[77]

Should we conclude that the voters erred in not seeing through the gimmick of authenticity? Or on the contrary that Eder fell victim to an ingrained cynicism of reporters, unable to recognize an honest man when they see one? Clearly, Mitterand did not impress this particular observer, and I must admit that his reasons for being sceptical ring

[75] *Ibid.* p. 1035.   [76] *New York Times*, 16 April 1981.
[77] *International Herald Tribune*, 11 May 1981.

true. In particular, the insistence that politics should not be well-oiled, if correctly reported, is definitely suspect. People with integrity and character may not be very good at building smoothly functioning political machines. Pierre Mendès-France comes to mind as an example. Yet I believe that such people will be the first to regret their inability, not flaunt it as an asset. The scepticism may not be justified in this case, but the general point will surely be conceded that faking integrity runs a strong risk of being detected by some of the people some of the time. For another contrast to the questionable integrity of Mitterand, take the unquestioned integrity of de Gaulle, to whom one may fittingly apply Paul Veyne's observation that 'le galimatias a toujours été le signe des dieux, des oracles et des "patrons" '.[78] Someone capable of finely calculating the impression he makes on others could hardly behave as unreasonably stubbornly as did de Gaulle on many occasions. One reason why he was so successful was that his interlocutors correctly perceived that he would not listen to reason, and so he had better get his way. In a game of 'Chicken' – the paradigm for most negotiations – a clearly irrational person will usually get his way.[79] It has been said that Richard Nixon deliberately cultivated the image of someone who was capable and liable to act irrationally in a crisis, so as to dissuade the Russians from creating one. More plausibly, perhaps, his adviser did not mind him exhibiting his erratic and unpredictable ways, and may well have encouraged them. In any case faking unpredictability is too demanding, since it involves acting arbitrarily in innumerable small ways, not just grand-standing on occasion.

For any actor, then, there is some potential spectator clever enough to see through him. Christianity rests on the idea that there is one spectator clever enough to see through any actor, viz. God. Hence Pascal's wager argument must take account of the need to induce a real belief, since faking will not do. Moreover, the fact of God's clairvoyance explains why good works cannot bring about salvation if performed for the sake of salvation. The state of grace is essentially (or at most) a by-product of action. Let me record an objection to the wager argument. What kind of God is it that would be taken in by a genuine belief with a suspect past history – i.e. belief ultimately caused, even if not proximately justified, by instrumental rationality? Pascal's own

[78] Veyne (1976), p. 676.   [79] Schelling (1960), p. 143 and *passim*.

attack in *Les Provinciales* on Jesuit casuistry shows that he is open to this objection. Here he argues against the Jesuit doctrine of *directing the intention,* i.e. the idea that an action which is blameable when performed on one intention may not be so if performed on another, so that the confessor should direct his attention to the intention behind the behaviour rather than to the behaviour itself.[80] The obvious objection is that even if – contrary to the general argument of the present chapter – one were to succeed in changing the intention, the blameable intention behind the change of intention would contaminate the action that was performed on the new intention. Yet a similar argument would seem to apply to the reasoning behind the wager: how could present belief not be contaminated by the mundane causal origin?

Artistic disorder is much like studied indifference in that it is difficult to make it look like the real thing. Watching films or plays one sometimes gets the impression that the stage instructions have called for 'disorder', and that the director has tried to carry them out by more or less ingenious attempts to arrange chairs, newspapers etc. in some casual layout. This of course easily fails, for whenever there is a human intention at work it tends to leave a pattern that can in principle be detected by some other intention. To create order is easy; to create disorder is impossible; to create the appearance of disorder may be more or less difficult, depending on the sophistication of the observer and the ingenuity of the means employed to fool him. Von Neumann once observed that 'Anyone who considers arithmetical methods of producing random digits is, of course, in a state of sin.'[81] Similarly, the artificial ruins – constructed from scratch – dear to earlier generations of landscape architects rarely succeeded in producing the desired impression of picturesque decrepitude. (See also the comments on the Gothic revival in the following section.)

The things that are difficult to fake are usually also hard to learn. Here are some aphorisms on this problem. 'We are told that one of the most capable ministers of Louis XVI, M de Marchault, noticed this possibility and indicated it to his master. In such enterprises, however, one cannot act on advice: to be able to carry them out, one must be able to conceive them.'[82] Or again, 'Some things are such that if you do not

[80] See notably *Les Provinciales,* Septième Lettre: 'De la méthode de diriger l'intention, selon les casuistes'.

[81] Quoted after Goldstine (1972), p. 297.

[82] Tocqueville (1952), p. 215.

understand them immediately, you never will.'[83] And finally there is Bourdieu's observation that the essence of culture is to possess it without ever having acquired it.[84] This is but one of a series of acute comments by Bourdieu on the hopeless attempts of the petty bourgeoisie to acquire, imitate or fake upper class habits. They fail because, fearing to do too little, they invariably do too much.[85] One might add that their undoing is the tendency to do just a little too much, since extravagant deviations from their own unwritten rules are quite in character for the upper classes. The deliberate deviations from the rule can usually be distinguished from the involuntary deviations that stem from the deliberate adherence to it, 'going by the book' in the mistaken belief that the book covers all cases. (See also the discussion in II.3 of scrupulosity.)

Could there also be cases in which successful faking is downright impossible, because it requires the qualities needed to bring off the real thing? An obvious example could be the attempt to simulate originality and creativity in art or science. Such efforts may fool the public, but fellow artists or scientists will not be taken in. More to the point, perhaps, it may be impossible to simulate mediocrity in art. I know of no example in which an author of stature has successfully turned his talents to the production of best-sellers. Many have tried, but the result invariably is either too good or too bad, because the serious writer will be unable to hit the right note of mediocrity. (This is also an essential idea in Zinoviev's analysis of the Soviet system: the competent are persecuted for doing good work, and they cannot compete with the incompetent in doing bad work.[86]) My tentative claim is that faking in such cases is not just psychologically difficult, but involves some kind of conceptual impossibility. Which kind, I do not know. I would like the reader to reflect for himself on the predicament of an imaginative author setting out to write a best-seller. He cannot just truncate his talents, using for instance his skill in constructing a story while pulling his punch in character analysis or dialogue. He has to turn himself into

[83] Mme de Sévigné, quoted after Bourdieu (1979), p. 77.
[84] Bourdieu (1979), p. 381. Bourdieu instructively compares the born facility of the aesthete which stems from 'l'apprentissage total, précoce et sensible' (*ibid.* p. 70), the pedantic rigidity of the professor whose knowledge derives from 'l'apprentissage tardif, méthodique et *accéléré*' (*ibid.* p. 71) and the helpless confusion of the self-educated who 'ignore le droit d'ignorer que confèrent les brevets de savoir' (*ibid.* p. 379).
[85] Bourdieu (1979), pp. 274, 283, 382.
[86] Zinoviev (1979), p. 64.

a different sort of writer altogether, blunting his perception, coarsening his language, using three words whenever two would have done. Although by assumption he is able to understand other people, this does not mean he can turn himself into them to the extent of writing their books.

Lastly, the attempt to simulate may be self-defeating, if it ends up by inducing the very state that one is faking. Aristotle argued that by acting as if one were virtuous, one would in time come to be so. I am less impressed by this argument than I used to be, because it is not clear that following rules turns one into a person capable of transcending them when necessary. Waiving this objection, however, the argument would presumably also apply to cases in which one fakes virtue to impress others and not to become virtuous. In I.5 above a similar argument was suggested with regard to the impact on oneself of paying lip-service to the common interest. In fact, could not faking be more efficient than character planning in bringing about the states that cannot be induced at will, such as sincerity, public spirit, belief or virtue? If one fakes belief and as a result ends up believing, the outcome is a by-product of the faking, the main purpose being to impress or fool others. This means that one can, as it were, slide into belief without noticing it, whereas the more deliberate planning of belief advocated by Pascal must solve the self-eraser problem if it is to succeed. Needless to say, however, faking would lose this advantage if chosen because of it.

II.7   CHOICE AND INTENTION IN ART

Making a work of art is an intentional action, a series of choices guided by a purpose. Very generally speaking, the purpose is to condense and convey some specific aspect of human experience within the discipline created by a technical framework. To engage successfully in this activity is utterly satisfactory, and the result may be utterly impressive, but in both cases only and essentially as by-products. The artist fails if he is distracted from his real purpose by the pseudo-goals of self-realization or of making an impression on others. Narcissism and bravura are equally incompatible with what should be the constant aim of the artist, viz. 'getting it right'. This is not to say that an artist does not work with an audience in mind, but the audience is one of potential critics, not of admirers. His public are fellow artists, internalized in his own professional conscience. Looking for a wider audience often is an effective way of losing it.[87]

In this section I shall first suggest a general account of choice in art, and then link it up with the main theme of the present chapter. It cannot be stressed too strongly that the account is highly incomplete and tentative. I find the problem of understanding aesthetic value hauntingly difficult, and I am far from confident in my general approach to it. The remarks offered below are all at a very formal level, and perhaps do not come to grips at all with the really important issues.

Let me first state without argument two presuppositions of the analysis. First, artistic or aesthetic value is timeless, in the sense that the value of a work of art does not depend on the time it was created or exposed to the public. Secondly, the best judge of what is a good work of art is the good artist, and even the mediocre artist is a better judge than most others. These assumptions suggest that to find out what constitutes aesthetic value, we should look at the actual practice of the artist. I am not suggesting that he makes his artistic decisions according to conscious criteria of value, rather that such criteria (which I assume to exist) can best be reconstructed by looking at what artists do (which I suppose to be the best guide).

I suggest that artistic creation involves maximization under constraints, and that good works of art are local maxima of whatever it is that artists are maximizing. I shall not say anything about the nature of this maximand, and in this sense my account is indeed formal and unconcerned with the substance of aesthetics. I argue that the practice of artists can be understood only on the assumption that there is something which they are trying to maximize, by 'getting it right', and that their behaviour in this sense falls under the general heading of rational action. As in other cases the formal character of rationality is compatible with a wide range of substantive goals, about which I have nothing to say.

Artists working in any medium initially confront an infinity of possible configurations of the elementary units of their art, such as letters or words, notes, brushes of paint. The feasible set is not only

---

[87] Cp. the following comment by Anthony Smith, Director of the British Film Institute, on the surprising success of the British film *Chariots of Fire* in America: 'Gigantic sums have been lost by British producers in recent years toiling in pursuit of empty delusions of trans-Atlantic riches. Their films sink somewhere in mid-Atlantic, while success in America goes to those European films which deal most penetratingly with their own national problems and histories and characters' (*The Sunday Times*, 4 April 1982).

large, but also of extremely large variety – i.e. large in each of a large number of dimensions. Hence the size of the set of possible works of art imposes the need for a two-step strategy of choice. First, the artist must cut down the feasible set to a more manageable size, by imposing additional constraints. Secondly, he has to exercise his creative gift proper, by choosing within the reduced feasible set some specific configuration of elementary units that represents a local maximum of his objective function. To choose directly within the full feasible set would not be rational, for there are just too many possibilities to survey. The idea is expressed in a meta-sonnet by Edna St Vincent Millay:

> I will put Chaos into fourteen lines
> And keep him there; and let him thence escape
> If he be lucky; let him twist, and ape
> Flood, fire, and demon – his adroit designs
> Will strain to nothing in the strict confines
> Of this sweet Order, where, in pious rape,
> I hold his essence and amorphous shape,
> Till he with Order mingles and combines.
> Past are the hours, the years of our duress,
> His arrogance, our awful servitude:
> I have him. He is nothing more nor less
> Than something simple not yet understood;
> I shall not even force him to confess,
> Or answer. I will only make him good.[88]

Strictly speaking, the reduction of the feasible set need not take place by the deliberate choice of specific constraints; indeed this may be the exception rather than the rule. When an artist embraces a technique, defined among other things by strict constraints on the means of expression (rhyme, metre, tone scales, colour schemes), this need not be a conscious choice between alternatives. Often there is not much of an alternative. One should not fall into the trap of thinking that good art has to involve a break with tradition, nor a conscious reaffirmation of it. Racine, Mozart and Jane Austen are examples of supremely creative artists who felt happy within a framework wholly created before them. The artists who took the road less travelled by did so because they did not feel that the traditional constraints allowed sufficient scope for their specific gift for choosing within the feasible set (disregarding the ones who did so out of a misguided desire for originality). What often happens, I believe, is that the exercise of a tradition defined by certain formal constraints comes to create

[88] Edna St Vincent Millay (1975), Sonnet clxviii.

substantive constraints on what can be said within it, so that too *little* freedom for choice is left.

Tradition is not the only source of constraints. In addition there may be technical, physical or administrative limitations that have the (unintended) effect of cutting the feasible set down to a manageable size. Before the advent of sound tracks, silent movies had one dimension less to care about; similarly for films shot in black and white before the introduction of colour photography. The great era of jazz records came to an end, in my opinion, with the invention of the long-playing record. Jazz improvisation at a high level of quality is so hard to sustain that the '78' record with three minutes' playing time was just about optimal, permitting the incredible perfection of Armstrong in the twenties, Lester Young in the thirties and Charlie Parker in the forties. With more recording time came more freedom, too much in fact for the same intensity of focus to be maintained. (To be sure the deterioration may also be part of a more general trend towards 'character' at the expense of 'structure'.) Similarly, the financial or ideological constraints placed on an architect by the builder may liberate rather than trammel his creative imagination, provided of course that they are laid down before the work begins and not added along the way.

And finally there are the self-imposed and freely chosen restrictions of freedom, such as Woody Allen's use in *Manhattan* of black and white photography when colours were also available, financially no less than technically. Other examples, chosen at random, could be the choice of miniature painting or the haiku outside the settings where these are traditional forms; Bach's decision to work his own name into *The Art of the Fugue*; or – to take an extreme example – Georges Perec writing a novel in which the letter 'e' is nowhere used. If we regard an action very generally as the outcome of a *choice within constraints*,[89] then typically the choice will represent an element of freedom and the constraints an element of necessity. If, however, the constraints are themselves freely chosen, the element of necessity is to some extent mastered and harnessed to a purpose. Humankind cannot bear very much freedom, and hence there must be constraints, but one may choose them freely in one fell swoop and still have freedom left for choice within them.

I now turn to the principles guiding the choice within the given or

---

[89] See also Elster (1979), Ch. III.6, for an elaboration of this view.

chosen constraints. I shall argue that the artist is trying to achieve a *local maximum*, a notion in need of clarification. This I shall provide by quoting a pioneering observation by Eilert Sundt, a nineteenth century Norwegian sociologist who applied to boat construction some of the principles underlying Darwin's theory of evolution:

A boat constructor may be very skilled, and yet he will never get two boats exactly alike, even if he exerts himself to this end. The variations arising in this way may be called *accidental*. But even a very small variation usually is noticeable during the navigation, and it is then *not accidental* that the sailors come to *notice* that boat which has become improved or more convenient for their purpose, and that they should recommend this to be *chosen* as the one to *imitate* . . . One may believe that each of these boats is perfect in its way, since it has reached perfection by one-sided development in one particular direction. Each kind of improvement has progressed to the point where further development would entail defects that would more than offset the advantage . . . And I conceive of the process in the following way: when the idea of new and improved forms had first been aroused, then *a long series of prudent experiments*, each involving extremely small changes, could lead to the happy result that from the boat constructor's shed there emerged a boat whose like all would desire.[90]

The two ideas to be retained from this passage are that of a *local maximum* and that of *small variations*. By experimenting with small changes the boat constructors came up with a type in which all features were balanced optimally against each other, so that further change of any of them would lead to a worse overall performance. In another lecture Sundt contrasted this evolutionary mechanism, which he found at work in Northern Norway, with the discontinuous changes he found in the boat forms of Western Norway. Here, by non-incremental change, the constructors were able to reach superior local maxima that would not have been attainable through small stepwise improvements from a given initial type.

A first argument for seeing artistic creation as a process of local maximization is the frequently invoked cliché that in a good work of art 'nothing can be added and nothing subtracted' without loss of aesthetic value. A second, somewhat more forceful, consideration is that by looking at the process in this way we can make sense of the notion of a 'minor masterpiece' – a low-level local maximum. Similarly we can make sense of a distinction sometimes expressed as that between 'good bad art' and 'bad good art' – the first being a low-level local maximum and the second an imperfect approximation to a higher-level maximum. My central argument, however, comes from the extreme

---

[90] Sundt (1862), pp. 211–12. For a somewhat fuller discussion, see Elster (1982a), Ch. 6.

importance of drafts, sketches etc. in the artistic process. Poets typically play around with small variations, trying out one word, rejecting it, substituting another, until finally they decide that they have got it right. The sketch books of painters provide ample evidence for the same approach. Such practices show at the very least that the notion of 'better than' is one that makes important sense for the artist. They do not by themselves show that the artist tries to achieve 'the best', since he might conceivably be involved in a process of satisficing rather than of maximizing. Artists probably differ in this respect. Some employ variations that are so minute that they must be evidence for a concern with fine-tuned optimization. For obvious reasons, they also tend to work within rather strong formal constraints. Other artists impose weaker constraints on themselves, and are correspondingly less obsessed with perfection within them. Yet these are matters of fineness or coarseness of grain, that do not destroy the broad generalization I am trying to establish. Purposive choices are always made, *of* and *within* constraints.

On this background, I want to consider the question: What's wrong with conceptual art? Why cannot an artist achieve anything of value by taking a rucksack or a railway car and placing them on show? Or rather, why is it that whatever value such performances have cannot be an aesthetic one? Conceptual art may impress as a freak of nature can, or a woman preaching according to Dr Johnson. Yet surprise, although an important part of the linear arts,[91] cannot be the whole of art.

Conceptual art certainly violates the principle that the aesthetic value of a work of art should not depend on the time at which it is offered to the public. Once Andy Warhol had exposed his soup can, no one could have stolen his thunder by proving that unknown to the public he had done the same a long time ago. Conceptual art must always go beyond what is *currently* seen as the frontiers of invention. Moreover, conceptual art offers no scope for the specifically artistic gift of experimenting with small variations. In fact, the conceptual artist is

---

[91] By this I mean the arts that are one-dimensional because their elements are perceived in a given temporal order. Pure cases are music and oral literature, whereas written poetry already has an element of two-dimensionality that is crucial in many cases. Surprise occurs when a given element differs importantly from what the sequence leading up to it has made us expect, as in false endings in music. In the visual arts there can be no surprises in this internal sense, although there may be surprise in the external sense that the work of art does not conform to what we would expect from that artist or from that particular school or period. While internal surprise is essential to the aesthetic experience in the linear arts, external surprise in my opinion has no such function, contrary to what is argued by Wollheim (1980), pp. 146ff.

involved in game without an equilibrium point, since it is always possible to go one better and think of an even more stunning effect. It is in this respect like hyperinflation (I.2) with no holds barred. Similarly it is hard to see how the closely related minimal art offers any scope for small variations, for surely the choice between empty canvases of different shapes and sizes or between periods of silence of varying duration offers little scope for artistic choice and creation. The conceptual as well as the minimal artist sets out to impress through surprise, but this is not compatible with the creation of a *lasting* impression.

Richard Wollheim has attempted to make sense of conceptual and minimal art by suggesting that their importance lies in showing up in isolated and pure form elements of the artistic process that are usually found only in inextricable combination with other elements.[92] In any process of creation there comes a moment when one has to decide that the work is finished. According to Wollheim conceptual art isolates and as it were represents this decision, since it takes the actual content as given from outside. (On the present account, by contrast, the decision follows upon finding a local maximum.) Similarly all art involves an element of destroying conventional perception, as a prelude to the more constructive task of creating an alternative vision. Wollheim argues that minimal art isolates and holds up this negative and destructive phase. (On my account, however, this phase corresponds to the shaping of the feasible set, prior to the actual selection within it.) My objections to conceptual and minimal art are not affected by Wollheim's defence, for how can the operations he describes be carried out in more than one way? What is the scope offered to the conceptual or minimal artist for choices between different solutions, one of which emerges as *better* than the nearby alternatives? Conceptual art appears to be either a hopeless *fuite en avant* or a statement that can be made essentially once. In neither case does it offer the artist a manageable feasible set within which meaningful comparisons and choices can be made.

Conceptual and minimal art caters to a public whose main desire is expressed by Diaghilev's 'Etonne-moi!' (II.4). In one sense it is clear that it sometimes succeeds in following that injunction. Some of the effects deployed by conceptual art are stunning indeed. Yet I would

[92] Wollheim (1974), Ch. 5.

submit that there is a bored quality to the surprise it generates. It shows that surprise – the real thing, the perception of the world 'wie am ersten Tag' – is essentially a by-product. Surprise in this sense has to do with what Emily Dickinson refers to as 'a sudden expectation' or 'a flying attitude'.[93] Only by surprising himself can the artist surprise others in this sense. And when the surprise wears off, as inevitably it must do, something remains – for a new layer of perception has been added to our repertoire. With the appearance of the next sensation in conceptual art, however, nothing of permanence remains of the previous summit.

A brief digression into Victorian aesthetics may provide added illustrations.[94] The Victorians were obsessed by the picturesque and the striking effect, and not surprisingly developed a school of theorists providing recipes for effect building. These usually included advice on how to make the effect less obtrusive. In the words of Owen Jones, 'Those proportions will be most beautiful which it will be most difficult for the eye to detect.'[95] He therefore advised his readers to use the proportions 3:7 or 5:8 rather than the obvious 3:6 or 4:8. Presumably the next generation, being by now imbued with Jonesque sophistication, would need even subtler stuff such as 7:15 or 9:16. As above, focusing on the effect rather than on the work itself leads to one-upmanship and *fuite en avant*. For another example, consider Christopher Dresser's argument that

Curves will be found to be more beautiful as they are subtle in character. (1) The arc is the least beautiful of curves; being struck from one centre the origin is instantly detected, and the mind requires that a line the contemplation of which shall be pleasurable, must be in advance of its knowledge and call into activity its investigative powers. (2) A portion of the boarding line of an ellipse is more beautiful as a curve than the arc, for its origin is less apparent, it being struck from two centres. (3) The curve which bounds the egg-shape is more beautiful than the elliptic curve, for it is struck

---

[93] These phrases are from Dickinson (1970), no. 77. The preceding poem offers the following, self-descriptive, characterization of the aesthetic experience:

> Exultation is the going
> Of an inland soul to sea,
> Past the houses – past the headlands –
> Into deep Eternity –
>
> Bred as we, among the mountains,
> Can the sailor understand
> The divine intoxication
> Of the first league out from land?

[94] For information on this topic I am indebted to my wife, Elisabeth Elster. A rather different interpretation of the Gothic Revival is found in Watkin (1977).

[95] Jones (1856), p. 6.

from three centres. (4) The curve boarding the cartioid is more beautiful still, as it is struck from four centres.[96]

Against such absurd pedantry struggled Augustin Welby Pugin and John Ruskin. Pugin, in his first work *Contrasts,* strongly deplored the use of the ugly four-centred curve in the place of the pointed arch.[97] In his next work, *True Principles of Christian or Pointed Architecture,* he went on to make some general remarks on intention and effect in architecture:

When modern architects avoid the defect of regularity, they frequently fall into one equally great with regard to irregularity; I mean when a building is *designed to be picturesque,* by sticking as many ins and outs, ups and downs, about it as possible. *The picturesque effect of the ancient buildings results from the ingenious methods by which the old builders overcame local and constructive difficulties.* An edifice which is arranged with the principal view of looking picturesque is sure to resemble an artificial waterfall or a made-up rock, which are generally so *unnaturally natural* as to appear ridiculous.[98]

Ruskin fully endorsed this general appreciation of Gothic buildings. He added that the picturesque, although unacceptable as the main intended effect of architecture, was acceptable as a foreseen and desirable side effect:

And it is one of the chief virtues of the Gothic builders that they never suffered ideas of outside symmetries and consistencies to interfere with the real use and value of what they did. If they wanted a window, they opened one; a room, they added one; a buttress, they built one; utterly regardless of any established conventionalities of external appearance, knowing (as indeed it always happened) that such daring interruptions of the formal plan would rather give additional interest to its symmetry than injure it.[99]

The last remark fits in with the point made in II.3 above, that an action is not defeated by the agent anticipating that as a result of it a state will come about that is essentially a by-product, as long as it is not turned into the chief aim of the action. Yet I feel slightly uneasy about Ruskin's choice of words, for they suggest that the artist may relax his standards because any defects or imperfections will only add charm to the finished product. Not all violations of a plan add interest to the whole. The public often pays a snobbish attention to imperfections, which bear witness to the antiquity and therefore to the rarity of the work of art. If the artist himself is smitten by this attitude, cuteness and self-indulgence are the predictable results.

[96] Dresser (1862), quoted after Bøe (1956), pp. 168–9.
[97] Pugin (1836), p. 3.
[98] Pugin (1841), p. 52.   [99] Ruskin (1853), §38.

II.8 THE IMPOTENCE OF POWER

I have been concerned with cases in which an individual tries to set up, in himself or in another person, a mental state that is essentially a by-product. I now turn to cases in which a régime for similar reasons proves incapable of bringing about certain social and political states. There are states of society that may well come about by drift or by accident, yet resist any attempt to bring them about deliberately. The impossibility in such cases tends to inhere in the actor, rather than in the state he tries to realize. Let us call a state *inaccessible* if it cannot be brought about by intelligent and intentional action, and *inescapable* if one cannot intentionally and intelligently succeed in leaving it.[100] If an actor sets for himself only goals that are inherently inaccessible, his situation becomes inescapable. Yet there are also actors such that whatever goal they set for themselves is inaccessible *for them*, because they are the kind of actors who are unable to escape their situation. Whatever they touch turns into lead, and their every step into a stumble. When we do not find them in the role of Sisyphos, they occupy that of Tantalos. This is how Alexander Zinoviev views the Soviet régime, for reasons soon to be explained. Less dramatically, there are political agents that are unable to bring about states that may yet come about by accident, not because their situation is inescapable or the state inherently inaccessible, but simply because the nature of the régime is such that they lack the legitimacy to bring it about.

According to Zinoviev, the Soviet régime is both omnipotent and impotent: omnipotent in its power to destroy and to block action, impotent because of its inability to construct and to create.[101] (There may be an inconsistency here, because some of the causes – discussed below – that explain the inability to construct also make for reduced

---

[100] Elster (1978a), Ch. 3, suggests a formal framework for the analysis of these notions, interpreting the concept of 'political possibility' as a modal operator. I now believe, however, that this conceptualization is seriously inadequate, for reasons indicated by Kenny (1976) and further discussed in Elster (1980b). Briefly, the difficulty is that political possibility – like ability, which is the object of Kenny's analysis – does not obey the modal law of the distribution of possibility over disjunction: while it may be politically possible to bring about a state described as one in which either the Soviets or the central committee have all the power, each of the disjuncts may be politically impossible.

[101] Zinoviev (1979), p. 483. Similarly, Tocqueville argued that centralization 'excels at preventing, not at doing. When it is a question of deeply stirring society or of setting it at a rapid pace, its strength deserts it. Once its measures require any aid from individuals, this vast machine turns out to be astonishingly feeble; suddenly it is reduced to impotence' (Tocqueville 1969, p. 91).

destructive efficiency.) The fundamental principle of the régime is that 'people who want to make a change never change anything, while changes only are effected by people who had no intention of doing so'.[102] The formulation is misleading and somewhat ambiguous, at least in translation. It is misleading, because it is clear from what Zinoviev writes elsewhere that he does not exclude that the people who want to make a change also do bring about change – only that they succeed in bringing about the change they intended to. In his memorable phrase, Soviet institutions do not embody solutions to problems: they are the result of the search for solutions.[103] And it would be fully in his spirit to add that an institution that actually emerged as the solution to a problem could do so only in a non-standard way (II.3). The quoted formulation is also ambiguous, in that it is not clear whether 'had no intention of doing so' should perhaps be read as 'had the intention of not doing so'. Since Zinoviev's work both as a logician and as a satirist turns upon this distinction, it is highly unlikely that he wrote without paying attention to it. His other work makes it likely that the second reading corresponds to his intentions: the people who want to preserve the basic structure of society are in fact agents of change. To be precise, Zinoviev argues that the attempt to preserve society will lead to a retrogression towards a 'third serfdom'.[104]

Zinoviev suggests, moreover, that this offers an ironic illustration of the principle of the negation of the negation – provided that we here understand negation in the external sense, i.e. the sense in which it is simply cancelled when iterated. If negation is taken in the internal sense, iteration will not bring us back to the point of departure. Even assuming that the step from serfdom to communism was an intentional one, the reverse move back to serfdom can occur only by drift or by accident. The revolution against the revolution against X never brings us back to X.[105] In spite of the verbal symmetry, counterrevolutions are not the inverse operation of the revolutions that precede them. Had this been the case, the end state of the counterrevolution would be one in which a new revolution became possible, whereas the goal of the counterrevolutionaries is to render it impossible. The pre-revolutionary state is essentially a by-product. More generally, this holds for

[102] Zinoviev (1979), p. 198.   [103] *Ibid.* p. 750.
[104] The argument, if not explicit, is at least informally suggested in Zinoviev (1979).
[105] Cp. the following comment by Giscard d'Estaing, made soon after he was elected President: 'There is certainly no question of returning to the pre-1968 situation, if only for the reason that the pre-1968 situation included the conditions that led to 1968.' (*Le Monde*, 8 January 1975)

all attempts to revert to or imitate an earlier state that has as an essential component lack of awareness of what would follow. Pre-revolutionary France was not simply France before the Revolution, but France without the very notion of a revolution.[106] Similarly, although the Soviet rulers may by small steps bring the nation into a pre-revolutionary state, no one will recognize it as such until the process has come very far.

The most fundamental reason why the Soviet rulers are unable to achieve their goals is found in the lack of reliable information. The omnipotence-cum-impotence of despotism in this respect is classically captured by Tocqueville: 'the sovereign can punish immediately any faults he discovers, but he cannot flatter himself into supposing that he sees all the faults he should punish'.[107] In the Soviet Union reliable information does not exist, or if it does, cannot be reliably distinguished from the unreliable. The flaw of the system is that all acts tend to have an immediate political significance, which means that information degenerates into informing and so becomes worthless for planning purposes. Or else the information is offered that the informant believes his superiors want to hear, even if they insist on information that reflects the world as it is rather than the world as they would like it to be. The tradition of punishing or at least not rewarding the bearer of bad news is too ingrained for such insistence to be taken seriously. Both the KGB and Gosplan suffer accordingly. To take another Soviet-type society, it is impossible to believe that the North Korean rulers are told by their foreign representatives how utterly ridiculous they are made to appear by their full-page self-congratulating ads in the Western press.

Among the other obstacles to intelligent and intentional action Zinoviev mentions the tendency to believe that any important problem must also be a difficult one.[108] Problems are a source of power for the bureaucracy, not a hurdle to be passed with only the minimal clearance. Moreover, there is a widespread tendency to shape the problems so as to fit the politically feasible solutions rather than the other way around. If the goal is to reduce the crime rate, defined operationally as the maximization of the ratio of crimes solved to crimes committed, it is in the interest of the authorities to arrest as many innocent people as possible and then declare them guilty of fictitious crimes, since each such person will increase the maximand.[109]

[106] Tocqueville (1952), p. 197.   [107] Tocqueville (1969), p. 206.
[108] Zinoviev (1979), p. 572.   [109] Zinoviev (1978), p. 79.

If the goal is to reduce black market trafficking in certain commodities, the easiest solution is to cease production of them.[110] Finally there is the universal propensity to assume the worst, a generalized maximin behaviour that might be called paranoid were it not so justified.

Zinoviev's work obviously has its share of grotesque exaggerations. No country that has put a man in space can be wholly based on wishful thinking and paralysing distrust. Yet it would be wrong to dismiss it on this ground, for the world he constructs is too coherent to be only a figment of his imagination. It is certainly a distorted image of the Soviet system, but an image that nevertheless preserves the basic topological features, as when a piece of rubber is stretched without breaking. In particular I believe that the casual evidence one can gather – other evidence being hard to come by – confirms that the Soviet rulers no less than their subjects are prisoners of the system. To some extent one can apply to Soviet Russia a classic characterization of tsarism, as autocracy tempered by inefficiency. One can accept much of this, and yet remain sceptical about Zinoviev's assertion that the subjects no less than the rulers are responsible – morally and causally – for the system. In his view the creation of Soviet Man – the passive rather than the active negation of rationality and humanity – has been so successful that the system can endure almost indefinitely, by its ability to quench any spark of reform in an ocean of mediocrity.[111] Against this I would like to suggest that social systems are more malleable than the individuals who make them up, and that great changes will occur once the lid is taken off. Perhaps one could even hope for a drift towards freedom.

In modern democratic societies we also observe the occasional impotence of the powerful, although for quite different reasons. To identify the mechanism, we can start with an observation by Tocqueville, apropos compulsory military service: 'A democratic government can do pretty well what it likes, provided that its orders apply to all and at the same moment; it is the inequality of burden, not its weight, which usually provokes resistance.'[112] In other words, in democratic societies we observe the breakdown of the axiom 'Qui peut le plus, peut le moins,' since the government may be able to impose

---

[110] Zinoviev (1979), p. 804.
[111] Elster (1980a) surveys the various passages in which Zinoviev explains his theory of mediocrity. For a sample, see note 21 above.
[112] Tocqueville (1969), pp. 651–2.

hardships on the whole population without having the power to do so on a proper subset of the citizens.[113] The idea is that resistance is provoked not by the state in which the citizens find themselves, but by the causal process in which it originated. Social and economic inequalities that result from the impersonal play of market forces are much more acceptable than those that visibly stem from government discrimination. Imposed hardships are tolerable if shared by all, not if suffered by a minority – even when there is no point in more than a minority suffering them. The democratic government can get away with a wage-and-price freeze much more easily than with more efficient and more discriminatory measures. Welfare benefits are sometimes absurdly diluted because they cannot be offered to someone without being offered to everyone. Redistribution is most feasible in times of economic growth, where the differences in wage increases are to some extent swamped by the fact that everybody receives some increase. Hence governments become skilled at inventing policies whose first effect hits everybody equally, while the net effect is suitably unequally distributed. The paradigm case is income redistribution through equal nominal wage rises in an inflating economy with progressive taxation. To the extent that the causality remains opaque, the changes can be attributed to fate. If in ancient societies the rulers could get away with overt discrimination, it was not only because they had superior force at their disposal, but also because their behaviour could no more be assumed to be just and rational than one would expect a hurricane to be, and hence did not create resentment among the subjects.[114]

To summarize, when a person or a group in power attempts to bring about some desired state of society, the effort may be blocked by several kinds of obstacles. Some of these have to do with the states in question, others – the ones that concern me here – with the attempt to bring them about. The subject may not resist or even mind if the state comes about, and yet resist the attempt to bring it about deliberately. Or the effort to bring it about may create a counter-current of obstruction among the subjects or channel their reactions to the attempt in such a way that it will be frustrated. In the latter case one might ask whether the authorities could not anticipate these reactions and harness them to their purpose. Assume that if the government tells its agents and the

[113] The belief that what is possible in all cases is also possible in each case *separately and exclusively* is a good candidate for the 'fallacy of division', considered as the converse of the fallacy of composition as understood in Elster (1978a), pp. 97ff.

[114] Veyne (1976), p. 314; cp. also Tocqueville (1969), p. 549.

population that the goal is to bring about a state x, then the impact of the announcement will be that $f(x)$ in fact comes about. There may well be some x^* such that $f(x^*) = x^*$, i.e. some state that could be brought about by fluke, intentionally but not intelligently, but by assumption the reaction function will not be the identity function. We then ask whether for given x' there is some x'' such that $f(x'') = x'$. This could well be the case, but if the lack of reliable information is what makes the reaction function differ from the identity function, then *a fortiori* the government will not be able to collect the information required to ascertain the shape of the reaction function. To use an overworked analogy that may be somewhat more appropriate here than in other contexts, there is a genuine uncertainty principle at work that cannot be overcome by correcting for the impact of the announcement on the state of society.

II.9   Self-defeating political theories

In this section I shall discuss and criticize a certain view of politics, the theory that the main benefit and indeed purpose of a political system can be found in the educative and otherwise useful effect on the participants. I should give notice that I share the view that political participation is good for those who participate, at least if the proper institutional design is chosen (I.5). What I object to is the idea that these benefits can be the main or even the sole point of the system. This would be to turn into the main purpose of politics something that can only be a by-product. It can indeed be highly satisfactory to engage in political work, but only on the condition that the work is defined by a serious purpose which goes beyond that of achieving this satisfaction. If that condition is not fulfilled, we are left with a narcissistic theory of politics. True, many people who over the last decades have engaged in consciousness-raising activities of various kinds, with little or no purpose beyond that of achieving self-respect or self-realization, would protest strongly. They would insist that even activities that have no hope of success in the sense of achieving their official goal can yet succeed in changing the participants. To this I have two answers, each of which may be appropriate on different occasions. Some people may indeed have changed, but for the worse. Others may have succeeded in achieving political maturity through a process guided by no other goal, but only by fluke – intentionally and non-intelligently. I am not denying that bootstrap-pulling can occur, only that one can rationally count on it to occur.

In any case, I am more concerned with political theorists than with activists. I shall argue that certain arguments for political constitutions and institutions are self-defeating, since they justify the arrangements in question by effects that are essentially by-products. Here an initial and important distinction must be drawn between the task of justifying a constitution *ex ante* and that of evaluating it *ex post*. I show below that Tocqueville, when assessing the democratic system in America, praised it for effects that are essentially by-products. As an analytical attitude after the fact, and at some distance, this makes perfectly good sense. The difficulty arises when one invokes the same arguments before the fact, in public discussion. Although the constitution-makers may secretly have such side effects in mind, they cannot coherently invoke them in public.

Kant proposed a *transcendental formula of public right:* 'All actions affecting the rights of other human beings are wrong if their maxim is not compatible with their being made public.'[115] Since Kant's illustrations of the principle are obscure, I turn instead to John Rawls, who imposes a similar condition of publicity as a constraint on what the parties can choose in the original position: 'they must assume that they are choosing principles for a public conception of justice'.[116] Not only must the principles of justice hold for all; they must be known by all to hold for all. Rawls then goes on to argue that this constraint tends to favour – other things being equal – his own conception of justice compared to that of the utilitarians.[117] If utilitarian principles of justice were openly adopted, they would entail some loss of self-esteem, since people would feel that they were not treated fully as ends in themselves. A loss of self-esteem is also, other things being equal, a loss of average utility. It is then conceivable that public adoption of Rawls's two principles of justice would bring about a higher average utility than public adoption of utilitarianism, although a lower average than under a secret utilitarian constitution introduced from above. The latter possibility, however, is ruled out by the publicity constraint. A utilitarian could not then advocate Rawls's two principles on utilitarian grounds, although he might well applaud them on such grounds. The fact that the two principles maximize utility would

---

[115] Kant (1795), p. 126.   [116] Rawls (1971), p. 133.   [117] *Ibid.* pp. 177 ff., esp. p. 181.

essentially be a by-product, and if chosen on the grounds that they are utility-maximizing they would no longer be so. Utilitarianism would then be self-defeating in Kant's sense: its maxim would not be compatible with its being made public.

Derek Parfit has raised, and tried to meet, a similar objection to Act Consequentialism (AC):

This gives to all one common aim: the best possible outcome. If we try to achieve this aim, we may often fail. Even when we succeed, the fact that we are disposed to try might make the outcome worse. AC might thus be indirectly self-defeating. What does this show? A consequentialist might say: 'It shows that AC should be only one part of our moral theory. It should be the part that covers successful acts. When we are certain to succeed, we should aim for the best possible outcome. Our wider theory should be this: we should have the aims and dispositions having which would make the outcome best. This wider theory would not be self-defeating. So the objection has been met.'[118]

There is an ambiguity in the word 'should' in the penultimate sentence. Is the suggestion that it would be better if we were to have certain aims and dispositions, or that we should aim at having them? If the latter, we run into the problem that having certain aims and dispositions – i.e. being a certain kind of person – is essentially a by-product. When instrumental rationality is self-defeating, we cannot choose to take leave of it on instrumentalist grounds – any more than we can fall asleep by deciding not to try to fall asleep. If always opting for the best outcome creates a calculating attitude that is destructive of interpersonal relations, then it would indeed be best not to opt for the best outcome. Yet to recognize this ideal is not the same as to achieve it. I am not saying that it is totally impossible to plan instrumentally for a non-instrumental attitude, but the objections stated in II.3 certainly apply. The analogy with Rawls's objection to utilitarianism is clear: an Act Consequentialist might well applaud the non-instrumental attitude, yet it might be self-defeating were he to advocate it.

Tocqueville, in *Democracy in America,* was concerned to evaluate the social consequences of American institutions. The following methodological principles can be extracted from his work (i) One must look at the consequences that emerge when the institution in question is widely used rather than marginal. It should come as no surprise that the occasional love marriage in an aristocratic society ends in disaster, but this does not imply that it is an argument against democracy that it

---

[118] Parfit (1981), p. 554.

would encourage such marriages.[119] (ii) Any given institution will have many consequences, some of them opposed in their tendency. It is imperative, therefore, to look at their net effect. There may be more fires in democratic societies than elsewhere, but they are also more quickly extinguished.[120] (iii) One should not evaluate a given institution or constitution according to its efficiency at each moment of time, but rather look at the long-term consequences. Democracies tax more heavily, but also create more taxable income.[121] (iv) One should not confuse the transitional effect of introducing an institution with the steady-state effect of having it. The initial effect of a revolution may be loose morals, yet the steady-state effect may be to impose stricter morals.[122] (v) The four principles just indicated can only be applied after the fact, to trace the consequences of a system that has been in operation for some time.[123] Our knowledge about social causality is too slight to permit confident predictions about the effects of an as yet untried system.[124] (vi) After the fact we can often perceive that the main

[119] Tocqueville (1969), p. 596. Another important argument of the same form is put forward in Tocqueville (1953), p. 111: even though the institution of the Etats Particuliers had been harmless in an individual province such as Languedoc, the king miscalculated when he thought the Etats Généraux at a national scale would be equally innocuous.

[120] Tocqueville (1969), p. 723.

[121] Tocqueville (1969), pp. 208–9. As a defence of democracy, the argument will not carry weight with those, like Buchanan and Brennan (1980), who believe that taxation is theft anyway. To take the converse case, Marx (1879–80, p. 359) fully acknowledged that the capitalist 'does not only "deduct" or "rob" but forces the production of surplus, and thus helps to create what is deducted', yet did not think this could justify exploitation. By the same token, if government in other circumstances brings about a loss of taxable income by intervening this need not be an argument against intervention.

[122] Tocqueville (1969), p. 599. The distinction between transitional effects and steady-state effects is often found in Tocqueville's work. The most explicit statement is the following: 'One must be careful not to confuse the fact of equality with the revolution which succeeds in introducing it into the state of society and into the laws. In that lies the reason for almost all the phenomena which cause our surprise' (Tocqueville 1969, p. 688). Writing on the abolition of slavery (Tocqueville 1962, pp. 45, 55) he also takes care to point out that the predictable difficulties arising from abolition will be temporary only. In his notes for the second volume of the *Ancien Régime,* he argued that the purported positive influence of despotism on literature is due only to the introduction of a despotic regime and not to its steady-state nature (Tocqueville 1953, pp. 345–6). For the general problem of steady-state causality see also Elster (1982a), Ch. 1.

[123] This idea is not, as a matter of fact, stated in *Democracy in America.* Yet we observe that whenever Tocqueville suggests possible future developments of American democracy, be it towards the tyranny of the majority, despotic centralization or plutocracy, he does so in a very tentative and hypothetical manner. In his writings on the French Revolution he often points to the contrast between the total confidence with which the political actors predicted the course of events and the monotonous regularity with which they were proved wrong (e.g. Tocqueville 1953, p. 151).

[124] Moreover, it will not do to argue with Edmund Burke (1955, p. 198) or Popper (1957, pp. 64ff.) that trial-and-error or piecemeal social engineering can be a substitute for well-founded predictions, since these methods fail to respect principles (i) through (iv). By requiring initial and local viability of institutional reform, the incremental method neglects the fact that

advantage of the constitution is found in effects other than those which are its official purpose and in terms of which it makes sense to the participants.

The last proposition finds its principal application in the following argument. Tocqueville suggests, in a seeming paradox, that democracies are less suited than aristocracies to deal with long-term planning, and yet are superior in the long run to the latter. The paradox dissolves once it is seen that the first statement involves time at the level of the actors, while the second concerns the temporal consequences of their behaviour as seen by the observer. On the one hand, 'a democracy finds it difficult to cordinate the details of a great undertaking and to fix on some plan and carry it through with determination in spite of obstacles. It has little capacity for combining measures in secret and waiting patiently for the result.'[125] On the other hand, 'in the long run government by democracy should increase the real forces of a society, but it cannot immediately assemble, at one point and at a given time, forces as great as those at the disposal of an aristocratic government'.[126] This latter view is further elaborated in a passage from the chapter on 'The Real Advantages Derived by American Society from Democratic Government':

That constantly renewed agitation introduced by democratic government into political life passes, then, into civil society. Perhaps, taking everything into consideration, that is the greatest advantage of democratic government, and I praise it much more on account of what it causes to be done than for what it does. It is incontestible that the people often manage public affairs very badly, but their concern therewith is bound to extend their mental horizon and to shake them out of the rot of ordinary routine . . . Democracy does not provide a people with the most skillful of governments, but it does that which the most skillful government often cannot do: it spreads throughout the body social a restless activity, superabundant force, and energy never found elsewhere, which, however little favoured by circumstances, can do wonders. Those are its true advantages.[127]

The advantages of democracies, in other words, are mainly and essentially by-products. The avowed aim of democracy is to be a good system of government, but Tocqueville argues that it is inferior to aristocracy viewed purely as a decision-making apparatus. Yet the very

institutions which are viable in the large and in the long term may not be so in the small and in the short term. This is, in fact, the main objection that Tocqueville (1953, pp. 340ff.) makes to Burke's evaluation of the French Revolution.
[125] Tocqueville (1969), p. 229. Moreover, not only is democracy a bad system for long-term decision-making, it also tends to foster myopic attitudes in the individual (*ibid.* p. 536).
[126] Tocqueville (1969), p. 224. For a similar defence of capitalism, see Schumpeter (1954, p. 83) – further discussed in Elster (1982a), Ch. 5.
[127] Tocqueville (1969), pp. 243–4.

activity of governing democratically has as a by-product a certain energy and restlessness that benefits industry and generates prosperity. Assuming the soundness of this observation, could it ever serve as a justification for introducing democracy in a nation that had not yet acquired it? The question is somewhat more complex than one might be led to believe from what I have said so far, since instrumental efficiency is not the only argument that is relevant for the choice of a constitution. Considerations of *justice* could also be decisive. Yet the following conclusion seems inescapable: if the system has no inherent advantages in terms of justice or efficiency, one cannot coherently and publicly advocate its introduction because of the side effects that would follow in its wake. There must be a *point* in democracy as such. If people are motivated by such inherent advantages to throw themselves into the system, other benefits may ensue – but the latter cannot by themselves be the motivating force. If the democratic method was introduced solely because of its side effects on economic prosperity, and no one believed in it on any other grounds, it would not produce them.

Tocqueville suggests a similar argument for the jury system: 'I do not know whether a jury is useful to the litigants, but I am sure that it is very good for those who have to decide the case. I regard it as one of the most effective means of popular education at society's disposal.'[128] Here again the justification for the institution is found in side effects that probably were not the main purpose of those who created the system, and in any case cannot be that of the participants. A necessary condition for the jury system to have the educational effects on the jurors for which Tocqueville recommended it is their belief that they are doing something that is worth while and important, beyond their own personal development. Their minds are concentrated wonderfully by the knowledge that someone may hang as a result of their decision. But this effect would be spoilt if the jurors thought that the effect on their own civic spirit was the main purpose of the proceedings.

Tocqueville is content with observing that all the great achievements of democracy are realized 'without it and outside it',[129] although also because of it. We need to distinguish between this case and that – more in the spirit of Marx or of Zinoviev – in which an institution is justified because of what is achieved *against it and because of it*. A conceivable

[128] *Ibid.* p. 275.
[129] *Ibid.* p. 244 (translation modified).

although not very plausible justification for authoritarian ways of bringing up children could be that it tends to develop the very independence that it tries to stifle. Consider also the notion that 'it is because constitutional monarchs tend to be enemies of democracy that constitutional monarchs promote democracy'[130] – an observation similar to Zinoviev's comment that the dissident opposition is fortified by persecution. This might in the eyes of some be a justification for constitutional monarchy, but hardly one that would encourage the monarch to throw himself into the work. In such cases the gap between official purpose and sociological justification would be extremely striking, since the actual consequences of the institution are directly opposed to the intended ones. The Tocquevillian case is subtler, since the by-products of the democratic process may be highly welcome. The acknowledgement of these by-products will not by itself do away with the motivation to perform the actions of which they are the by-products (II.3), but there will be a lack of incentive if it is also believed that the institution performs its official purpose rather badly, since the by-products only arise if the participants believe it is performing well.

John Stuart Mill – and Carole Pateman who quotes him to this effect – also argue that the main effect of a political system is to educate the participants, and that 'the merely *business* part of human affairs' is of secondary importance.[131] And Pateman, in her gloss on Mill, adds that 'the two aspects of government are interrelated in that a necessary condition of good government in the first, business, sense is the promotion of the right kind of individual character'.[132] I would emphasize the inverse link, the importance of the merely business end for the development of the character of the citizens. Politics derives its educational quality from the business end: the more important the decision, and the more seriously one takes it, the more one can learn from it.

---

[130] Cohen (1978), p. 171. The idea is suggested to explain, by analogy, how pre-capitalist relations of production could be 'forms of development' for the productive forces, even though they are inherently conservative.

[131] Mill (1859), p. 106. Hirschman (1982), p. 82, suggests, on the basis of Mill's argument, that 'the benefit of collective action for an individual is not the difference between the hoped-for result and the effort furnished by him or her, but the *sum* of these two magnitudes'. I do not know what the proper functional form would be, but it follows from my general argument that the effort furnished by the individual brings a benefit only if the hoped-for result is non-zero – contrary to what would be the case if the interaction was additive as suggested by Hirschman.

[132] Pateman (1970), p. 29.

A similar comment applies to the following, somewhat ambiguous, passage from Hannah Arendt's *On Revolution*:

The Americans knew that public freedom consists in having a share in public business, and that the activities connected with this business by no means constituted a burden but gave those who discharged them in public a feeling of happiness they could acquire nowhere else. They knew very well, and John Adams was bold enough to formulate this knowledge time and again, that the people went to the town assemblies, as their representatives later were to go to the famous Conventions, neither exclusively because of duty nor, and even less, to serve their own interests but most of all because they enjoyed the discussions, the deliberations, and the making of decisions.[133]

This may be quite unexceptionable, but it can also be read as a statement of the narcissistic theory of politics. The town assembly sounds more like Plato's *Symposium* than an arena of compromise, trade-offs and choice between evils. True, the decision-making aspect of politics is mentioned, but not in the centrally important role it should have. Political discussion and deliberation may be deeply enjoyable or satisfactory, but only when and because they are guided by the need to make a decision. Discussion is subordinate to decision-making, not on a par with it as suggested by Arendt's wording. In her discussion of Greek democracy she explicitly states that 'politics is never for the sake of life'[134] – contrary to the view of Moses Finley that the Athenian people 'recognized the instrumental role of political rights and were more concerned in the end with the substantive decisions'.[135] It is admittedly unclear whether she refers to the theorists of Greek democracy or – as does Finley – to the way in which it actually functioned, but this is irrelevant for the point I am making, since in any case she embraces the non-instrumental conception of politics. In so doing she comes dangerously close to seeing politics as the plaything of an already-educated elite, rather than as an educative process.

As a final example of this self-defeating view of politics I shall take the ideology underlying the various campaigns for nuclear disarmament over the last decades. Needless to say, my comments have no implications for the substantive issues involved. I shall take my cue from a recent symposium on participation initiated by Stanley Benn.

---

[133] Arendt (1973), p. 119.
[134] Arendt (1958), p. 37. A more elaborate statement is the following: 'The public realm . . . was reserved for individuality; it was the only place where men could show who they really and inexchangeably were. It was for the sake of this chance, and out of love for a body politic that made it possible to them all, that each was more or less willing to share in the burden of jurisdiction, defence and administration of public affairs' (*ibid.* p. 41).
[135] Finley (1976), p. 83.

He first raised the vexed question of why one should bother to vote or otherwise participate in politics, since the chance of one individual influencing the outcome is virtually nil in modern democracies, while the costs of participation are at least noticeable.[136] In his answer he then suggested that

> political activity may be a form of moral self-expression, necessary not for achieving any objective beyond itself (for the cause may be lost), nor yet for the satisfaction of knowing that one had let everyone else know that one was on the side of the right, but because one could not seriously claim, even to oneself, to be on that side without expressing the attitude by the actions most appropriate to it in the paradigm case.[137]

In his comments on Benn's contribution, Brian Barry developed an argument similar to that put forward above concerning Hannah Arendt:

> Politics is a serious business. In any state with well-developed administrative competence it determines, by activity or default, the distribution of food, housing, medical and educational services, etc., and (in interaction with other states) whether weapons of destruction are to be unleashed. I believe that Benn thinks so too and is anxious to show that it is rational to play one's part in a serious way. But unfortunately the form of justification he has offered, in terms of self-expression, is a charter for frivolity. It offers aid and comfort to the politics of the beautiful people – the radical chic of the Boston-Washington corridor and the London-Oxbridge triangle . . . Ritualistic activity does exist in politics and provides a lot of unjustifiable self-satisfaction to those who take part in it. The last years of the Campaign for Nuclear Disarmament provide a perfect illustration.[138]

Sympathetic as I am to this characterization, I would add that we need to distinguish between acting out of self-respect and using political actions as a means to achieving self-respect. Like Benn, I believe that the former is a legitimate preoccupation; like Barry, if I understand him well, that the latter involves putting the cart before the horse. And like Barry I believe that the campaigns for nuclear disarmament have illustrated this form of 'middle class radicalism'[139] quite well. The 1982 campaigns were in many respects an exception, since they certainly had an impact on public opinion and on policy. Yet one of the leaders of

[136] Cp. Barry (1979) for an extensive discussion of this issue. Veyne (1976), pp. 415ff., explains that in Rome the incentive to vote was even less, since in addition to the small chance of having an influence on the outcome, the outcome made little difference for the voters. But there was no secret ballot, so that votes could be bought; also voting was a social occasion not to be missed. This suggests that one would not expect to see the simultaneous presence of (i) a small chance to influence the outcome, (ii) small importance of the outcome for the voters, (iii) secret ballot and (iv) high, voluntary participation.

[137] Benn (1978), p. 19.

[138] Barry (1978), p. 47.

[139] Parkin (1968), quoted by Barry (1978).

these campaigns has provided the best statement of the self-defeating view of political behaviour that I have yet come across. In an interview, E. P. Thompson was asked, 'Look, suppose that meeting in Trafalgar Square doesn't achieve anything?' Thompson's answer, supposing it to be correctly and completely reported, is quite extraordinary:

That's not really the point, is it? The point is, it shows that democracy's alive. People aren't just inclined to accept what politicians tell them. A rally like that gives us self-respect. Chartism was terribly good for the Chartists, although they never got the Charter.[140]

The implication can only be that, if asked whether they thought all those efforts to achieve the Charter would really get them anywhere, the Chartists would have answered, 'That's not really the point, is it?' But this is an absurd notion. Self-respect, like self-expression, self-realization and their companions, are essentially by-products. There is no such activity or *kinesis* as 'acquiring self-respect', in the sense in which one may speak of the activity of 'learning French', although other activities such as that of uniting in the struggle for a common goal may have self-respect as a side effect.[141]

We are dealing here with the same confusion as when artists declare that the process and not the end result is the real work of art; when Eduard Bernstein asserted that in his view the goal of socialism was nothing, the movement itself everything;[142] or when a chess player asserts that he does not play to win, but for the sheer elegance of the game. There are only elegant and inelegant ways of winning, but no such thing as an elegant way of losing.[143] If Gentlemen are those who play to play, and Players those who play to win, then it is not surprising that decline follows when the sons of Players are turned into Gentlemen, as in one recent interpretation of late nineteenth century economic development in Britain.[144] E. P. Thompson, it would seem, is a Gentleman.

---

[140] *The Sunday Times*, 2 November 1980.
[141] See Kenny (1963) for the sense of *kinesis* invoked here.
[142] Bernstein (1899), Ch. V.
[143] Elegance in chess is lexicographically subordinate to winning. This is also the trend in ski jumping, graded by the two criteria of length and style. There used to be a trade-off between these two criteria, but increasingly judges seem reluctant to accord good marks for style to short jumps, so that style is only used to differentiate between jumps of considerable and approximately equal length.
[144] Coleman (1973).

II.10   THE OBSESSIONAL SEARCH FOR MEANING

'Any defect or fault in this garment is intentional and part of the design.' This label on a denim jacket I bought in San Francisco some years ago summarizes the intellectual and moral fallacies discussed in the present chapter. It embodies a widespread tendency to *search for meaning* in all phenomena – a tendency that can express itself either as an attempt to *find* meaning or as an effort to *create* meaning. If some action or pattern of action has good consequences, it is tempting to see them as providing a meaning and hence an explanation for the behaviour. One may also form an intention to engage in such behaviour in order to gain these benefits. If, however, the consequences in question are essentially by-products, the explanation will usually fail, and the intention prove self-defeating. I shall first discuss the explanatory issue at some length, and then more briefly the moral issues that have already been explored in some detail.

The explanatory issue is a special case of a more general problem: when is it legitimate to explain a phenomenon in terms of its consequences? Consequence-explanations in this sense are extremely widespread, although rarely well-founded. I shall first discuss the pre-theoretical form of such explanations, the form in which they are embedded in everyday life and perception. I then look at some theoretical defences of consequence-explanations, before proceeding to the more specific issue of explanation in terms of consequences that are essentially by-products.

In everyday life – in politics, in the family or at the work-place – one constantly encounters the implicit assumption that any social or psychological phenomenon must have a meaning or significance that explains it: there must be some sense or some perspective in which it is beneficial for someone or something – and these benefits also explain the presence of the phenomenon. This way of thinking is wholly foreign to the idea that there could be such a thing as sound and fury in social life, unintended and accidental events that have no meaning whatsoever. It takes for given that although the tale may appear to be told by an idiot, there always exists a code that, if found, would enable us to decipher it. This attitude also pervades the more unthinking forms of functionalist sociology, some samples of which are given below. It is reinforced, or so I believe, by the widespread diffusion of psychoanalytic notions. Whenever 'latent function' will not provide the meaning of behaviour, 'unconscious intention' may serve as a substitute. And if neither succeeds, conspiracy theories can always be invoked. I have already quoted Scheler's comment about *envy*, which arises when our factual inability to get something is explained as the result of a positive action against our desire. Another example to show the practical importance of this attitude is the Stalinist notion of 'objective complicity' – most recently illustrated by the Red Guards during the Cultural Revolution in China.[145]

The attitude has two main roots in the history of ideas. (It may also have deep roots in individual psychology; some of the mechanisms discussed in Ch. III below could well be relevant.) The first is the theological tradition and the problem of evil.[146] Within Christian theology there emerged two main ways of justifying evil, pain and sin – they could be seen either as indispensable causal conditions for the optimality of the universe as a whole, or as inevitable by-products of an optimal package solution. The first was that of Leibniz, who suggested that monsters had the function of enabling us to perceive the beauty of the normal. The second was that of Malebranche, who poured scorn on the idea that God had created monstrous birth defects 'pour le bénéfice des sages-femmes', and argued instead that accidents and mishaps are the cost God had to pay for the choice of simple and general laws of nature. In either case the argument was intended to show that the actual world was the best of all possible worlds, and that every feature of it was part and parcel of its optimality. Logically speaking, the theodicy cannot serve as a deductive basis for the sociodicy: there is no reason why the best of all possible worlds should also contain the best of all possible societies. The whole point of the theodicy is that suboptimality in the part may be a condition for the optimality of the whole, and this may be the case even when the part in question is the corner of the universe in which human history unfolds itself. If monsters are to be justified by their edifying effects on the midwives that receive them, could not the miseries of humanity have a similar function for creatures of other worlds or celestial spheres? But even though the theodicy cannot serve as a premise for the sociodicy, one can

---

[145] Tsou (1980) brings out well how 'functional analysis can be placed in the service of radicalism as well as conservatism'. In China, he argues, the 'misuse of functional analysis as a political weapon contributed to the loss of a generation of educated youth, scientists, engineers, physicians, humanists, social scientists, writers, artists and other specialists'.

[146] This paragraph draws heavily on Elster (1975).

use it as an analogy, as did Leibniz, although with some timidity. He argued, for instance, that luxury could be justified as a regrettable but inevitable by-product of prosperity, leaving it for Bernard Mandeville to argue more boldly that luxury was actually conducive to prosperity, through the effect on employment. The legacy of the theological tradition was a strong presumption that private vices are public benefits.

Secondly, the search for meaning derives from modern biology.[147] Pre-Darwinian biology also found a pervasive meaning in organic phenomena, but this was a meaning derived from the divine creator, not one that could serve as an independent inspiration for sociology. When Darwin rooted biological adaptation firmly in causal analysis, he not only destroyed the theological tradition, but also provided a substitute. Formerly, biodicy no less than sociodicy derived directly from the theodicy, but after Darwin sociodicy could invoke an independent biodicy. Once again, the biodicy did not – with the exception of social Darwinism and recent sociobiological thought – serve as a deductive basis for sociology, but as an analogy. In forms sometimes crude and sometimes subtle, social scientists studied society as if the presumptions of adaptation and homeostasis were as valid there as in the animal realm. Now even in the latter, these principles have less than universal validity, since for example pleiotropic by-products of adaptive features need not themselves be adaptive. In the social realm the principles suffer a complete breakdown. There is no mechanism, comparable in generality and power to natural selection, that could ensure social adaptation and social stability. This objection notwithstanding, the grip of the organic analogy on social actors and on the social scientists studying them remains strong.

For these historical reasons, there has been a close link between consequence-explanation and sociodicy, in the sense that the defects of society have been explained by their globally beneficial consequences for stability, integration or prosperity. Among the phenomena justified and explained in this way are economic inequality,[148] social conflict[149] or political apathy.[150] Yet the link is not a necessary one, since the

---

[147] This paragraph draws heavily on Elster (1979), Ch. I, and Elster (1982a), Ch. 2.

[148] Davis and Moore (1945). As observed by Boudon (1977), Ch. VI, the argument reappears among the empirical premises of Rawls (1971).

[149] Coser (1971), p. 60, argues for instance that 'Conflict within and between bureaucratic structures provides the means for avoiding the ossification and ritualism which threatens their form of organization.'

[150] In the vein of Mandeville, Berelson (1954, p. 316) writes that 'the voters least admirable when measured against individual requirements contribute most when measured against the

explanation can also invoke consequences that are globally negative, as in the following passage from Michel Foucault's *Discipline and Punish*:

> But perhaps one should reverse the problem and ask oneself what is served by the failure of the prison; what is the use of these different phenomena that are continually being criticised; the maintenance of delinquency, the encouragement of recidivism, the transformation of the occasional offender into a habitual delinquent, the organisation of a closed milieu of delinquency. Perhaps one should look for what is hidden beneath the apparent cynicism of the penal institutions, which, after purging the convicts by means of their sentence, continues to follow them by a whole series of 'brandings' (a surveillance that was once *de jure* and which is today *de facto*; the police record that has taken the place of the convict's passport) and which thus pursues as a 'delinquent' someone who has acquitted himself of his punishment as an offender? Can we not see here a consequence rather than a contradiction? If so, one would be forced to suppose that the prison, and no doubt punishment in general, is not intended to eliminate offences, but rather to distinguish them, to distribute them, to use them; that it is not so much that they render docile those who are liable to transgress the law, but that they tend to assimilate the transgression of the laws in a general tactics of subjection. Penality would then appear to be a way of handling illegalities, of laying down the limits of tolerance, of giving free rein to some, of putting pressure on others, of excluding a particular section, of making useful another, of neutralising certain individuals and of profiting from others.[151]

This lengthy quotation serves well to bring out the following characteristic features of this mode of explanation. (i) The consequence-explanation is suggested rather than explicitly stated. Foucault uses the technique of the rhetorical question; Bourdieu the device of stating that 'tout se passe comme si' cultural behaviour can be explained by its efficacy in keeping outsiders out.[152] (ii) The explanation is suggested in a cascade of verbs without a corresponding subject, corresponding to free-floating intentions that cannot be imputed to any individual. (iii) There is a presumption that the question *Cui bono?* is not only one of many that could usefully guide the investigation, but that it is somehow a privileged one. (iv) The suggested explanation on closer analysis emerges as sheer fantasy – an arbitrary and frictionless account that may be concocted by anyone with a modicum of eloquence and ingenuity. Leibniz curtly remarked of the neo-Confucian philosophers: 'I strongly doubt whether they have the vain subtlety of admitting sagacity without also admitting a sage.'[153]

aggregate requirements for flexibility . . . they may be the least partisan and the least interested voters, but they perform a valuable function for the entire system' (quoted after Pateman 1970, p. 7).

[151] Foucault (1975), p. 277. See also Elster (1982d).

[152] I counted 15 occurrences of this phrase in *La Distinction* (Bourdieu 1979, pp. 33, 35, 45, 161, 175, 234, 335, 358, 371, 397, 405, 467, 508, 515, 552).

[153] Quoted after Bodemann (1895), p. 105.

Foucault, Bourdieu and their likes certainly do not recoil from the subtlety of postulating a diabolical plan to which there corresponds no devilish planner.

Not all consequence-explanations, however, are of this crude variety. Among the more sophisticated ways of justifying such explanations are the following. (i) Behaviour can be explained by its consequences when these were intended by the actor.[154] (ii) Even when the consequences are unintended, they may explain the behaviour if there is some other agent who (a) benefits from the behaviour, (b) perceives that he benefits from it and (c) is able to maintain or reinforce it in order to get the benefits.[155] (iii) A similar explanation may be invoked when the agent himself recognizes that the behaviour has unintended and beneficial consequences which then tend to reinforce it.[156] (iv) Even when the consequences are unintended by the agents producing them and unrecognized by the agents benefiting from them, they may explain the behaviour if we can specify a feedback mechanism from the consequences to the behaviour. Natural selection is one such mechanism of outstanding importance.[157] (v) Even if none of the above conditions obtains, consequences may be invoked with explanatory force if we have general knowledge that ensures the existence of some feedback mechanism, even though we may be unable to specify it in each case.[158] (vi) Or the explanation might dispense with intention, recognition or feedback altogether, and rest instead on a well-established *consequence law*.[159]

I cannot here discuss these varieties of functional explanation, except to state that (i) through (iv) have broad application in the social sciences, whereas (v) and (vi) have a more dubious status.[160] Let me turn instead directly to the issue of explanation in terms of

---

[154] This is a misleading formulation, since it is the intended rather than the actual consequence that has explanatory power, even in the cases when the two coincide non-accidentally.

[155] Elsewhere (Elster 1979, Ch. I.5) I have proposed the term a 'filter-explanation'. Artificial selection as practised by animal breeders could be one mechanism underlying explanations of this form.

[156] See also Skinner (1981) and van Parijs (1981), Ch. 4 (and *passim*).

[157] For discussion of natural-selection models in the social sciences, see van Parijs (1981), Ch. 3, and Elster (1982), Ch. 6.

[158] Stinchcombe (1974, 1980) argues that social change can be modelled as a Markov-chain with absorbing states, enabling us to explain social institutions by their stabilizing effect (or absence of de-stabilizing effect) even when we do not have detailed knowledge about the mechanisms that brought them about.

[159] Cohen (1978) advocates this idea at some length.

[160] For a fuller discussion, see Elster (1982a), Ch. 2.

consequences that are essentially by-products of the explanandum. Pierre Bourdieu's work raises this problem in a most acute form, since it has such explanations at its very core. If we disregard an occasional lapse, he well understands that the ability to impress and to achieve distinction is incompatible with the intention to do so. The symbolic behaviour of the petty bourgeoisie is explained, for instance, in terms of the self-defeating intention to impress.[161] Yet the general theme of *La Distinction* is that behaviour which succeeds in impressing can also be explained in terms of this success, as an objective or unconscious strategy harnessed to this goal. It remains unclear, however, what is meant by an objective strategy. We are never told how to distinguish between behaviour that only by accident serves the agent's interest – for surely Bourdieu would agree that there are such cases? – and behaviour that can be explained by the fact that it does so.

Hence my objection to Bourdieu is not his explanatory use of consequences that are essentially by-products, only his lack of concern for a mechanism. There could well be a non-intentional mechanism that brought it about that behaviour emerges or persists because of certain consequences that are essentially by-products. Consider again Veyne's analysis of evergetism. If uncalculated magnificence is a condition for winning the affections of the people, and the latter a condition for getting or retaining power, then the calculatingly magnificent and the thrifty will not be found in positions of power. This would enable us to explain a certain behavioural pattern – the magnificence of the powerful – by consequences that are essentially by-products, through a mechanism of type (ii) above. According to Veyne the explanation would be incorrect, because the second premise is false. Generosity was not essential for power, at least not initially; and even when it became essential, lack of calculation was not indispensable.[162] Yet this objection is less important, for my purpose, than the fact that in the suggested explanation at least a mechanism is sketched, so that it fails on honourable empirical grounds. My main criticism is directed to the explanations that offer no mechanism, nor an argument that one may dispense with mechanisms, but simply proceed on the unthinking assumption that if generous behaviour has these eminently desirable results, then surely this must explain the generosity. This account fails dishonourably, since it proceeds from the misguided search for meaning.

[161] Bourdieu (1979), Ch. 6, esp. pp. 422ff.   [162] Veyne (1976), p. 327.

The hypothetical explanation cited above invoked artificial selection as the mechanism whereby unintended consequences can serve to explain their causes. Another possible mechanism could be reinforcement within the individual, i.e. case (iii) above. As mentioned in I.2, people often engage in rewarding activities *because* they are rewarding, but this is not to say that they do so *in order to* get the reward. When the rewards belong to the states that are essentially by-products, this distinction becomes crucial. Even though, say, the feeling of gratification or self-realization is essentially a by-product and hence could not *be* the motivation for action, it could *reinforce* the motivation to undertake the activities of which they are the by-products. This, presumably, is why artists are artists, scientists scientists and so on. They do not engage in art or science to get a thrill, but to 'get it right', and yet the thrill they get when they get it right strengthens their motivation to do this kind of work. Here we invoke the states that are essentially by-products in order to explain (causally) the motivations that explain (intentionally) the activity, which is very different from saying that the states *are* the goals that explain the behaviour.

Hence the explanatory fallacies that arise in this context are of two kinds, that may be associated with the names of Veblen and Bourdieu respectively (see also II.5). First, there is the attempt to explain intentionally the bringing-about of states that are essentially by-products; secondly, the idea that such states can be explained simply by pointing to their usefulness, without providing a mechanism. Or again, one may fail either by pointing to an inappropriate mechanism or by not suggesting any mechanism at all.

Of these two intellectual fallacies, the first is also closely linked to what I have called the moral fallacy of by-products – a misplaced or self-defeating form of instrumental rationality. It is the fallacy of striving, seeking and searching for the things that recede before the hand that reaches out for them. In many cases it takes the form of trying to get something for nothing, to acquire a character or become 'a personality' otherwise than by 'the ruthless devotion to a task'.[163] In other cases it is accompanied by self-indulgence, when one is led to tolerate errors or imperfections in one's work because one knows that they sometimes prove useful or fertile. In particular, many will have come across the brand of scientist who excuses the one-sidedness of his

[163] Weber (1968), p. 591.

work by the need for fertile disagreement in science.[164] And above all this attitude goes together with a form of self-monitoring whose corrosive effects I have been concerned to bring out.

It is sometimes said that all the good things in life are free: a more general statement could be that all the good things in life are essentially by-products. As in Albert Hirschman's recent work, this could be explained by the fact that by-products have no 'disappointment potential', since we never have any expectations about them in the first place.[165] We can also explain their attraction in more positive terms, by pointing to the value we attach to freedom, spontaneity and surprise. Most centrally, by-products are linked to what befalls us by virtue of what we *are*, as opposed to what we can achieve by effort or striving.

---

[164] For an example, see Scheff (1966), p. 27, critically discussed in Gullestad and Tschudi (1982). A systematic defence of this disastrous practice is offered by Mitroff and Mason (1981).

[165] Hirschman (1982), Ch. 1.

III

SOUR GRAPES

Certain Renard gascon, d'autres disent normand,
Mourant presque de faim, vit au haut d'une treille
  Des Raisins mûrs apparemment
  Et couverts d'une peau vermeille.
Le galant en eût volontiers fait un repas;
  Mais comme il n'y pouvait atteindre:
'Ils sont trop verts, dit-il, et faits pour des goujats.'
    Fit-il pas mieux que de se plaindre?
      (La Fontaine, *Fables* XXX.xi)

God grant us the serenity to accept the things we cannot change, courage to change the things we can and wisdom to know the difference. (*Alcoholics Anonymous prayer*[1])

Le 'ces raisins sont trop verts' de la fable serait du bon bouddhisme si le résultat n'était obtenu par une illusion sur l'objet alors qu'il faut au contraire dénoncer l'illusion du désir. (*S.-C. Kolm*[2])

III.1 INTRODUCTION

My goal in this chapter will ultimately be to throw light on a problem arising in the foundations of utilitarian theory. It is this: why should individual want satisfaction be the criterion of justice and social choice when individual wants themselves may be shaped by a process that preempts the choice? And in particular, why should the choice between feasible options only take account of individual preferences if people tend to adjust their aspirations to their possibilities? For the utilitarian, there would be no welfare loss if the fox were excluded from consumption of the grapes, since he thought them sour anyway. But of course the cause of his holding them to be sour was his conviction that he would be excluded from consuming them, and then it is difficult to justify the allocation by invoking his preferences.

[1] Quoted after Bateson (1972), p. 334.   [2] Kolm (1979), p. 530.

I shall refer to the phenomenon of sour grapes as *adaptive preference formation*, or adaptive preference change, as the case may be. Preferences shaped by this process I shall call adaptive preferences.[3] I set out by trying to clarify the notion of adaptive preferences: first by contrasting it with some other notions to which it is closely related and with which it may easily be confused (III.2); and then by interpreting it in the light of a long-standing controversy over the meaning of freedom (III.3). On the background provided by this analysis I then look at the substantive and methodological implications of adaptive preference formation for utilitarianism, ethics and justice (III.4). The idea of sour grapes appears to me just as important for understanding individual behaviour as for appraising schemes of social justice. Hence the conceptual analysis in III.2 and III.3 is intended to be of interest in its own right, and not merely a preparation for the ethical issues raised in III.4.

Sour grapes can be seen as a way of reducing cognitive dissonance. Hence the influence of Leon Festinger will make itself felt in what follows, both directly and indirectly through the work of Paul Veyne, which is heavily indebted to Festinger, while also going beyond him in important respects.[4] In particular Veyne introduces the important idea of 'over-adaptation' to the possible, which again is related to his general notion that people tend to overshoot in their choices and go to extremes not required by the situation. But Festinger's work, although important, does not have adaptive preferences as its only or main theme. Sour grapes is one mechanism for dissonance reduction among others. Indeed, I do not believe there has been any systematic discussion of the notion. This is largely so, I believe, because one has not made the crucial distinction between the causally induced and the intentionally engineered adaptation of preferences to possibilities. *Amor fati*, 'making a virtue out of necessity' and similar phrases lend

---

[3] The term 'adaptive utility' is used by Cyert and DeGroot (1975), but in a sense more related to what I here call endogenous preference change due to learning. They also use it to refer to what might better be called 'strategic utility', i.e. the need for a rational man to take account in the present of the fact that his preferences will change in the future (see also Tocqueville 1969, p. 582). I do not know of any discussions in the economic literature of adaptive preferences in the sense of the term used here, but some insights can be drawn from the economic analysis of Buddhist character planning in Kolm (1979), pp. 531–5.

[4] See Veyne (1976), pp. 706ff., for his general theory of choice, based on the ideas that (i) options come in bundles that cannot be disassembled and reassembled at will, (ii) that people tend to go to extremes and (iii) that the choices, once made, retroactively influence the preferences.

themselves to both interpretations, and not much of interest can be said without making it clear which of them one has in mind.[5]

III.2   A CONCEPTUAL MAP

Our minds play all sorts of tricks on us, and we on them. To understand the particular trick called 'sour grapes' we need to locate it more precisely on the map of the mind. I shall first contrast adaptive preferences to one mechanism that in a sense is its direct opposite; and then to a number of mechanisms that either have similar causes or bring about similar effects.

(a)   Counteradaptive preferences. The opposite phenomenon of sour grapes is that of 'forbidden fruit is sweet', which I shall call counteradaptive preference formation. If when I live in Paris I prefer living in London to living in Paris, but prefer Paris over London when in London, then my wants are shaped by the feasible set, as with adaptive preference formation, but in exactly the opposite way. This perverse mechanism of want formation shows the reality of the distinction between *desires* and *drives*, which in many other cases is hard to draw unambiguously. In I.5 I made a distinction between conformism and conformity based on the difference between desires and drives, but clearly it may be hard to detect in actual cases. Similarly, although I shall argue below that one can distinguish operationally between intentional adjustment of preferences to possibilities by meta-desires and the similar causal adjustment by drives, actual cases may not be clearcut enough to persuade sceptics of the reality of this distinction. Counteradaptive preferences, however, can hardly be shaped by a meta-desire to frustrate satisfaction of first-order desires. I argue below that frustration may be part of happiness and to that extent the object of preference planning, but it cannot be all of happiness. True, one could point to the side benefits of counteradaptive preferences, linked

---

[5] Bourdieu (1979) has 'le choix du nécessaire' as a central notion in his theory of choice and taste, but the idea remains vague because of the lack of this conceptual clarification. He makes fun (p. 326) of the academics who substitute Romanian carpets for the expensive Persian ones, a practice that is to be understood 'comme une manière de faire de nécessité vertu'. But there is nothing in his argument to indicate that they actually come to prefer the Romanian carpets, or at least think them equally good; nor any indication that these two alternatives might correspond to unconscious adaptation and to deliberate preference adjustment respectively. On the other hand he provides several good examples of sour grapes, as when he observes (p. 406) that the very fact of being able to cite a work of art which one does not personally like is a sign of upper-class origin: the culturally deprived cannot afford this luxury.

to the incentive effects created by a moving target. Through sheer restlessness one may acquire wealth, experience and even wisdom and the ability to come to rest. But these benefits would essentially be by-products, and thus could not be achieved through rational character planning.

Do counteradaptive preferences pose a similar problem to social choice theory as that created by adaptive preferences? Should one, that is, discount wants that have been shaped by this mechanism? If someone wants to taste the forbidden fruit simply because it is forbidden, should we count his exclusion from it as a welfare loss? And would it be a welfare gain to give him access, when this would make him lose his taste for it? An ordinal-utilitarian theory of social choice offers no answers to these questions. This indeterminacy in itself points to an inadequacy in that theory, although we shall see in III.4 that counteradaptive preferences are less troublesome for ethics than adaptive ones, since they do not generate a comparable conflict between autonomy and welfare.

(b) Preference change through learning. 'It is commonplace that choices depend on tastes and tastes on past choices.'[6] When in a set of alternatives I prefer an option of which I have little experience, trying it out may make me change my mind and rank it below some of the alternatives initially rejected. How are we to distinguish such preference change through learning and experience from adaptive preference change? Consider the case of job preferences. Imperfect regional mobility may lead to dual labour markets, e.g. to income in agriculture being systematically lower than in industry. Such income gaps may reflect the agricultural labourer's preference for being his own master, or for certain commodities that are cheaper in the countryside than in the city. The labourer may prefer to stay in the countryside rather than move to the city, even if the demand for agricultural goods is too small to enable him to earn the same monetary income as a factory worker. What are the welfare implications of this state of affairs? The standard answer is that a transfer of the labourer to the city would involve a loss in welfare for him and *ceteris paribus* for society. Consider, however, an argument proposed by Amartya Sen:

Preferences about one's way of life and location are typically the result of one's past experience and an initial reluctance to move does not imply a perpetual dislike. The

[6] Gorman (1967), p. 218.

distinction has some bearing on the welfare aspect of employment policy, since the importance that one wishes to attach to the wage gap as a reflection of the labourer's preferences would tend to depend on the extent to which tastes are expected to vary as a consequence of the movement itself.[7]

On a natural reading of this passage, it would seem to imply that (in some cases at least) the transfer is justified if the *ex post* evaluation of city life makes it preferable to the country life that was more highly valued *ex ante*.[8] We then need to ask, however, about the exact nature of the induced preference change. One possibility is that the transfer would imply learning and experience, another that the change would be due to habituation and resignation (adaptive preferences). On the first hypothesis the process is irreversible, in the sense that it cannot be reversed simply by a transfer back to the countryside. (It could, to be sure, be reversed by learning even more about life in the city, or by some quite different mechanism.) On the second hypothesis reversal could occur simply by going back to the initial feasible set.

Preference change due to learning can be fitted into an extended utilitarian framework, in which situations are evaluated according to *informed* preferences and not just according to the given preferences. One should attach more weight to the preferences of someone who knows both sides of the question than to someone who has at most experienced one of the alternatives. These informed preferences are, of course, those of the individual concerned, not of some superior body. They are informed in the sense of being grounded in experience, not in the sense of being grounded in the meta-preferences of the individual. They differ from given preferences only (or at most[9]) in their stability

---

[7] Sen (1975), p. 54.

[8] In an earlier work (Elster 1979), pp. 82–3, I interpreted the quoted passage as justifying 'seduction', i.e. as arguing that *ex post* preferences justify forcible violation of the *ex ante* ones. Sen (1980–1, p. 211, note 41) takes exception to this reading, and argues that nothing more is implied in the passage than that the welfare analysis should take account both of the *ex ante* and of the *ex post* preferences, not only of the former as on the standard view, but also not only of the latter as on the view he believes that I impute to him. I agree that my brief comment on his equally brief original statement could be read as if I impute to him the view that *ex post* preferences always override the *ex ante* ones, and that this (implausible) view is not in fact supported by the passage. Yet my original criticism stands. Assuming that Sen by the phrase 'depend on' means that the welfare evaluation of *x* vs. *y* is enhanced by *ex post* preferences for *x* over *y*, and that *ex post* preferences are not lexicographically subordinate to *ex ante* preferences, then there must be cases in which *ex ante* preferences can be overridden. If there is a welfare trade-off between *ex ante* and *ex post* preferences, this must mean that *ex ante* preferences can *sometimes* be overridden, but not, of course, that they *always* will be. My view, however, is that preference reversal by itself *never* justifies forcible violation of *ex ante* preferences.

[9] In fact, stability and irreversibility are neither sufficient criteria for the preference change being

and irreversibility. Informed preferences could be implemented in social choice by a systematic policy of experimentation, that gave individuals an opportunity to learn about new alternatives without definitely committing themselves to one of them. This would leave them with more information, but also with less character.[10] Individuals reared every second year in the city and every second in the countryside could make a more informed choice, but they would have less substance as persons.

Be this as it may, it appears clear that preference change through habituation and resignation cannot even be fitted into this extended utilitarianism. If preferences are reversibly linked *to* situations, then preferences *over* pairs of situations appear in a very different light. If an initial preference for city life could be reversed by extended exposure to the countryside and *vice versa*, then one could justify any *status quo* by what might appear as 'informed' preferences. This, however, would not be an extension of utilitarianism, but its breakdown. At least this holds for ordinal utilitarianism. Cardinal utilitarianism, in its classical version, is perfectly capable of handling the problem, by comparing total want satisfaction of countryside life with countryside preferences to total want satisfaction of city life with city preferences. But, as will be argued below, cardinal utilitarianism then has to face other, even more serious problems.

(c) Precommitment. Adaptive preferences bring it about that my preferred alternative in the feasible set also is my preferred option within a larger set of conceivable alternatives. The same result may also be brought about through precommitment, i.e. by the deliberate shaping of the feasible set for the purpose of excluding certain possible choices.[11] Some people marry for this reason: they want to create a barrier to prevent them from leaving each other for whimsical reasons. Other people abstain from marriage because they want to be certain that their love for each other (or lack of desire to leave each other) is not due to adaptive preference formation. It does not seem possible to ensure both that people stay together for the right reasons, and that

due to learning (since addictive preferences also have these properties), nor necessary criteria (since preference reversal may occur by learning even more about the alternatives).

[10] For the importance of character, see Williams (1981), Ch. 1.

[11] Elster (1979), Ch. II, has a survey of such techniques of precommitment. The goal of precommitment may either be to make certain options permanently unavailable, or to make them permanently undesirable as a result of their having been temporarily unavailable. The latter would be precommitment in the service of character planning, whereas here I am concerned with the first variety.

they do not leave each other for the wrong reasons. If one deliberately restricts the feasible set, one also runs the risk that the preferences that initially were the reason for the restriction ultimately come to be shaped by it, in the sense that they would have been different had they not been so restricted. As also argued by George Ainslie in a somewhat different context, the devices for coping with impulsiveness may end up as prisons.[12]

Another example showing the need for this distinction is the desire for submission to authority. As argued at length by Paul Veyne, the mechanism of sour grapes may easily lead the subjects to glorify their rulers, but this is then an ideology induced by and posterior to the actual submission, not a masochistic desire that generates the submission.[13] Again, we need to distinguish between preferences being the cause of a restricted feasible set and their being an effect of the set. The oppressed may spontaneously invent an ideology justifying their oppression, but this is not to say that they have invented the oppression itself. Veyne's account of ideology and hegemony may have the appearance of blaming the victims, but on reflection one must agree when he says that an explanation of ideology in terms of indoctrination and manipulation is no more flattering to the subjects.[14] And in fact the latter idea also is inherently implausible, as I now go on to argue.

(d) Manipulation. Sour grapes may make people content themselves with what little they can get. This, no doubt, will often be to the benefit of other people, who can get away more easily with exploitation and oppression. But this should not lead one into assuming that resignation generally is induced by those who benefit from it. Consider the following passage:

A may exercise power over B by getting him to do what he does not want to do, but he also exercises power over him by influencing, shaping or determining his very wants. Indeed, is it not the supreme exercise of power to get another or others to have the desires you want them to have – that is, to ensure their compliance by controlling their thoughts and desires? One does not have to go to the lengths of talking about *Brave New World*, of the world of B. F. Skinner, to see this: thought control takes many less total and more mundane forms, through the control of information, through the mass media and through the processes of socialisation.[15]

There is an ambiguity in this passage, for does it propose a purposive or a functional explanation of wants? Do the rulers really have the power

[12] Ainslie (1984) shows how certain mental 'book-keeping' arrangements, deviced to overcome weakness of will and impulsiveness, may lead to excessive rigidity of character.
[13] Veyne (1976), pp. 660ff. See also IV.3 below.
[14] Veyne (1976), p. 89.   [15] Lukes (1974), p. 23.

to induce deliberately certain beliefs and desires in their subjects? Or does the passage only mean that certain mental states have consequences that are good for the rulers? And if so, could these consequences still explain their causes? As explained in Ch. II, the purposive explanation is implausible since the states in question are essentially by-products, and a non-intentional explanation in terms of consequences will not work unless some feedback mechanism is specified. In any case, the notion of sour grapes involves a strictly endogenous causality, as opposed to these exogenous explanations in terms of the benefits for others. It is good for the rulers that the subjects are resigned to their situation, but what brings about the resignation – if we are dealing with sour grapes – is that it is good for the subjects.

This is not to say that the behaviour of the rulers is irrelevant for the beliefs and desires created in the subjects. On the contrary, when acting with fervour rather than with calculation the ruling classes can succeed in reaching and shaping the minds of their subjects, with consequences beneficial to their rule. Consider the importance of Methodism during the Industrial Revolution in England, when it served '*simultaneously* as the religion of the industrial bourgeoisie . . . and of wide sections of the proletariat',[16] i.e. as the 'religion of both the exploiters and the exploited'.[17] It was the religion of the exploiters both in the sense described by Weber, that Methodism, as all doctrines with an element of Calvinism, was conducive to rational economic activity,[18]and in the sense that it transformed the workers by turning them into their own slave-drivers and thus reduced the need for supervision and force.[19] (Observe that neither of these consequences of Methodism provides any explanation of why the bourgeoisie believed in it. The issue is briefly raised in IV.2 below.) It was also the religion of the exploited, for three sets of reasons set out by E. P. Thompson.[20] First, there was direct indoctrination through Sunday schools and other institutions of 'religious terrorism'; secondly, Methodism provided some kind of community to replace the older communities that were being destroyed; and thirdly, many working people turned to

---

[16] Thompson (1968), p. 391.   [17] *Ibid.* p. 412.

[18] Conducive in the sense that Calvinism can only be sustained psychologically by 'inner-worldly asceticism', not in the sense that such asceticism is commanded by, or follows logically from, the doctrine. As is evident from Thompson (1968), p. 38, Calvinism is an instance of Newcomb's Problem (Nozick 1969), i.e. of the confusion between causal and diagnostic criteria for salvation. See also Tversky (1982).

[19] Thompson (1968), pp. 392–3.   [20] *Ibid.* pp. 412ff.

religion as a consolation. The indoctrination, however, was successful only because the religious terrorists believed in what they were preaching. It is ambiguous to refer to this as 'the supreme exercise of power', in the sense of getting other people to have the desires one wants them to have. I may want you to have certain desires because they will make you act in a way that is to my benefit, or because they will have benefits for yourself in the form of salvation. To be sure, it would be naive to assume that the bourgeoisie were not aware and appreciative of the benefits to them of working class Methodism, but equally naive – or overly sophisticated – to believe that this is what nurtured their fervour in preaching it. Side effects may be known and welcome and yet have no explanatory power – either because as a matter of fact they are not strong enough to motivate the action or because, as in the present case, they are essentially by-products.

(e) Character planning. The notion of adaptation is crucially ambiguous, lending itself to a causal as well as to an intentional reading. Sour grapes is a purely causal process of adaptation, taking place 'behind the back' of the person concerned. Very different indeed is the intentional shaping of desires advocated by the Stoic, Buddhist or Spinozistic philosophies,[21] by psychological theories of self-control[22] or the economic theory of 'egonomics'.[23] In both cases the process begins with a state of tension between what you can do and what you might like to do. If the escape from this tension takes place by some causal mechanism of dissonance reduction, we are dealing with sour grapes; if it is engineered by conscious 'strategies of liberation',[24] with character planning. It is the difference between preferences being shaped by drives or by meta-preferences.

Sour grapes and character planning differ in many respects, morally as well as phenomenologically. Nietzsche spoke of *ressentiment* – a phenomenon closely linked to sour grapes – as a mentality suitable for

[21] See Kolm (1979) and Wetlesen (1979) for Buddhist and Spinozistic theories of character planning. Wetlesen's reading of Spinoza is also heavily influenced by Buddhist thought, as is evident from the title of his book.
[22] For a survey, see Mahoney and Thoresen (eds.) (1974).
[23] The term was coined by Schelling (1978); see also March (1978), Thaler and Shefrin (1981) and Schelling (1984), chs. 3 and 4.
[24] Wetlesen (1979), Ch. 4, has a valuable discussion, with the emphasis on a distinction between gradual and instantaneous strategies of liberation, the former having as subvarieties liberation by social control and liberation by self-control. On his interpretation, Spinoza did not believe that gradual strategies could lead to the highest form of freedom; this would seem to be opposed to the views of Kolm (1979) discussed in II.3 above.

slaves.[25] By contrast he argued that *amor fati* as a self-conscious attitude was a 'formula for the greatness of man'.[26] We can reject this aristocratic view, and yet agree that it is better to adapt to the inevitable through choice than by non-conscious resignation. This in turn is linked to the important phenomenological differences which I shall now describe.

First, there is the tendency of adaptive preferences to overshoot or, more generally, to miss the mark one way or another:

> For power and prestige are not the direct cause of obedience. There is an intermediate mental operation, an act of legitimation, which consists in bringing about a consonance with the possibilities. This is why the real social relationships do not coincide exactly with the relations of power. By virtue of this mental operation they tend to fall slightly short of the latter, or to go somewhat beyond them, leading at times to revendications and at other times to exaggerated submission. It is this exaggeration which is the basis for status societies.[27]

By character planning one may, at least in principle, shape one's wants so as to coincide exactly with – or differ optimally from – one's possibilities, whereas adaptive preferences do not lend themselves to such fine-tuning. Without the 'wisdom to know the difference' between what one can do and cannot do, one will either try too much or too little. Veyne emphasizes the excess of humility more than the opposite, overshooting more than under-adaptation, and rightly so I believe, since the underlying mechanism is the general tendency of the human mind to go to extremes. This tendency, in turn, may be explained by 'lack of toleration for ambiguity',[28] by stereotypical thinking[29] or the 'primitive mentality' which, failing to distinguish between external and internal negation, assumes that when not everything is possible, nothing is (I.3). Tocqueville believed that it was a peculiarity of the Frenchman that 'he finds pleasure in doing more than what is commanded of him; he goes beyond the spirit of servitude as soon as he has entered it',[30] but I think Veyne is right in seeing it as a universal phenomenon – generating discontinuous classes out of continuous distributions of life chances.[31] To be sure, this is largely speculation on

[25] Nietzsche (1887), I.10; also Nietzsche (1888), pp. 410ff. Scheler (1972) has a fascinating and somewhat repelling analysis of this phenomenon.

[26] Nietzsche (1888), p. 428.

[27] Veyne (1976), pp. 312–13.

[28] Loevinger (1976) sees toleration for ambiguity as a characteristic feature of the autonomous person.

[29] For surveys, see Jones (1977), Ch. 3, and Nisbett and Ross (1980), Ch. 5 and pp. 238ff.

[30] Tocqueville (1953), p. 331.

[31] Since 'going to extremes' would seem to make best sense in terms of 'going to the closest

my part, based on little else than casual evidence. But the hypothesis that preference adaptation tends to overshoot could certainly be empirically tested. For example, one might ask whether pure time preferences, net of income and uncertainty effects, could yet be correlated with income. The poor, that is, might over-evaluate the present over and above the extent to which this is rational for them to do as a result of their poverty.

Secondly, whereas adaptive preferences typically take the form of downgrading the inaccessible options, deliberate character planning would tend to upgrade the accessible ones. Given that dissonance is created by positive attributes of rejected options and/or negative attributes of chosen ones, reduction of dissonance might occur by emphasizing negative attributes of rejected or positive attributes of chosen alternatives.[32] In a less than perfect marriage I may adapt either by stressing the defects of the wise and beautiful women who refused me, or by cultivating the good points of the one who finally accepted me. The latter adaptation, if I can bring it off, clearly is better in terms of cardinal want satisfaction. Moreover, it would enable me to avoid the moral self-poisoning often associated with sour grapes, which easily shades over into envy, spite, malice etc.[33]

Thirdly, character planning and adaptive preference formation have very different consequences for *freedom*, as I argue in more detail below. It would hardly do to say that the free man is one whose wants have shrunk to the vanishing point out of sheer resignation, but there is a respectable and I believe valid doctrine that explains freedom in terms of the ability to accept and embrace the inevitable.

extreme', there will typically be some threshold mechanism which creates discrete 'sociétés à ordres' out of continuous mobility prospects.

[32] Wicklund and Brehm (1976), Ch. 5, offers evidence on this issue. It should be mentioned here that many findings of the Festinger school imply that dissonance is reduced by increased attractiveness of the chosen alternative, contrary to my suggestion that this is more likely to occur with deliberate character planning than with non-conscious adaptation. It is, for example, a well-known fact (Festinger 1957, p. 49) that people tend to be avid readers of advertisements for products in their own possession, although this would hardly make sense as a deliberate strategy for upgrading the chosen alternative. I believe, however, that this may to some extent be explained by the distinction between state-dependent and possibility-dependent preference formation (see below). Having bought a car, it may be easier to dispel doubts about the wisdom of the choice by reading ads telling you how good it is than by looking for negative assessments of rival brands. Before the choice, however, your feeling of envy or bitterness induced by the expensive cars you cannot afford may be more amenable to dissonance reduction by sour grapes.

[33] This is strongly emphasized by Scheler (1972) in his discussion of 'the impulse to detract', quoting Goethe to the effect that 'against another's great merits, there is no remedy but love'.

(f) Prior change of attribute weights. Adaptive preferences involve a retroactive change of weights in the attributes of the options: 'Once the choice has been made, or accepted, the interests it turns out to satisfy assume a more than proportional importance'.[34] What may have been a close race at the time of choice is after the fact transformed into a clearcut superiority of the option that – perhaps only by accident – was in fact chosen. It takes Cartesian clarity of mind to follow an arbitrarily chosen course without coming to believe that it is in fact superior to the alternatives.[35] This should be distinguished from the cases in which a change in the attribute weights – or even the formulation of new attributes[36] – takes place before the choice, to permit avoidance of the unpleasant state of mind associated with a close race between the options. It has been suggested that in such cases one unconsciously looks around for a framework within which one option (no matter which) has a clear advantage over the others, and that, having found such a framework, one adopts it for the time being and chooses the option which it favours.[37] The proper fable for this mechanism is not the fox and the grapes, but Buridan's ass and the two bunches of hay. If, contrary to the hypothesis, there had been some perspective in which one bunch was superior to the other, the ass would not have starved to death.

Why should the state of mind associated with a close decision be unpleasant? An obvious answer is the sheer strain of weighing the pros and the cons. In the case of Buridan's ass this may be the whole answer. But in other cases the tension stems from anticipated regret, i.e. from an anticipation of the kind of dissonance that will induce the retroactive change of weights postulated by Festinger. If the initial advantage of one option is fairly large, one is more immune to the new information that could otherwise reverse the preferences and induce regret.[38]

(g) Addiction. Preference change may occur endogenously because

---

[34] Veyne (1976), p. 708.

[35] See Elster (1979), Ch. II.4, for a discussion of Descartes' maxim to be, 'le plus ferme et le plus résolu en mes actions que je pourrais, et de ne suivre pas moins constamment les opinions les plus douteuses, lorsque je m'y serais une fois déterminé, qui si elles eussent été très assurées' (Descartes 1897–1910, vol. VI, p. 24).

[36] For the importance of attribute selection, see Aschenbrenner (1977). His concern, however, is only with randomness in attribute formulation, not with the more systematic bias discussed here.

[37] Shepard (1964), p. 277; Ullmann-Margalit and Morgenbesser (1977), p. 780.

[38] Of course, people might also prefer making close decisions, because of the thrill of responsibility. But I agree with Fellner (1965, p. 33) that such cases probably are rare.

people get hooked on certain goods, which they then consume
compulsively. A satisfactory model of addiction would have to
incorporate the following elements. First, addiction should be
distinguished from learning. It does not seem useful to talk of people
developing a 'beneficial addiction' to music; this in my view is more like
a learning process.[39] Secondly, addiction may, but does not necessarily,
go together with a divided self, one part struggling against the
addiction and one part revelling in it.[40] (Note, however, that sour
grapes *never* goes together with this kind of internal conflict.) It is surely
a mistake to believe that addiction must go together with occasional
pangs of conscience or regret. Thirdly, addiction differs from sour
grapes in the severity of the withdrawal symptoms. Although I have
argued that adaptive preference change is reversible, I do not believe
that the reversal occurs instantaneously. There may well be a period of
regret before one has completely readjusted to the old feasible set. But
excluding the object of addiction from the feasible set does not lead to
regret, but to violent physical reactions. Addiction, in fact, is much
more specific than sour grapes: it is to be explained more by the nature
of the object of addiction than by the tendency of the human mind to
adapt to whatever objects are available. Fourthly, there is a dynamic of
addiction, in that the craving for the object of addiction becomes
increasingly strong.[41] The reason why love, for example, is not
addictive is that it tends to wear off by itself when satisfied, or at least to
assume less compulsive forms. In fact love, unlike most other desires,
becomes compulsive and self-reinforcing only when *not* satisfied.[42]
Addictive preferences, like adaptive ones, are induced by the choice
situation rather than given independently of it, but there the
resemblance seems to end.

   (h) State-dependent preferences. In the standard theory of individual or
social choice, preferences are taken as *given* independently of the choice
situation (I.5). The alternative conceptualization, explored here, is to
see preferences as causally shaped by the situation. The term

[39] Stigler and Becker (1977) and Winston (1980) accept as meaningful the notion of beneficial
   addiction. An important reason for rejecting this idea is related to the specificity of addiction:
   one can develop 'beneficial addiction' to virtually any activity, but addiction in the
   non-metaphorical sense is much more specific.
[40] Winston (1980) and Thaler and Shefrin (1981) postulate a split mind in their accounts of
   addiction.
[41] Thus the analysis of alcoholism in Ainslie and Schaefer (1981) explains the *state* of being
   addicted to alcohol, but not the dynamics of addiction.
[42] See Elster (1979), Ch. IV.3, for comments on this pathological and common phenomenon.

'situation', however, is ambiguous. As observed by Serge Kolm,[43] the notion of situation-determined preferences may be understood either as *state-dependency* or *possibility-dependency* of preferences. In the standard theory of endogenous preference change–which is itself non-standard with respect to the economic theory of choice – tastes are assumed to be shaped by the current or past *choices*, not by the whole feasible set.[44] But the latter interpretation is equally plausible. My current preferences for, say, reading may be shaped not only by the book I currently read, but equally by the books currently on my bookshelf. My preferences for spouses may be shaped by my current spouse or by the set of women who could conceivably accept my proposal. And sour grapes may be taken to involve either a down-grading of the options not chosen or of the options not available. Veyne, in a phrase cited earlier, includes both possibilities when he says that retroactive change of attribute importance may emerge when the choice is 'made or accepted'. The Festinger experiments mostly interpret dissonance reduction as a reaction to actual choices, whereas my main focus has been on the shaping of preferences by the feasible set.

The distinction is a real one, and could be important for many purposes. I want, however, to point to two considerations that tend to reduce its salience in the kind of situations with which I am mostly concerned. First, the actual choice of one option can make the alternatives less accessible than they were, because of the costs of choice reversal. When I buy a car of brand A for £3,000, a car of brand B at the same price becomes just as inaccessible as was formerly a car of brand C costing £4,000, if the most I can get by a second-hand sale of my new car is £2,000. Hence after buying car A I will tend to downgrade car B just as much as before the purchase I may have tended to downgrade car C. The former downgrading could be described as state-dependent, but the comparison shows that it may equally be seen as possibility-dependent. Secondly, the distinction between state and feasible set may turn upon the way in which the situation is described. Consider again the city–countryside example. To live in the city may be considered globally as one state which (when in the city) I prefer over the countryside, considered as another global state. With a more fine-grained description of the states, however, it is clear that there are many modes of farming, all accessible to me when in

---

[43] Personal communication.
[44] This, for example, holds of all the works cited in Elster (1979), p. 77, note 68.

the countryside, and many modes of city life I can choose when in the city. Adaptive preferences then imply that according to my city preferences my globally best alternative is some variety of city life, but there may well be some varieties of countryside life that I prefer to some city lives.

(i) Rationalization. Sour grapes is a mechanism for dissonance reduction that operates on the preferences by which options are graded. An alternative mechanism works on the cognitive elements, shaping the perception rather than the evaluation of the situation. In some cases adaptive preferences and adaptive perception (i.e. rationalization) can hardly be distinguished from each other. In the French version of the sour grapes, cited in the epigraph to this chapter, the fox is deluded in his *perception* of the vermillion grapes, wrongly believing them to be green. In the English version he wrongly believes them to be sour, a matter of taste rather than of belief.[45] Similarly for counteradaptive preferences, where to 'Forbidden fruit is sweet' there corresponds 'The grass is always greener on the other side of the fence.' But in many cases the phenomena are clearly distinct. If I do not get the promotion I have coveted, I may ease the tension by saying that 'my superiors fear my ability' (misperception of the situation) or 'the top job is not worth having anyway' (misformation of preferences). Or again I may change my life-style so as to benefit from the leisure permitted by the less prestigious position (character planning).

For a more substantial example in which both mechanisms were observed, we may take Joseph Levenson's account of China's humiliating encounter with the West in the nineteenth century. On the one hand there were the *t'i-yung* rationalizers who believed it possible to retain the Chinese substance, or *t'i*, while assimilating Western function or *yung*. But of course this was sheer wishful thinking, since the attempt to get industrialization without modernization invariably leads to the worst of both worlds, rather than to the best of both as intended.[46] Moreover, this use of the *t'i-yung* formula in fact betrayed it; to look at the function as a mere means to the substance was already to

---

[45] Actually the matter is somewhat more complex. 'Vert' in French can mean lack of ripeness generally, and is used, for instance, about wines that have not attained maturity. Moreover, the idea that the grapes were sour can be a question of belief, if held of these *particular* grapes. Only if the fox came to believe that grapes *in general* were sour could their inaccessibility be said to have induced a change of taste *sensu stricto*.

[46] Half-hearted attempts to industrialize tend to create social upheaval without the economic growth that could justify it. For a good discussion, see Knei-Paz (1977), pp. 100ff.

be infested by Western thinking.[47] On the other hand there were Wo-jen and other anti-westernizers who, perceiving the fallacy behind the *t'i-yung* formula, had recourse to sour grapes for their dissonance reduction. Western techniques represented an option that China had considered and then rejected; they were not worth having anyway.[48] Accordingly they made Chinese culture rather than the Chinese nation into the focus of their loyalty; and it was left for the Kuomintang to discard both wishful thinking and sour grapes, in their choice of the nation as a main value, with culture relegated to a merely instrumental function.[49]

In the short run, wishful thinking and adaptive preference formation lead to the same outcome, viz. reduction of tension and frustration. In the long run, however, the two mechanisms are not equivalent and may even work in opposite directions, as can be shown by considering the classical finding from *The American Soldier* that there was a positive correlation between possibilities of promotion and level of frustration over the promotion system.[50] In the services where promotion chances were good, there was also more frustration over promotion chances. In Robert Merton's phrase, this paradoxical finding had its explanation in that a 'generally high rate of mobility induced excessive hopes and expectations among members of the group so that each is more likely to experience a sense of frustration in his present position and disaffection with the chances for promotion'.[51] We might also, however, envisage an explanation in terms of sour grapes. On this view, frustration occurs when promotion becomes sufficiently frequent, and is decided on sufficiently universalistic criteria, that there occurs a *release from adaptive preferences*. On either hypothesis the increased objective possibilities for well-being bring about decreased subjective well-being, be it through the creation of excessive expectations or by the inducement of a new level of wants. In III.4 I touch upon the relevance of this distinction for ethics and social choice.

---

[47] Levenson (1968), vol. i, pp. 65ff.
[48] *Ibid.* pp. 69ff.
[49] *Ibid.* pp. 107–8.
[50] Stouffer *et al.* (1949). The finding is sometimes called the 'Tocqueville effect', after the analysis in Tocqueville (1952), pp. 222–3.
[51] Merton (1957), p. 237. Boudon (1977), Ch. V, offers a rather different explanation, in terms of rational rather than irrational expectations: when chances of promotion go up, the number of people who *ex ante* find it worth their while to make an extra effort to get promotion rises even more, leading to more disappointment and frustration *ex post*.

III.3   POWER, FREEDOM AND WELFARE

From the external characterization of adaptive preferences through the contrasts explored above, I now turn to the internal structure of the phenomenon. I shall take a somewhat oblique route to the goal, by considering how not only the notion of welfare, but also those of power and freedom, are affected by the idea that preferences can be shaped by the feasible set. In fact, all of these notions have been defined in terms of 'getting what one wants', and the possibility that wants may be shaped by what one can get raises similar problems for all of them. I shall have least to say about power, which is somewhat peripheral to the present concerns, but more about freedom and how it is related to welfare.

Alvin Goldman, having noted that getting what one wants must be central to the concept of power, adds the following comment:

> It would be wrong to conclude, however, that whenever one gets what one wants one must have power in the matter . . . Even a person who *regularly* gets what he wants need not be powerful. The Stoics, and Spinoza as well, recommended that one form one's desires to accord with what can realistically be expected to happen in any case; they regarded freedom as conformity of events with actual desires, or rather, as conformity of desires with events. But as an account of power this is inadequate. To take an extreme example, consider Robert Dahl's case of the 'chameleon' legislator who always correctly predicts beforehand what the legislature is going to decide, and then forms a desire or preference to accord with this outcome. The chameleon always gets what he wants, but he is not one of the more powerful members of the assembly.[52]

The passage embodies the confusion that haunts many of the analyses of freedom and power, that between adaptation by character planning (advocated by Spinoza and the Stoics) and adaptive preference formation (practised by the chameleon legislator). We will encounter a similar confusion in Isaiah Berlin's analysis of freedom. Also I have half a quarrel with Goldman's contention that the case of the chameleon shows 'that an analysis of power cannot simply concern itself with what an agent actually wants and actually gets, but must concern itself with what he *would* get on the assumption of various *hypothetical* desires'.[53] The first part of this sentence clearly is true, but not the second. If an agent brings it about that *p*, in the face of resistance from other agents who do not want this outcome, and he also brings it about in the intended way (i.e. not by fluke), then he has power with respect to *p*. And this holds even if *p* would have been brought about in any case by some other agent. There is nothing

[52] Goldman (1972), p. 223.   [53] *Ibid.*

insubstantial or shadowy about preemptive power. Moreover, his power is not affected by the assumption that his desire to bring about p is caused by his knowledge that p will be brought about in any case, e.g. because he wants to show off to his rival power-holder. And, finally, his power to bring about p is not lessened one iota by his inability to bring it about that q rather than p, should his desire to spite his rival take that form. In other words, I believe that Goldman's reliance on non-causal subjunctive conditionals is doubly misplaced. Power must be understood in terms of causality; and the case of preemptive power shows that counterfactuals are not sufficient in any case for understanding power statements.

Turning now to the analysis of freedom, I want to discuss four notions of increasing complexity: being free to do something, being free with respect to something, being a free man and living in a free society. The basic building block of the analysis will be the notion of being *free to do something*. This I shall take more or less as unanalyzed, except to point to some ambiguities that a fuller analysis would have to resolve. First, and most important, there is the distinction between formal freedom and real ability, the latter but not the former implying that a desire to perform the action in question will in fact be realized.[54] Secondly, the obstacles to freedom in this strong sense can be either internal (psychic constraints) or external; if external, natural or man-made; if man-made, accidental or deliberate.[55] And thirdly, we need to understand the relation between freedom in the distributive and in the collective senses: even if any individual is free to do some particular thing, not all may be free to act similarly.[56] Much of what follows makes sense, I believe, both on the reading of freedom as formal absence of constraints of some specified type and on the reading of freedom as full ability, provided, of course, that the same meaning is kept in mind throughout.

[54] On the other hand ability, while more than freedom in the formal sense, is yet less than power. If in the actual world you are able to achieve x, this means that in all the possible worlds that differ from the actual one at most in your desire to achieve x, you get x. Power, however, is defined with respect to a larger set of possible worlds, including those in which there is some resistance to your getting x.

[55] My view is that unless the obstacles have deliberately been created for the purpose of preventing one from doing x, one has the formal freedom to do x. Moreover, I believe that this formal freedom is a valuable thing, even if it does not go together with full ability. This is so for at least two reasons: it is a good thing in itself not to be subject to another person's will; and when one is not so subject, the chances are better that one may be able to achieve something substantially equivalent. If I cannot afford to buy a book, I can borrow it from the library; if the government forbids its sale, it will also forbid its being available in the library.   [56] See Cohen (1979).

What is freedom, freedom *tout court*, being a free man? We may distinguish between two extreme answers to this question. One is that freedom consists simply in being free to do what one wants to do, irrespective of the genesis of the wants. In a well-known passage Isaiah Berlin argues against this notion of freedom: 'If degrees of freedom were a function of the satisfaction of desires, I could increase freedom as effectively by eliminating desires as by satisfying them; I could render men (including myself) free by conditioning them into losing the original desire which I have decided not to satisfy.'[57] And this, in his view, is unacceptable. By this argument Berlin was led to the other extreme in the spectrum of definitions of freedom: 'It is the actual doors that are open that determine the extent of someone's freedom, and not his own preferences.'[58] Freedom is measured by the number and importance of the doors and the extent to which they are open.[59] Disregarding the last clause, which appears to conflate formal freedom and real ability, this means that freedom is measured by the number and the non-subjective importance of the things one is free do do. True, Berlin suggests that the notion of importance should also take account of the centrality of the freedoms to the individual, but this would seem to smuggle in preferences again, contrary to his main intention.[60] Importance, in his view, must be divorced from the individual's own evaluation of importance. What the non-subjective importance involves is not explained by Berlin, but it surely makes sense, for example, to say that the freedom to worship is more important *even to the non-worshipper* than the freedom to turn right against the red light.[61]

In other words, by the possibility of conditioned desires Berlin is led into downgrading the importance of actual wants, and to stress the things one is free to do irrespective of whether one wants to do them. There is, however, a crucial ambiguity in the argument. By 'conditioning men' (including oneself) into losing the desires that cannot be satisfied one may mean either manipulation and indoctrination (of other people), character plannning (in the case of oneself), or perhaps even sour grapes (although then the intentional language used by Berlin would not be appropriate). But these senses differ radically in their implications for freedom. Character planning, although neither a

---

[57] Berlin (1969), p. xxxviii.   [58] Berlin (1963–4), p. 193.
[59] Berlin (1969), p. 130, note 1; Berlin (1963–4), p. 191.
[60] 'Some doors are much more important than others – the goods to which they lead are far more central in an individual's or society's life' (Berlin 1963–4, p. 191).
[61] Taylor (1979) makes a similar point.

necessary nor a sufficient condition for autonomy (I.3), is at least much more compatible with autonomy than are either manipulated preferences or adaptive ones.

I do in fact suggest that the degree of freedom depends on the number and importance of the things that one (i) is free to do and (ii) autonomously wants to do. This takes care of two central intuitions about freedom. First, freedom must involve some kind of unconstrained movement. If I live in a society that offers me a great many important opportunities, which do not at all overlap with what I want to do, then I suggest it would be perverse to say that I have a great deal of freedom. But, secondly, intuition also tells us that it is perverse to say of a man that he is free simply because he is made to content himself with little, by manipulation or adaptive preference formation. By defining freedom in terms of autonomous wants – rather than in terms of any want or not in terms of wants at all – we can accommodate both of these intuitions. I am not thereby committed to the extreme rationalistic view discussed and rejected by Berlin,[62] that there is only one thing that the autonomous man could want to do in any given situation. True, given my confessed lack of ability to give a positive characterization of autonomy (I.3), I cannot refute this view. Moreover, since part of my case for autonomy rests on the analogy with judgment, and since one might want to argue that there is only one thing that a man endowed with judgment could believe in any given situation, it could appear that I am close to the rationalistic view. But I am not sure about the unambiguous character of judgment,[63] and in any case I strongly believe that autonomy – unlike judgment – is so closely linked to the idiosyncracies of *character* that it not only allows, but positively demands, diversity and plurality.[64]

It will be objected that this definition of freedom is useless if it does not go with a criterion for autonomy, so that for practical purposes we have to fall back on Berlin's definition, which surely represents the lesser evil. But I think we can do better than this. We can exclude operationally at least one important variety of non-autonomous wants, viz. adaptive preferences, by requiring freedom to do otherwise. If I want to do x, and am free to do x, and free not do x, then my want cannot

[62] Berlin (1963–4), p. 185.
[63] Cp. the argument for satisficing in I.3 above.
[64] For this anti-Kantian idea I again refer the reader to Williams (1981), Ch. 1. If character stems from past choices, and if many choices are largely arbitrary or at least based on satisficing rather than optimizing, the idea of a 'rational character' makes little sense.

be shaped by necessity. (At least this holds for the sense of 'being free to do x' in which it implies 'knowing that one is free to do x'. If this implication is rejected, knowledge of the freedom must be added as an extra premise.) The want may be shaped by all other kinds of disreputable psychic mechanisms, but at least it is not the result of adaptive preference formation. Other things being equal, one's freedom is a function of the number and importance of the things that one (i) is free to do, (ii) is free not to do and (iii) wants to do. The freedom to perform or abstain from performing an action may also be called *freedom with respect to that action*, so that, say, the Australians, while free to vote, are not free with respect to voting, since it is compulsory for them to vote.[65] And then one's freedom depends on the number and importance of the things one wants to do and with respect to which one is free.

An alternative proof that my want to do x is not shaped by the lack of alternatives would be that I am not free to do x. It would be absurd to say that my freedom increases with the number and importance of the things I want to do, but am not free to do, but as briefly mentioned in I.5 above, there is a core of truth in this paradoxical statement. If, namely, there are many things that I want to do, but am unfree to do, then this indicates that my want structure, including the things that I want to do and am free to do, but not free not to do, is not in general shaped by adaptive preference formation. This in turn implies that all my satisfiable wants should count in my total freedom, since there is a reason for believing them to be autonomous or at least non-adaptive. The reason is weaker than that provided by the freedom to do otherwise, but it still is a reason of a sort. I conclude that given two persons with exactly the same things they both want to do and are free to do, then (*ceteris paribus*) the one is freer or more likely to be free who is free not to do them; also (*ceteris paribus*) the one is freer or more likely to be free who wants to do more things that he is not free to do.

I shall argue below that these last considerations also carry over to welfare, but first I would add the fourth level to the structures of freedom discussed above. This is the notion of *a free society*, a notoriously ideological notion with ominous right-wing connotations. There is no reason, however, to let this notion be the monopoly of libertarians. Socialists should more than others, not less, be concerned about freedom as a value that could conceivably conflict with other values.

[65] Cohen (1979).

But first we need to know what freedom means at the aggregate level. I would suggest that aggregate social freedom is a function of (i) the total sum of the amounts of freedom of the individuals, calculated on the basis sketched above; (ii) the distribution of freedom among the individuals; and (iii) the extent to which the individuals value their freedom. The first two determinants of a free society raise the question of a trade-off between the total amount of freedom and its distribution, suggesting the same range of solutions as in the similar case of aggregate welfare.[66] The extent to which the individuals value freedom depends in turn on their attitude to responsibility[67] (the other side of the coin of freedom) and on other factors that might discourage them from using their freedom. In particular, a freedom which all have distributively might be little used and valued because the individuals concerned do not have it collectively.[68] (Needless to say, this notion of the value of freedom is not related to Rawls's discussion of the worth of liberty, which turns on the distinction between formal freedom and real ability.[69]) So, broadly speaking, a free society would tend to be one in which there is much individual freedom, evenly distributed and highly valued. It ought to go without saying that the apparent precision of this analysis is misleading. I am not suggesting one could ever construct a formal theory of freedom analogous to welfare economics, but the arguments I have invoked could find application in sufficiently clearcut cases.

The objects of welfare differ from the objects of freedom in that, for some of them at least, it makes little sense to speak of not being free to abstain from them. It makes good sense to say that freedom to worship is enhanced by the freedom not to worship (and *vice versa*), but hardly to say that the welfare derived from a certain consumption bundle is enhanced by the option of not consuming the bundle, since one always has that option. Nevertheless the arguments of the paragraph before the last carry over to the extent that (i) the larger the feasible set and (ii) the more your wants go beyond it, the smaller is the probability that your wants are shaped by it. Or to put it the other way around: a small

---

[66] One might argue, that is, for an egalitarian distribution of freedom, for a maximin distribution or for a distribution that maximizes the sum-total of freedom. Rawls (1971, pp. 231ff.) extends the maximin principle from welfare to freedom, while Nozick (1974, pp. 28ff.) basically takes an egalitarian view of freedom.

[67] Cp. the discussion of Amos Tversky's work on 'costs of responsibility' towards the end of I.4 above (and especially note 72 to Ch. I).

[68] Cohen (1979).

[69] Rawls (1971), p. 204.

feasible set more easily leads to adaptive preferences, and even with a large feasible set one may suspect adaptive preferences if the best element in the feasible set is also the globally best element.

On the other hand, preferences may be autonomous even if the best feasible element is also the global best, viz. if they are shaped by deliberate character planning. The question then becomes whether we can have evidence about this beyond the (usually unavailable) direct evidence about the actual process of want formation. Very tentatively I would suggest the following *condition of autonomy for preferences:*

If S_1 and S_2 are two feasible sets, with induced preference structures R_1 and R_2, then for no x or y (in the global set) should it be the case that xP_1y and yP_2x.[70]

This condition allows preference to collapse into indifference and indifference to expand into preference, but excludes a complete reversal of preferences. Graphically, when the fox turns away from the grapes, his preference for strawberry over raspberrry should not be reversed. The condition permits changes both in intra-set and inter-set rankings. Assume x,y in S_1 and u,v in S_2. Then xP_1u and xI_2u could be explained as a deliberate upgrading of the elements in the new feasible set. Similarly xP_1y and xI_2y could be explained by the lack of need to make fine distinctions among alternatives that have become inaccessible. Also, uI_1v and uP_2v could be explained by the need for such distinctions among the elements that have now become available. By contrast, xP_1u and uP_2x would indicate an upgrading of the new element or a downgrading of the old beyond what is called for, corresponding to the tendency of adaptive preferences to overshoot. Similarly, xP_1y and yP_2x (or uP_1v and vP_2u) are blatantly irrational phenomena, for there is no reason why adjustment to the new set should reverse the internal ranking in the old.

For a conjectural example of preference change violating this autonomy condition, I might prefer – in my state as a free civilian – to be a free civilian rather than a concentration camp prisoner, and to be a camp prisoner rather than a camp guard. Once inside the camp, however, I might come to prefer being a guard over being a free civilian, with life as a prisoner ranked bottom. In other words, when the feasible set is (x,y,z) I prefer x over y and y over z, but when it is reduced to (x,y) I prefer z over x and x over y. In both cases the best element in

---

[70] Here and in the following I use 'P' for strict preference ('better than'), 'R' for weak preference ('at least as good as') and 'I' for indifference.

the feasible set is also the globally best, not in itself a sign of non-autonomy. But in addition the restriction of the feasible set brings about a reversal of preferences, violating the condition. If the restricted set had induced indifference between x and y, both being preferred to z, this would have been evidence of a truly Stoic mastery of self. For another example, consider the labourer who after a transfer to the city comes to reverse his ranking of the various modes of farming, preferring now the more mechanized forms that he previously ranked bottom. Thirdly, observe that modernization does not merely imply that new occupations are interpolated at various places in the prestige hierarchy, but that a permutation of the old occupations takes place as well.

When a person with adaptive preferences experiences a change in the feasible set, one of two things may happen: adaptation to the new set or release from adaptive preferences altogether. An indication of the latter would be if the globally best element was no longer within the feasible set. And even if the feasible best remained the global best, release from adaptation might be conjectured if no reversal of the preferences took place. Adaptation to the new set was illustrated in the city–countryside case, whereas release from adaptation is exemplified below in the case of the Industrial Revolution. Here the release is diagnosed through the first criterion, that the global best is outside the feasible set. The second criterion – the feasible best remaining the global best, with no preference reversal – presumably would not have widespread application, since conscious character planning is a relatively rare phenomenon.

Does lack of autonomy detract from welfare, or is autonomy orthogonal to welfare so that we would rather have to consider trade-offs? The answer to this question depends on whether we consider welfare in an ordinal or a cardinal perspective. I believe that *if* one can talk meaningfully about cardinal want satisfaction in the full classical sense, involving interpersonally comparable and additive utilities, then the issue of autonomy is irrelevant for the measurement of welfare. Want satisfaction is want satisfaction, irrespective of the genesis of the wants. If, however, we restrict ourselves to the ordinal framework of social choice theory, I believe that the issue of autonomy is relevant for welfare. Within the ordinalist language, we cannot meaningfully distinguish between the case in which the change from yRx to xPy occurs by upgrading x and the case where it is due to downgrading of y. If, however, the preference change violates the autonomy condition, we may suspect that it has taken place by downgrading y, so that, cardinally speaking, the person is not better off with x after the change than he was before. In other words, the autonomy condition, stated in purely ordinal language, provides a cue to the underlying cardinal structure of the preferences. I now turn to some more substantial remarks on this issue.

III.4 Sour grapes and social choice

To discuss the relevance of adaptive preferences for utilitarianism, I shall consider the question whether the Industrial Revolution in Britain was on the whole a good or a bad thing. In the debate among historians over this question,[71] two issues have been raised and somtimes confused. First, what happened to the welfare level of the British population between 1750 and 1850? Secondly, could industrialization have taken place in a less harsh way than it actually did? (And if the latter, would it have been better for it to have taken place in a more or in a less capitalist manner than it did?[72]) Focussing here on the first issue, what kind of evidence could be relevant? Clearly the historians are justified in singling out the real wage, mortality, morbidity and employment as main variables: their average values, dispersion across the population and fluctuations over time. But if we are really concerned with the question of welfare, we should also inquire into the level of wants and aspirations. If the Industrial Revolution made wants rise faster than the capacity for satisfying them, should we then say that the Pessimist interpretation was correct and that there was a fall in the standard of living? Or, following the non-Pessimist[73] interpretation, that an increased capacity for want satisfaction implies a rise in the standard of living? Or, following Engels,[74] that even assuming a fall in the material standard of living, the Industrial Revolution should be welcomed because it brought the masses out of their apathetic vegetation and so raised their dignity?

---

[71] Elster (1978a), pp. 196ff., has further references to this debate.

[72] In fact, it does not appear that anyone holds the view that the actual course was optimal, so that the debate is rather between those who – like T. S. Ashton or F. Hayek – believe it was insufficiently capitalist in character and those – like E. Hobsbawm or E. P. Thompson – who believe that the misery was due to its excessively capitalist character.

[73] As argued in Elster (1978a), p. 220, note 35, the term 'optimism' vs. 'pessimism' are misleading. The issue of pessimism vs. non-pessimism is the factual one discussed here, and the question of optimism vs. non-optimism the counterfactual one of alternative and better ways of industrialization.   [74] Engels (1845), pp. 308–9. Cp. also Marx (1857–8), pp. 162, 488.

The problem is analogous to that of *The American Soldier,* and as in that case there is also the possibility that frustration, if such there was, stemmed from excessive expectations and not from rising aspirations. If that turned out to be true, the utilitarian might not want to condemn the Industrial Revolution. He could say, perhaps, that frustration derived from irrational beliefs should not count when we add up the sum total of utility: if we require preferences to be informed, then surely it is also reasonable to require beliefs to be well-grounded? But I do not think the utilitarian could say the same about frustration derived from more ambitious wants, and if this proved to be the main source of discontent, he could be led into a wholesale rejection of the Industrial Revolution. I assume in the sequel that there was indeed some frustration due to a new level of wants, and try to spell out what this implies for utilitarianism. Later I return to the problem of excessive expectations.

Imagine that we are in pre-industrial state x, with induced utility functions $u_1 \ldots u_n$. We may think of these as either ordinal and non-comparable, i.e. as short-hand for continuous and consistent preferences (I.2), or as fully comparable in the classical cardinal sense. I shall refer to the two cases as the ordinal and the cardinal ones, but the reader should keep in mind that the crucial difference is that the latter permit, as the former do not, to speak unambiguously of the sum total of utility.[75] Assume now that industrialization takes place, so that we move to state y, with induced utility functions $v_1 \ldots v_n$. In addition there is a possible state z, representing a society in which more people enjoy the benefits of industrialization, or all people enjoy more benefits. Given the utility functions, we assume that there is some kind of utilitarian device for arriving at the social choice or the social preference order. In the ordinal case this must be some kind of social choice function (I.4); and in the cardinal case we simply choose the state that realizes the greatest sum-total of utility. We then make the following assumptions about the utility functions $u_1 \ldots u_n$:

Ordinal case: According to the pre-industrial utility functions, x should be the social choice in (x,y,z).
Cardinal case: According to the pre-industrial utility functions, the sum total of utility is larger in x than it would be in either y or z.

---

[75] Sen (1970), Ch. 7, has a good discussion of the problems of utility aggregation. The recent discussion in d'Aspremont and Gevers (1977) highlights the informational requirements of various approaches to comparison and aggregation of utilities.

We also stipulate the following for the utility functions $v_1 \ldots v_n$:

Ordinal case: According to the industrial utility functions, the social choice function ranks z over y and y over x.
Cardinal case: According to the industrial utility functions, there is a larger sum of utility in z than in y, and a larger sum in y than in x.

Finally we add for the

Cardinal case: The sum-total of utility in x under the pre-industrial utility functions is greater than the sum-total of utility in y under the industrial utility functions.

This means that before industrialization, in both the ordinal and the cardinal cases, the individuals live in the best of all possible worlds. After industrialization, this is no longer true, as the social choice would now be an even more industrialized world. Yet the industrial state is socially preferred over the pre-industrial one, although – assuming cardinality – people are worse off than they used to be. The intuitive meaning is that for everybody z is better than y on some objective dimension such as actual or expected income and y better than x; indeed, y is sufficiently much better than x to create a new level of desires and z sufficiently much better than y to engender a level of frustration that actually makes people cardinally worse off in y than they were in x, although, to repeat, the social choice in y is y rather than x. 'We were happier before we got these fancy new things, but now we would be miserable without them.' Clearly the story is not an implausible one.

What in this case should the utilitarian recommend? The ordinal utilitarian has, I believe, no grounds for any recommendation at all. State x is socially better than y according to the x-preferences and y better than x according to the y-preferences, and no more can be said. The cardinal utilitarian, however, would unambiguously have to recommend x over y on the stated assumptions. And this, I submit, is unacceptable. It cannot be true that the smallest loss in welfare always counts for more than the largest increase in autonomy. There must be cases in which the autonomy of wants overrides the satisfaction of wants, and in which frustration, unhappiness and revolt should be positively welcomed. And the release from adaptive preferences in the case described has exactly these consequences: inducement of frustration and creation of autonomous persons. We do not want to solve social problems by issuing vast doses of tranquillizers, nor do we want people to tranquillize themselves through adaptive preference change. Engels may have overestimated the mindless bliss of pre-industrial society and underrates the mindless misery, but this does not detract from his observation that 'this existence, cosily romantic as it was, nevertheless was not worthy of human beings'.[76]

I am not basing my argument on the idea that frustration in itself may be a good thing. I believe this to be true, in that happiness requires an element of consummation and an element of expectation that reinforce each other in some complicated way.[77] In fact, 'To be without some of the things you want is an indispensable part of happiness.'[78] But a utilitarian would then be happy to plan for optimal frustration. My argument is that even more-than-optimal frustration may be a good thing if it is an indispensable part of autonomy. Nor am I arguing that the search for ever larger amounts of material goods is the best life for man. There certainly may come a point beyond which the frustrating search for material welfare no longer represents a liberation from adaptive preferences, but rather enslavement to addictive preferences. But I do argue that this point is not reached in the early stages of industrialization. Only the falsely sophisticated would argue that the struggle for increased welfare was non-autonomous from its very inception. The Rawlsian emphasis on primary goods as a means – in itself neutral – to realization of a chosen life plan seems to me absolutely correct, as does also his observation that at some stage further increase in material welfare becomes less urgent.[79] Whether it comes to be experienced as less urgent is another and very different matter.

I should now explain exactly how this example provides an objection to utilitarianism. Generally speaking, a theory of justice or of social choice should satisfy two criteria (among others). First, it should be a guide to action, in the sense that it should enable us to make effective choices in most important situations. If in a given case the theory tells us that two or more alternatives are equally and maximally good, then this should have a substantive meaning and not simply be an artifact of the theory. The latter is true, for instance, of the Pareto principle that x

---

[76] Engels (1845), p. 309.

[77] Cp. Ainslie (1984) for a discussion of 'premature satiation'. The person unable to control this basic tendency of human beings 'returns to the sterile omnipotence of infancy and acquires a species of Midas touch: His every appetite is gratified, but so quickly that the anticipation which is necessary to harvest full satisfaction for a drive never develops, and so briefly that he must repeat the process indefinitely'. Sour grapes in this respect has some of the qualities of masturbation.

[78] Bertrand Russell, quoted after Kenny (1965–6).   [79] Rawls (1971), §§15, 82.

is socially better than y if and only if one person strictly prefers x over y, and no one strictly prefers y over x, whereas society is 'indifferent' between x and y if some person strictly prefers x over y and some other person strictly prefers y over x. Even though this principle formally establishes a ranking, it is hopelessly inadequate as a guide to action. A theory should not tell us that some alternatives are non-comparable, nor try to overcome this problem by stipulating that society is indifferent between all non-comparable alternatives.[80]

Secondly, we must require of a theory of justice that it does not strongly violate our ethical intuitions in particular cases. If a theory suggests that people should take tranquillizers when the Coase theorem requires them to,[81] we *know* it is a bad theory. True, the proper role of such intuitions is not well-understood. If they are culturally relative, one hardly sees why they should be touch-stones for a non-relative theory of justice. And if they are culturally invariant, one suspects that they might have a biological foundation,[82] which would if anything make them even less relevant for ethics. Perhaps one could hope that persons starting from different intuitions might converge towards a unique reflective equilibrium by a process of the kind discussed in I.5 above. The outcome, then, would represent a man as a rational rather than a culturally or biologically determined being. But I have argued that it is not very likely that unanimous agreement on values would in fact emerge in this manner. Such problems notwithstanding, I do not see how a theory of justice can dispense with intuitions altogether.

My objection to utilitarianism, then, is that it fails on both of these counts. Ordinal utilitarianism in some cases fails to produce a decision, and cardinal utilitarianism sometimes generates bad decisions. The indecisiveness of ordinal utilitarianism is due, as in other cases, to the paucity of information about the preferences.[83] Cardinal utilitarianism allows for more information, and therefore ensures solutions to the decision problem. But even cardinalism allows too little information. Satisfaction induced by resignation may be indistinguishable on the hedonometer from satisfaction of autonomous wants, but I have argued that we should distinguish between them on other grounds.

Some of the distinctions proposed in III.2 may now be brought to bear on these issues. The reason why counteradaptive preferences are

[80] Cp. Sen (1970), Chs. 2 and 5.
[81] As suggested by Nozick (1974), p. 76n.
[82] Rawls (1971), p. 503, following Trivers (1971).
[83] See Sen (1979) on the relevance of information for ethics.

less problematic for ethics than adaptive ones is that release from counteradaptive preferences simultaneously improves autonomy and welfare. When I no longer possess – or no longer am possessed by – the perverse drive for novelty and change, the non-satisfaction of non-autonomous wants may turn into the satisfaction of autonomous ones. The destructive character of counteradaptive preferences was brought out in an example given in I.4 above, related to the idea of 'improving oneself to death'. Here a person obsessed by novelty is led to ruin by a series of stepwise changes, each of which is perceived as an improvement in terms of the preferences induced by the preceding step. Clearly, to be released from this obsession is both a good thing in itself and has good consequences for welfare. Release from adaptive preferences, however, may be good on the autonomy dimension while bad on the welfare dimension.

Similar remarks apply to character planning, which may improve welfare without loss of autonomy. I am not arguing that character planning *ipso facto* makes for autonomy (I.3), but surely it could never detract from it. One should note that character planning may improve welfare compared both to the initial situation of dissonance and to the alternative solution, i.e. adaptive preference change. First, recall that character planning tends to upgrade the possible, and that this – cardinally speaking – is a better solution than that of downgrading the impossible. Both solutions reduce dissonance, but character planning leaves one cardinally better off. Secondly, observe that the strategy of character planning is fully compatible with the idea that for happiness we need to have wants somewhat (but not too much) beyond our means. True, this notion is incompatible with the Buddhist version of character planning, which sees in frustration *only* a source of misery. But I believe this to be bad psychology, and that Leibniz was right in that 'l'inquiétude est essentielle à la félicité des créatures'.[84] Character planning, then, should aim at optimal frustration, which makes one better off than in the initial situation (with more-than-optimal frustration) and also better off than with adaptive preferences, which tend to limit aspirations to, or even below, the level of possibilities, resulting in a less-than-optimal level of frustration.

Endogenous preference change by learning not only creates no problems for ethics, but is positively required by it. If trying out something you believed you would not like makes you decide that you

---

[84] Leibniz (1875–90), vol. v, p. 175.

like it after all, then the latter preferences should be made the basis for the social choice, and social choice would not be adequate without this basis. This, of course, is subject to the qualifications that the newly formed preference should not be an addictive one, and that the need for knowledge may be overridden by the need for substance of character. In fact, these two qualifications are related: a person who decides that he wants to try everything once before he decides on his permanent long-term choice may lose what little character he has if he gets into one of the 'absorbing states' associated with addiction.

Hard problems remain, however, concerning the relation between misperception of the situation and misformation of the preferences. Consider again the alternative interpretation of the Industrial Revolution, in terms of excessive anticipations rather than of rising aspirations. From the work of Tocqueville, Merton and Veyne it would appear that below a certain threshold of actual mobility, expected mobility is irrationally low, in fact zero. Above this threshold, expected mobility becomes irrationally high, close to unity. And so in a society with little actual mobility, preferences may adapt to the perceived rather than to the actual situation, contributing to what I have called overshooting or over-adaptation. Similarly, once a society has passed the mobility threshold, irrational expectations are generated, with a correspondingly high level of wants. The intensity of the desire for improvement grows with the belief in its probability, and the belief in turn through wishful thinking feeds on the desire.

This view, if correct, implies that one cannot sort out in any simple way the frustration due to irrational expectations from that which is due to new levels of aspirations. Let us imagine, however, that there is no tendency to wishful thinking. Then the actual and the expected rates of mobility will coincide, or at least not differ systematically. Rational expectations will then generate a specific intensity of desire or level of aspirations, with a corresponding level of frustration. The utilitarian might then want to argue that in this counterfactual state of rational expectations there will not be generated so much frustration as to make people worse off after the improvement in their objective situation. For subjective welfare to fall in spite of, and because of, the rise in objective possibilities for welfare, wishful thinking is required.

I am far from sure that this last claim is true. Even when one knows that there is only a modest probability that one will get ahead, it may suffice to induce an acute stage of dissatisfaction. This, however, is a purely empirical issue, and as such should not be relevant for the assessment of utilitarianism. The utilitarian, when confronted with counterintuitive implications of his theory, cannot just answer that these are not likely to arise in actual cases. Rather, he would have to modify his account and propose a theory that is co-extensional with utilitarianism in actual cases *and* gives the correct answer in the cases where utilitarianism fails. True, our intuitions concerning hypothetical cases may be less strong and more pliable to theory than those concerning actual instances, which means that there is a small loophole left for the utilitarian after all. I leave it to the reader to assess for himself the importance of this difficulty.

I conclude with a methodological remark. The objection to utilitarianism sketched here is also a critique of a particular *end-state theory of justice*, in Robert Nozick's terminology. For the purpose of social choice theory, we should not take wants as given, but inquire into their rationality or autonomy. These, in the general case, are properties that cannot be immediately read off the wants themselves. Truth and goodness of beliefs and desires are end-state notions; properties that adhere to the mental states irrespective of their genesis. Rationality in the broad sense (I.3) depends on the way in which the states are actually formed. Two individuals may be exactly alike in their beliefs and wants, and yet we might assess them differently from the point of view of rationality, judgment and autonomy. This does not imply, however, that social justice should rest on given wants filtered through history. As argued at some length in I.5, there is also the alternative possibility of changing the wants through rational and public discussion. On the temporal axis, this is a forward-looking rather than a backward-looking procedure. The historical approach is needed for a diagnosis of what is wrong with the actual want structure, but the remedy may involve changing it.

IV

BELIEF, BIAS AND IDEOLOGY

IV.1 INTRODUCTION

An ideology is a set of beliefs or values that can be explained through the position or (non-cognitive) interest of some social group. I shall mainly discuss ideological beliefs, although at some points reference will also be made to ideological value systems. Ideological beliefs belong to the more general class of biased beliefs, and the distinction between position and interest explanations largely corresponds to a more general distinction between illusion and distortion as forms of bias. In social psychology a similar distinction is expressed by the opposition between 'cold' and 'hot' causation of beliefs,[1] or between 'psychologic' and 'psychodynamics'.[2]

The main goal of the chapter is to provide for belief formation what the preceding chapter did for preference formation, i.e. a survey of some important ways in which rational mental processes can be undermined by irrelevant causal influences. As briefly indicated in I.3 above, there are close similarities between irrational belief formation and irrational preference formation. In IV.2 I discuss the phenomenon of illusionary beliefs, an analogy to which is found in preference shifts due to framing.[3] Similarly, many of the phenomena discussed in IV.2 are due to dissonance reduction, and therefore closely parallel to sour grapes and similar mechanisms. One important disanalogy should be mentioned, however. Whereas the causal process of adaptive preference formation can be contrasted to intentional character planning, the causal process of wishful thinking has no similar intentional analogue, because it is conceptually impossible to believe at

[1] Abelson (1963) is at the origin of these notions.
[2] Nisbett and Ross (1980), Ch. 10.
[3] Tversky and Kahneman (1981) and Ainslie (1975) suggest how such perspectival effects can have an impact on preferences.

will. I shall argue that the notion of self-deception, which might appear to provide such an analogy, is in fact incoherent. Another disanalogy is that wishful thinking, unlike sour grapes, will in general give temporary relief only. When reality reasserts itself, frustration and dissonance will also reappear. True, there are cases in which wishful thinking has useful consequences. In IV.4 I discuss the general phenomenon of useful mistakes, arguing that since these are essentially by-products one cannot coherently make them into the basis of policy.

A secondary goal of the chapter is to provide micro-foundations for the Marxist theory of ideologies and, simultaneously, indicate how cognitive psychology could be made 'social' in a more real sense than the one offered by experiments with college students. I believe that the Marxist theory of ideology is potentially of great importance, and that its underdeveloped state is mainly due to misguided notions of what kinds of evidence and explanation are required. Some Marxists have been content to impute causal connection between beliefs and social structure on the basis of 'structural homologies', a solemn name for whatever arbitrary similarities the writer in question can think of.[4] Others have explained beliefs through their accordance with class interest, without pausing to define that term[5] or to sketch plausible mechanisms by which the beliefs can bring about their own fulfilment. Against the structural and the functionalist approaches I would like to insist on the need for an understanding of the psychological mechanisms by which ideological beliefs are formed and entrenched. This in turn is part of a broader argument that Marxist theory will continue in its stagnant state unless it explicitly espouses methodological individualism. In William Blake's phrase, 'He who would do good to another must do it in Minute Particulars, ... for Art and Science cannot exist but in minutely organized Particulars.'

These minute descriptions are provided by cognitive psychology, in rigorous controlled experiments. In what follows I shall draw in a quite general way on the work of the dissonance theorists, and in somewhat more detail on the work of Amos Tversky and others within the same

---

[4] For examples, see Borkenau (1934) (and the criticism in Elster 1975, pp. 18ff.) or Goldmann (1954) (and the criticism in Kolakowski (1978), vol. iii, pp. 336ff.).

[5] The term 'class interest' is a mere *flatus vocis* unless the following distinctions are drawn. (i) Does it refer to the interest of the class as a whole or to the interests of the individual members? (ii) Does it refer to short-term or to long-term class interest? (iii) If the reference is to the short term, is this to be understood as a steady-state effect or as a transitional one (III.9 above)? (iv) Does the term refer to subjective class interest, or to the objective or fundamental class interest that is ascribed to the class by outside observers?

tradition. In particular I have found very useful the recent synthesis by Richard Nisbett and Lee Ross, *Human Inference*. I believe that the experimental and the broadly historical approaches to belief formation could be cross-fertilizing: historians need social psychology to understand which of the observed patterns are accidental and which causally grounded, and social psychologists should look to history for examples that could stimulate their imagination.

IV.2   SITUATION-INDUCED BELIEFS

The Marxist theory of ideologies can be defended in two distinct ways: as a theory relating beliefs to class situation and as a theory explaining beliefs in terms of class interest. I shall be concerned with both of these, and also with the relation between them. Further on I shall explain what I mean by situation-induced beliefs, but let me begin with stating the first of a series of negative propositions that form an important part of my argument:

First proposition: There is no reason to suppose that beliefs shaped by a social position tend to serve the interests of the persons in that position.

And in particular, ideas shaped by class position need not serve class interest. This insight is clearly formulated by Leszek Kolakowski:

[When] Engels says that the Calvinistic theory of predestination was a religious expression of the fact that commercial success or bankruptcy does not depend on the businessman's intention, but on economic forces, then, whether we agree with his statement or not, we must regard it as asserting a merely causal connection: for the idea of absolute dependence on an external power (viz. the market in the 'mystified' shape of providence) does not seem to further the businessman's interest, but rather to set the seal on his impotence.[6]

The context shows that Kolakowski is not quite clear in his mind on this point, as he only makes a distinction between causal and teleological determination of beliefs, and not the further distinction between hot and cold causation. He seems to believe, wrongly in my opinion, that the phrases 'beliefs are caused by the interests of the class in question' and 'beliefs are what they are because of the situation of the class' are synonymous. On the other hand, he correctly perceives that the first of these is not synonymous with 'the beliefs serve the interests of the class in question'. In fact, the two distinctions between causal and teleological explanations of belief and between position and

[6] Kolakowski (1978), vol. I, p. 342.

interest explanations cut across each other, giving a total of three rather than two cases: causal position explanation, causal interest explanation and teleological interest explanation, or functional as I shall say here. Broadly speaking, they are at the centre of the present section, of IV.3 and of IV.4 respectively.

This ambiguity means that Kolakowski's observation could also be seen as an illustration of my third proposition (IV.3). But the example he cites from Engels clearly falls under the first proposition. This case also is interesting from a substantial point of view. It rests on the idea that agents in a competitive market tend to generalize the economic fact that their behaviour cannot influence prices, and so come to believe that they are equally powerless with respect to non-material elements that are important to them. Unlike Weber's analysis, this actually offers an explanation of why capitalist entrepreneurs believed in Calvinism, not only an analysis of the consequences of their doing so. For Weber, Calvinism sustained capitalism rather than the other way around, at least in the early stages of capitalist development when religion had to provide the element of compulsion that later was realized through the competitive market.[7] A corollary of Engels' analysis is that imperfectly competitive capitalism should tend to foster an 'illusion of control', so that agents that are more than quantity-adjusting price-takers should also come to believe that their actions make a difference for their salvation. And more generally, it would seem to follow that perfect, imperfect and strategic markets tend to develop, respectively, attitudes of dependence, control and inter-dependence that may be less justified in other areas.

The characteristic feature of this case, and of the instances to be discussed later, is that the believer generalizes certain features of his local environment, wrongly believing them to hold in a wider context. (Or, if the belief is in fact a correct one, it is so only by accident, not because it is grounded in evidence.) The believer observes that his small world obeys certain laws or falls under certain descriptions, and then unthinkingly assumes that this must also hold of the larger context. In the language of cognitive psychology, this could be called an inferential error due to sample bias and to excessive reliance on the 'availability heuristic',[8] but clearly this is an incomplete description that fails to capture the specificity of the phenomenon. It can best be captured, I think, by saying that the believer has a *partial* vision, in one

[7] Weber (1920), p. 203.   [8] Nisbett and Ross (1980), pp. 77ff.

of the two senses of that term, expressed in French by 'partiel' and 'partial' respectively. (The second sense is the topic of IV.3 below.) The important feature of the ideologies discussed here is that they embody an *understanding of the whole according to the logic of the part*.

An important special case is that of ideologies stemming from the *fallacy of composition*, the belief that causal mechanisms valid for any particular member of a set in isolation must also be valid for all members taken as a whole.[9] In II.9 I briefly mentioned an example of this fallacy, the belief (denounced by Tocqueville) that since love marriages tend to be unhappy in societies where they form the exception, this provides an argument against democracy in which they would be the rule. I now proceed to give a number of other instances of this fallacious mode of inference.

A particularly important case of ideological belief systems is the tendency of the oppressed and exploited classes in a society to believe in the justice or at least the necessity of the social order that oppresses them. This belief may be largely due to distortion, i.e. to such affective mechanisms as rationalization (IV.3). But there is also an element of illusion, of bias stemming from purely cognitive sources. Paul Veyne argues, convincingly to my mind, that any dependent man in Classical Antiquity had to believe that he owed his living and his security to his master: 'I owe my living and my existence to this master by the grace of God, for what would become of me without him, and that great domain which he owns and on which I live?'[10] The most despised of all was the Roman plebs 'parce que, n'étant à personne, elle n'est rien'.[11] Since I would be worse off without a master, it follows on this logic that a society without masters would be intolerable, for who would then provide employment and protection?[12]

A similar optical illusion may account for the theories that explain feudalism as a voluntary and mutually beneficial exchange between the serfs and the lord, the latter providing protection and receiving goods

---

[9] Elster (1978a), pp. 97ff.   [10] Veyne (1976), p. 554.

[11] *Ibid.* p. 696.

[12] In fact, the historian as well as the agents he studies is liable to this fallacy: 'In slavery days the cities and towns of the South, being neither numerous nor large, derived their support principally from plantation districts, where there were many slaves, rather than from small-farming regions, where there were few. It was chiefly the planters who bought, sold, borrowed, travelled and sent their children to academies and colleges. It seems quite certain, therefore, that *if it had not been for plantations and slavery, the cities and towns of the South would have been even fewer and smaller, resulting in even fewer opportunities for nonslaveholding whites*' (Russel 1966; italics added. See also the discussion in Elster 1978a, pp. 211ff.).

and labour services in return.[13] The illusion of a voluntary and rational arrangement disappears when one observes that the lord provided protection mainly against other lords, much as a gangster can justify his protection racket by pointing to the threat from rival gangsters. Feudalism may well have been a Nash equilibrium, in the sense that for each community subordination was optimal given that everybody else behaved similarly. But insubordination would also have been an equilibrium, for if all communities refused to sustain their lords, there would be no predatory lords to fear and therefore no need for protection.

A similar illusion, finally, underlies the neoclassical theory of capitalist exploitation and, more generally, all theories which argue that the workers should be paid according to what each of them produces in circumstances that, logically, have no place for all of them. Neoclassical theory says that labour is not exploited if paid according to marginal product,[14] i.e. if each worker is paid as if he were the last to be hired or, more to the point, the first to be fired. With individual wage negotiations each worker can in fact be made to see himself in this light, since the employer may threaten each of them with dismissal and plausibly say to each of them that he cannot pay more than the value of what he gets from them, at the margin. But not everybody can be at the margin, and since the infra-marginal product is typically larger than the marginal product, the argument breaks down when there is collective rather than individual bargaining. Similarly Marx argued that the capitalist could reap the profits from cooperation by paying each worker according to what he could make by himself, before entering into cooperation with other workers:

Being independent of each other, the labourers are isolated persons, who enter into relations with the capitalist, but not with each other . . . Because [the productive power developed by the labourer when working in cooperation] costs capital nothing, and because, on the other hand, the labourer himself does not develop it before his labour belongs to capital, it appears as a power with which capital is endowed by Nature.[15]

These examples show that because of their place in the social and economic structure, the oppressed and exploited tend to view social causality in a way that does not serve their interests. But, correspondingly, these beliefs certainly serve the interests of their

---

[13] For this argument, see North and Thomas (1971), ably criticized in Fenoaltea (1975).

[14] Bloom (1940) or Bronfenbrenner (1971), Ch. 8, are expositions of the neoclassical theory of exploitation. See also Elster (1978b, c).

[15] Marx (1867), p. 333.

masters. And there is indeed an important strand in the Marxist theory of ideology that argues for a systematic and explanatory correlation between the belief systems in a society and the interests of the ruling classes. Against this I advance my

Second proposition: There is no reason to suppose that beliefs shaped by a social position tend to serve the interests of the ruling or dominant group.

In particular, there is no reason to believe that ideas shaped by the position of the dominant class itself generally serve the interest of that class. The example from Engels discussed by Kolakowski illustrates this point. It can also be shown that the capitalist class, because of its place in the economic structure, is liable to optical illusions similar to those of the workers. Marx, for example, argued that the confusion between money and capital, characteristic of mercantilist thought, can be explained by the equivalence of the two for the practical capitalist:

He has the choice of making use of his capital by lending it out as interest-bearing capital, or of expanding its value on his own by using it as productive capital, regardless of whether it exists as money-capital from the very first, or whether it still has to be converted into money-capital. But to apply [this argument] to the total capital of society, as some vulgar economists do, is of course preposterous.[16]

The argument is indeed preposterous, and yet it was the foundation of mercantilist reasoning for several hundred years. We find the seventeenth century cameralists arguing that wars would never run an economy down as long as the money remained within the country, as if the soldiers could be fed on gold and silver.[17] According to the historian of mercantilism, this mode of thought still prevailed among German economists during World War I,[18] and no doubt still survives as an implicit assumption in some quarters. It follows fairly immediately from the actual choice situation of the capitalist entrepreneur, and yet is clearly adverse to the interests of the capitalist class.

For a final example, consider George Katona's argument that a manufacturer, when asked about the probable incidence of a general tax increase on the general price level, is liable to answer that prices will rise, since in his limited sphere of experience a tax increase is just like a wage increase in the effect on cost and pricing.[19] Keynesian reasoning

[16] Marx (1894), p. 377.
[17] See for example the texts by Leibniz quoted in Elster (1975), p. 115.
[18] Heckscher (1955), vol. II, p. 202.
[19] Katona (1951), pp. 45ff. The most famous example of this line of reasoning is probably Adam Smith's statement, 'What is prudence in the conduct of every private family can hardly be folly in that of a great kingdom.'

shows that the aggregate effect will be the opposite, since the tax will reduce aggregate demand and thus prices. And it is clearly the case that if the view of the typical manufacturer was made into a basis for policy, the effect on the manufacturing class would be negative. In fact, no extended arguments are needed to show that an illusionary perception of reality will not in general be conducive to an efficient manipulation of reality, although we shall see in IV.4 that there are exceptions to this statement. For the same reason, we may generally expect that the illusions of the oppressed classes work out to the benefit of the rulers, but in the absence of any explanatory connection this does not amount to much. In fact, the statement remains true if for 'oppressed classes' we substitute 'rulers' and *vice versa*.

I have argued that different social classes make different kinds of errors about social causality because they find themselves in different positions in the economic structure. Implicitly I have assumed that the proneness to unwarranted generalization is itself invariant across classes, but this might of course be questioned. It might be the case, that is, that not only social position, but also the tendency to generalize from local to global causality, vary with social class. This factor, if operative, would presumably be related to class origin rather than to current class situation. I have no ideas whatsoever as to the existence of such class-related differences in cognitive processing capacity, but they present a logical possibility that should not be ignored by the theory of ideologies. As in all cases in which an internal psychic apparatus interacts with an external situation to produce some outcome, e.g. a choice, a preference or a belief, the issue of social causation arises both for the subjective and for the objective elements of the situation.

IV.3   INTEREST-INDUCED BELIEFS

Beliefs often are distorted by affects, mainly perhaps through wishful thinking and rationalization, but also through more perverse mechanisms such as a tendency to excessive pessimism (the analogy, as it were, of counteradaptive preferences). I shall here limit my attention to wishful thinking and related phenomena. By wishful thinking I mean the tendency to form beliefs when and because I prefer the state of the world in which they are true over the states in which they are false. Let me sharply distinguish this phenomenon from that of believing at will, a deliberate choice rather than a causal process. The decision to believe is shaped by a conscious desire, wishful thinking by a non-conscious drive. Moreover, whereas nobody would deny the existence of beliefs derived from wishful thinking, one can argue (II.2) that a decision to believe will never successfully be carried out. As Sartre says somewhere, one drifts into bad faith as one drifts into sleep.

Similarly, wishful thinking should be clearly distinguished from self-deception, supposing the latter phenomenon to be at all possible. Many writers use these terms interchangeably,[20] but I shall argue that the notion of self-deception as commonly understood involves paradoxes that are absent from that of wishful thinking. It is not the fact that self-deception involves the simultaneous entertaining of two incompatible or contradictory beliefs that makes it impossible.[21] Rather, the root of the paradox is the peculiar feature that the self-deceiver intentionally hides one of his beliefs from himself and professes the other as his official view. The idea of successful self-deception therefore raises two closely related questions: How does one manage to *forget intentionally* what one 'really' (somehow, somewhere) believes? And, having achieved this impossible feat, how does one achieve that of *believing at will* what one also believes that there are no adequate grounds for believing? In II.2 I suggested that the decision to forget has the paradoxical feature that the harder you try to carry it out, the less likely it is to succeed; it is like an attempt to create darkness by light. And for related reasons believing at will also seems to be a feat beyond human ability.

However, as in the related case of weakness of will, the theoretical arguments for the incoherence of the notion of self-deception simply seem to evaporate in the face of massive clinical, fictional and everyday experience attesting to the reality of the phenomenon. And so there is a need for a theoretical analysis of self-deception: *wie ist es überhaupt möglich?* Among the better-known attempts to provide an answer are those by Freud, Schafer, Sartre and Fingarette, none of them in my view convincing since they all tend to reproduce the basic paradox in ever-subtler forms.[22] I would rather suggest a diversified strategy, explaining different cases of what superficially looks like self-deception

---

[20] E.g. Kolakowski (1978), vol. III, pp. 89, 116, 181; Levenson (1968), vol. I, pp. 59ff., 70.

[21] Fingarette (1969), Ch. 2, makes this point forcefully.

[22] It would require a book to justify this assertion. For Freud and Sartre, let me refer the reader to Fingarette (1969), Chs. V–VI and Pears (1974), as well as to such general accounts as MacIntyre (1958), Wollheim (1971) and Farrell (1981). For brief comments on the accounts proposed by Fingarette (1969) and Schafer (1976), see Elster (1979), p. 173.

along different lines.[23] Most of these will only be briefly mentioned, but the notion of wishful thinking – the most plausible alternative, in my view, to the notion of self-deception – will be discussed in somewhat more detail.

First, some cases may be unsuccessful *attempts* at self-deception and so no more paradoxical than other attempts to realize contradictory goals (I.2). Secondly, some cases may be understood by the distinction between higher-level and lower-level beliefs. I can deliberately choose not to acquire the lower-level beliefs that would give substance and body to my higher-level belief, thus making it less tolerable. ('I do not want to know the details.') Thirdly, some instances may be seen as unsuccessful attempts at character modification. In any description of one's own character there is some indeterminacy that can be exploited for the purpose of changing it, although one cannot know in advance exactly how much leeway one has. Each year sees the publication of innumerable manuals of popular psychology telling people that they can acquire self-confidence and pulling themselves up by the bootstraps simply on the will's saying so. These, although in general quite ridiculous, have a kernel of truth in that *some* progress can in general be made by a *Gestalt* switch induced by redescription of oneself. And since one cannot in general know beforehand *how much* progress is possible, one may by trying to achieve too much lay oneself open to the charge of self-deception. Fourthly, I may bring it about now that I come to believe something at a later time, if I can also and simultaneously bring about forgetfulness of the process itself. Self-deception of this variety would be an instance of *joint production*, as it were, one outcome of the process being a certain belief and another the obliteration of the process from memory which is necessary for that belief to take hold. True, one then may run into the hammock problem (II.3) and related difficulties, but these need not be insuperable in all cases. And fifthly, there is wishful thinking.

The distinction between self-deception and wishful thinking should be acceptable also to those who believe that the mind is capable – in a sense not exhausted by the strategies given above – of intentionally deceiving itself. My argument for the distinction is that by wishful thinking one may arrive at beliefs that are not only true (in fact, truth is irrelevant here) but also well-grounded, in the sense of corresponding to the available evidence. Wishful thinking by definition cannot be

23 The following draws on Elster (1979), Ch. IV.4.

causally grounded in evidence, but it may well be sustained by the evidence. Self-deception, by contrast, necessarily involves a duality between the belief that one officially holds and that which one believes to be grounded in evidence. For an example, consider a man who wishes to be promoted and by his wish is led to believe that he is about to receive promotion. We might speak of self-deception here if the evidence available to him points in another direction and he somehow is aware of this, and yet manages to hide this knowledge from himself and believe that promotion is imminent. But it might also be the case that the man has very good grounds for believing himself about to be promoted, but that he arrived at the belief by wishful thinking rather than by a considered judgment on these grounds. Here there is no duality, no opposition between the reality principle and the pleasure principle, between what the evidence tells me to believe and what my desires make me believe. There is no question of hiding from oneself an unpleasant truth or well-grounded belief, since the well-grounded belief is also the one that the believer wants to be true and indeed believes because he wants it to be true. He has good reasons for believing it, but it is not for those reasons that he believes it.[24]

This is not just an abstract possibility, but a configuration often met in everyday life. Surely we have all met persons basking in self-satisfaction that seems to be both justified and not justified: justified because they have good reasons for being satisfied with themselves, and not justified because we sense that they would be just as content were the reasons to disappear. Or, to take the opposite case, consider the congenital pessimist whose evaluation of the situation is for once justified by the evidence: he is right and justified, and yet we hesitate to say that he is right and justified. As argued in I.3, the criteria for rational beliefs involve looking at the actual *causal relation* between evidence and beliefs, the mere *comparison* between evidence and belief being insufficient. Or, should this language not be judged acceptable, we might distinguish between the rational formation of beliefs and the formation of rational beliefs.

I believe this argument to show that in some cases at least wishful thinking does not involve self-deception, the cases, namely, in which the belief born of desire is also borne out by the evidence. But then, why

---

[24] Cp. the point made in I.2 above, concerning the need to exclude 'coincidences of the first class' as well as 'coincidences of the second class' in the definition of rational action. The same idea applies to the definition of rational beliefs, as briefly mentioned at the beginning of I.3 above.

should not the same argument apply to other cases? Why could it not be the case that the wishful believer goes directly for the pleasant belief, instead of going through the four-steps process of (1) arriving at the well-grounded belief, (2) deciding that it is unpalatable, (3) suppressing it and only then (4) adhering to another and more tolerable belief? Or again, why should the repellent force of an unpleasant belief have explanatory privilege over the attracting force of a pleasant belief? I submit that in the absence of specific arguments to the contrary, wishful thinking is a more parsimonious explanation than self-deception. Indeed, I believe that the substitution of wishful thinking for self-deception is a first step towards the elimination of the Freudian unconscious as a theoretical entity – a highly desirable goal.

To give some substance to this general analysis, I shall consider two historical examples: the suppression of the truth about Hitler's 'final solution' and the Chinese encounter with the West in the nineteenth century. Other instances will be mentioned more briefly to illustrate specific points.

In *The Terrible Secret*, Walter Laqueur surveys extensively the reasons why the news of Hitler's genocide took so long in gaining acceptance among Germans, Allies, Neutrals – including Jews in all these countries. The following of his observations is especially relevant for the present concerns. First, although by the end of 1942 millions of Germans knew that the Jewish question had been radically solved, details were known only to a much smaller number.[25] As suggested above, the lack of specific knowledge may make the general knowledge more possible to bear. A related but different idea is that 'while many Germans thought that the Jews were no longer alive, they did not necessarily believe that they were dead'.[26] This is but an extreme instance of a fairly common phenomenon, viz. the failure to draw the logical conclusion from one's own beliefs.[27] The failure may be due to defective cognition or, as is probable in the present case, to affective pressures. The latter possibility offers a strong *prima facie* case for the existence of self-deception, as distinct from wishful thinking, for how could an unpleasant conclusion block the inference unless it had already somehow been drawn? I have no easy answer to this objection.

Secondly, there were cases in which the failure was not one of deductive logic, but rather of judgment and inference from the evidence. Here, clearly, there is much scope for wishful thinking, to

[25] Laqueur (1980), pp. 31–2.   [26] *Ibid.* p. 201.   [27] Veyne (1976), pp. 248ff., 669ff.

which the Jewry of many Nazi-occupied countries seem to have been prone. Even when – as in the Danish case – escape was easy, many Jews believed that 'it cannot happen here' and even that 'it did not happen there'. The rare letter from a deported relative counted for more than news about the German extermination;[28] and the absence of letters from the large majority of deported acquaintances was not allowed to count either.[29] Among the many possible mechanisms for wishful thinking in such cases one may list selective weighting of the evidence, selective scanning,[30] evaluation of new pieces of evidence separately rather than collectively[31] and the failure to take in negative evidence, i.e. the absence of the evidence one would expect if the favoured hypothesis were true. Where escape was difficult and the threat more obvious, as in Poland and Eastern Europe generally, the failure to understand looks more like self-deception. Laqueur compares it to the faith in miracle cures among dying men and women, and adds that the analogy is to some extent misleading, since the threatened Jews – unlike a man dying of cancer – would have benefited had they had a more realistic appraisal of their situation.[32] I believe that the case for self-deception is stronger in the dying man, in whom the belief in the miracle cure typically supplants earlier scepticism, or outright disbelief, to which nothing corresponds in the case of the Jews who believed themselves to be invulnerable. Also, the belief in the miracle cure may in some cases be a rational choice when all else has failed and there is nothing to lose. For these reasons, I do not think that the comparison with the dying can serve as a basis for ascribing self-deception (as distinct from wishful thinking) to the Eastern Jews.

Thirdly, the disbelief among Gentiles in allied and neutral countries

[28] Laqueur (1980), p. 153.   [29] *Ibid.* p. 146.

[30] The following mechanism, for example, would appear to be a plausible rendering of how judgment can be biased by optimism. When scanning the evidence, one goes on collecting new information until there comes a point at which the net effect of the evidence (with no bias in weighting) points in the desired direction, and then stops scanning, If there never comes any such point, one may go on scanning indefinitely, or other biasing mechanisms (e.g. biased weighting) may take over. The important point is that this mechanism does not imply a repressed knowledge about further, as yet unscanned, pieces of information that might reverse the judgment: it is a mechanism for wishful thinking, not for self-deception.

[31] On this hypothesis, one goes on collecting new pieces of evidence even after one has formed the preliminary judgment in the way outlined in the preceding note. But each new bit of information is balanced against all the evidence that went into that judgment, and – if by itself it is insufficient to reverse the judgment – discarded for good. The rational procedure, by contrast, would be to carry along such bits of negative information in the background on which further evidence is evaluated.

[32] Laqueur (1980), pp. 154–5.

stemmed in part from lack of evidence and in part from lack of ability to evaluate the evidence. The governments in many allied countries hesitated to make public what they knew, out of fear that this could distract attention from the war effort, have demoralizing consequences for the Jews in occupied countries, unleash latent anti-Semitism in the population and even actually induce disbelief. The last fear rested on the theory that as a result of wild stories about German atrocities in World War I people had become 'contra-suggestible' to horror tales.[33] Also, governments as well as individuals tended to believe that many reports were exaggerated, the outcome of Jewish imagination or provocation. In one specific instance Laqueur comments as follows about a non-Jewish witness: 'Those who knew him describe him as a somewhat unreliable witness, a man given to excitement and exaggeration. But, and this is all that matters, on this occasion he certainly did not exaggerate and his excitement was not misplaced.'[34] I must disagree. *At the time* it certainly did matter whether a person was known to be a reliable witness, for if he was not, his evidence could not provide independent confirmation. If the worst is true, a tendency to believe the worst may produce true beliefs, but the belief is not rationally grounded. And as observed above, this holds even when there are grounds for believing the worst, since *ex hypothesi* these grounds are not causally efficacious in producing the belief.

I have referred several times to Joseph Levenson's marvellous work, *Confucian China and its Modern Fate*. The first volume of this trilogy is largely a study in wishful thinking and its close relative, sour grapes. In III.2 above I drew attention to his analysis of the '*t'i-yung* fallacy', the belief that substance or essence can be kept intact through a transformation of function or appearance. In reality, 'Chinese learning had come to be prized as substance because of its function, and when its function was usurped, the learning withered.'[35] The infection of spirit by techniques, of *t'i* by *yung*,

> began in China, as one might expect, with emphasis on the bare means of military defence . . . to control the barbarians through their own superior techniques. Soon the list of indispensable superior techniques lengthened, to cover industry, commerce, mining, railroads, telegraph . . ., and essential traditional attitudes were almost casually dissipated by seekers after the useful techniques which were to shield the Chinese essence.[36]

Et propter vitam vivendi perdere causas.

[33] *Ibid.* p. 91.   [34] *Ibid.* p. 43.
[35] Levenson (1968), vol. I, p. 61.   [36] *Ibid.* p. 62.

Chinese traditionalists, foremost among whom was Wo-jen, 'recognized the *t'i-yung* dichotomy for what it was, a formula for self-deception about the implications of innovation'.[37] Instead they suggested that the Chinese culture be made into the focus of loyalty, since it was impossible to defend both nation and culture. In other words, a defence of the traditional Chinese culture was common ground between innovators and traditionalists, at least in the first wave of responses to the Western challenge. But the defence was only that: a defence, i.e. an apology. Commenting on this notion, Levenson makes an observation that fits neatly into the analysis suggested here:

> To speak of apologetics is not to suggest that Chinese thinkers, in vindicating the worth of Chinese culture against western pretensions, were saying anything untrue. What is true is no less true because apologists insist upon it. But apologists are no less apologetic because what they insist upon is true: it is the insistence that counts.[38]

In the hands of the apologist, good reasons are transformed into tools of persuasion. The recipient is in a bind, for should he listen to the reasons or to the tone of voice in which they are advanced? It takes more than ordinary good faith to be susceptible to good reasons advanced in bad faith.

Levenson argues that Wo-jen and his followers also were obscurantist and irrational in another, more complex sense:

> On their own proper ground, [the *t'i yung* rationalizers] had less feeling than the reactionaries for the ominous potentialities of Western methods imported solely 'for use'. Nevertheless, although the reactionaries might well plume themselves for sensing the logical inadequacies of that particular rationalization for innovation, their conclusion – that the innovation must be stopped, rather than the rationalization changed – was unsound. For they were obscurantist in failing to realize that innovation was inevitable, and that some rationalization, logical or not, was psychological necessity.[39]

I take this passage as stating that the traditionalists were fighting a hopeless rearguard action. This in itself does not make them obscurantist. But Levenson appears to argue that their failure to realize that their action was hopeless and that innovation was inevitable shows them to have been victims of wishful thinking no less than their *t'i-yung* opponents. This, however, is a delicate argument, to be employed with much circumspection. In politics the frontiers of the inevitable are the stakes of action and the outcome of action, not constraints that exist prior to action.[40] True, the frontiers are not indefinitely elastic. There

[37] *Ibid.* p. 70.   [38] *Ibid.* pp. 73–4.   [39] *Ibid.* p. 77.   [40] Elster (1978a), pp. 50–1.

exist outer bounds beyond which they cannot be moved. But can one always know *in advance* where on the political map these outer bounds are located? I believe that in some cases such knowledge is possible, and then it *is* obscurantist to strive for the impossible. But in other cases the appearance of wishful thinking (or self-deception) is due to the retroactive illusion that people at the time ought to have known what we perceive today. The phenomenon is related to what I described above as unsuccessful attempts at character modification, which also turn upon the *ex ante* uncertainty that surrounds the limits of what can be achieved by bootstrap-pulling.

Paralleling the first proposition in IV.2 above, I now argue for a

Third proposition: There is no reason to suppose that beliefs shaped by interests tend to serve these interests.

On quite general grounds, distorted beliefs cannot be expected, any more than illusionary beliefs, to be very helpful for goal achievement (but see IV.4 for an exception). If out of wishful thinking I form a belief that I am about to be promoted, my subsequent display of unwarranted self-confidence may destroy whatever chance of promotion I had. *Beliefs born of passion serve passion badly.*[41] The exploited and oppressed classes may be led by rationalization to believe that their fate is just and proper – a belief that may indeed give short-term gratification, but cannot be said to serve the interests of these classes well at all. And the same holds, of course, for the ruling classes. The Lysenko affair showed how disastrous may be the result when the authorities are led by wishful thinking to favour certain theories at the expense of others, an attitude unforgettably captured in *The First Circle*.

The examples just cited cannot be reduced to a single formula; and some distinctions may be useful. First, the tendency to engage in wishful thinking is in itself liable to lead one into trouble, independently of the actual beliefs. The promotion example can be modified to include the assumption that the belief in promotion is well-grounded, and yet the chances for promotion may be destroyed if the good reasons for believing in it are not what causes the belief. ('He would be promoted were he not so infernally confident that he would be promoted.') Secondly, of course, it is frequently the actual belief which, being

---

[41] 'Avant d'être des "couvertures", les idéologies sont des préjugés; la logique passionnelle des intérêts contribue à leur fausseté, mais elles les abusent en retour. Car les intérêts n'ont pas de sixième sens qui leur permettrait de percer l'obscure confusion du réel pour localiser immédiatement leur objectif' (Veyne 1976, p. 667).

distorted, is contrary to the interests that have distorted it. True beliefs about ends–means relationship are in general needed for promotion of one's interests, and although interest-induced beliefs may also be true, this will only happen by accident. Thirdly, the efficacy of the belief may turn more upon its being generally accepted than on its being true, and beliefs shaped by interest may for that very reason not gain acceptance. Thus self-serving theories of the need for inequality are rarely self-serving.[42] The interests of the upper class are better served by lower classes spontaneously inventing an ideology justifying their inferior status.

IV.4   THE BENEFITS OF BIAS

Biased beliefs are irrational, in the broad sense explained in I.3. To this characterization, the automatic response of many economists and philosophers would be to seek for some way of rationalizing the irrational. Although irrational in the genetic sense, could not the belief be rational in the sense of being useful, beneficial and even optimal, in the search for welfare or even for truth? And if the belief proved to have such beneficial consequences, could one not then take the further step and suggest that these consequences actually *explain* the belief? Before I look at some examples, let me briefly survey the varieties of claims that can be made, by the help of the following distinctions. (i) The claim for the deeper rationality of the apparently irrational could be made with respect to a given belief, or with respect to beliefs in general. (ii) The claim could be made with respect to illusions, to distortions, or both. (iii) The claim might be made with respect to the *utility* of the irrational belief, or with respect to the tendency of biased cognition to favour *truth*. (iv) If made on grounds of utility, the claim could rationalize the belief in terms of the useful consequences for the believer or in terms of the benefit provided to some other person or persons. (v) And finally the claim may either be explanatory or non-explanatory.

I shall first consider illusions that are either useful or conducive to truth. Nisbett and Ross offer some interesting observations on this 'dangerous notion', as they call it. First, they argue that illusions may

---

[42] In fact, there would seem to be two conditions for being a good propagandist. First, you should believe in the message you are preaching; and secondly, your belief in the message should not too obviously correspond to your narrow self-interest. Thus I would conjecture that the critique of capitalism by G. Fitzhugh (1857) had a greater impact than his defence of slavery, since the first could more easily be divorced from his position in the social system.

benefit the individual who is subject to them, by the effect on motivation: 'unrealistically positive self-schemas or other illusions about the self, together with the processing biases they can engender, may be more socially adaptive than are totally accurate self-perceptions'.[43] It is not totally clear, in the case on which they base this observation, that the erroneous self-perception is due to purely cognitive bias, without any element of wishful thinking. But elsewhere they argue convincingly that self-serving characterizations of self may stem from 'simple availability effects, rather than any motivational bias'.[44] One simply knows more about oneself than about other people, and so may be led into overestimating one's own efforts and actions. (To be sure, this also may lead to excessive feelings of guilt.) To the extent, then, that self-confidence has a positive effect on motivation and achievement, excessively positive self-perception due to cognitive bias may have good consequences, *even when it falls short of a complete self-fulfilling prophecy*. In many cases, I submit, the belief that one will achieve much is a causal condition for achieving anything at all.

Albert Hirschman has made a related point, in his argument for what he calls 'The principle of the Hiding Hand':

Creativity always comes as a surprise to us; therefore we can never count on it and we dare not believe in it until it has happened. In other words, we would not consciously engage upon those tasks whose success clearly requires that creativity be forthcoming. Hence, the only way in which we can bring our creative resources into full play is by misjudging the nature of the task, by presenting it to ourselves as more routine, simple and undemanding of creativity than it will turn out to be. Or, put differently: since we necessarily underestimate our creativity, it is desirable that we underestimate to a roughly similar extent the difficulties of the tasks we face so as to be tricked by these two offsetting underestimates into undertaking tasks that we can, but otherwise would not dare, tackle. The principle is important enough to deserve a name: since we are apparently on the trail here of some sort of invisible or hidden hand that beneficially hides difficulties from us, I propose *the Hiding Hand*.[45]

The book from which this passage is taken spells out in numerous case studies how the hiding hand works in development projects, by compelling the economic agents to exploit and invent unanticipated solutions to unanticipated problems. As always in Hirschman's work, these analyses are extraordinarily illuminating and open up a new range of approaches to the issues confronted. Let me point, however, to some problems inherent in the notion of the Hiding Hand. First, what is the nature and the status of the psychological mechanisms

[43] Nisbett and Ross (1980), pp. 198–9.   [44] *Ibid.* p. 76.   [45] Hirschman (1967), p. 13.

generating the tendencies to underestimate the difficulty of the problems and our ability to cope with them? Are they affective or cognitive? Do they represent general human propensities, or could the tendency to overestimate be equally widespread? Secondly, are there any explanatory overtones to the passage just cited and the book from which it is taken? In other words, could a reader be justified in thinking that Hirschman suggests that the tendency to underestimate the difficulty of the problem not only has the beneficial consequence of offsetting the tendency to underestimate our creativity, but in fact can be explained by that consequence?[46] Thirdly, and most importantly, would not the principle of the Hiding Hand be self-defeating once revealed to the world by Hirschman? Are not some of the 'side effects' by which he justifies development projects *essentially* by-products in the sense of Ch. II above, so that they could not be incorporated *ex ante* into the project design?[47]

Observe that in this case the illusions are beneficial to the very agent under their spell, e.g. the planning agency. There is also the possibility, however, that the illusions could be on the average detrimental to the agent, but beneficial to some wider group or to society as a whole. Nisbett and Ross observe, for example, that

The social benefits of individually erroneous subjective probabilities may be great even when the individuals pay a high price for the error. We probably would have few novelists, actors, or scientists if all potential aspirants to these careers took action based on a normatively justifiable probability of success. We also might have few new products, new medical procedures, new political movements, or new scientific theories.[48]

A similar argument is basic to Schumpeter's theory of the capitalist entrepreneur. The capitalist system, in his opinion, works so well because it induces unrealistic expectations about success and therefore draws out much more effort than would have been forthcoming from more sober spirits.[49] Unlike Nisbett and Ross, however, Schumpeter does not suggest that this socially beneficial over-estimation stems from a purely cognitive bias. And from what Schumpeter says elsewhere

46 See especially Hirschman (1967), pp. 21ff., for a number of formulations which are highly ambiguous in this respect, with repeated references to the Hiding Hand as a 'method' or 'technique' rather than just a 'mechanism'.
47 Hirschman (1967), pp. 168ff., discusses at some length whether attention should be paid to side effects in the choice between alternative development projects, but at no point refers to the possibility that to do so might be self-defeating. Perhaps this is because the condition of publicity (III.9) has not always been incorporated into such projects?
48 Nisbett and Ross (1980), p. 271.   49 Schumpeter (1954), pp. 73–4.

about the psychology of the entrepreneur, it would seem more probable that he views him as propelled by wishful thinking rather than by defective cognition.[50]

In addition to illusions that are individually or socially useful, Nisbett and Ross also discuss the idea that some illusions may be conducive to truth, either by correcting another illusion or by substituting for correct inference. For example, people seem to have great difficulties in understanding and applying the simple notion of regression to the mean, e.g. in seeing that extreme observational values are likely to prove atypical. This defect can lead to such harmful practical conclusions that punishment is more effective than reward in training, because on the average good performances (even when rewarded) will be followed by less good, while bad performances (even when not punished) will be followed by less bad.[51] Nisbett and Ross then point to no less than three mechanisms that, by compensation or substitution, may enable us to make correct predictions. (1) By diluting the information that leads to wrong prediction with additional *irrelevant* information, subjects are enabled to improve their score.[52] (2) The irrational 'gambler's fallacy', when interacting with the equally irrational 'fundamental attribution error', may give the net result of a rationally justified regression.[53] (3) As in other cases, a causal interpretation of what is essentially a sampling effect may lead to a correct result, as when the baseball trainer argues that the brilliant first-year player will be spoiled by all the attention he gets and not live up to his performance in the next season.[54]

Going now from illusion to distortion, is it possible that wishful thinking could be individually or socially beneficial? The arguments given by Hirschman and Schumpeter can be understood as providing

---

[50] Schumpeter (1934), pp. 91ff., has an eloquent character portrait of the entrepreneur which is certainly closer to this view.

[51] Tversky and Kahneman (1974).

[52] Thus 'non-diagnostic information about the target person, though logically irrelevant to the prediction task, has the capacity to render the target person less "similar" to that hypothetical individual who might be most likely to exhibit extreme and atypical responses' (Nisbett and Ross 1980, p. 155).

[53] The second of these two fallacies 'encourages people to assume that outcomes reflect stable dispositions of the actor and hence that future outcomes generally will resemble past ones', the first 'makes individuals believe that the future somehow compensates for unusual outcome patterns by reversing those patterns' (Nisbett and Ross 1980, p. 268). The net result may be a correct regression to the mean.

[54] Nisbett and Ross (1980), pp. 164–5. See also Feller (1968), p. 122, for the distinction between real after-effects and sampling effects.

an affirmative answer to this question. Hirschman has a striking quote from Kolakowski that illustrates the basic idea very well:

> The simplest improvements in social conditions require so huge an effort on the part of society that full awareness of this disproportion would be most discouraging and would thereby make any social progress impossible. The effort must be prodigally great if the result is to be at all visible ... It is not at all peculiar then that this terrible disproportion must be quite weakly reflected in human consciousness if society is to generate the energy required to effect changes in social and human relations. For this purpose, one exaggerates the prospective results into a myth so as to make them take on dimensions which correspond a bit more to the immediately felt effort ... [The myth acts like] a Fata Morgana which makes beautiful lands arise before the eyes of the members of a caravan and thus increases their efforts to the point where, in spite of all their sufferings, they reach the next tiny waterhole. Had such tempting mirages not appeared, the exhausted caravan would inevitably have perished in the sandstorm, bereft of hope.[55]

And elsewhere Kolakowski argues that Lenin's success in fact was due to a number of 'fortunate errors' that he made in judging and misjudging the strength of the revolutionary movement: 'His mistakes enabled him to exploit the possibilities of revolution to the full, and were thus the cause of his success.'[56] Similarly I have quoted Levenson to the effect that Wo-jen and his followers were obscurantist in not understanding the need in China for some rationalization that would enable the Chinese to deal psychologically with the inevitable modernization. These are cases in which the overestimation of chances of success were necessary for taking action. In other cases overestimation of dangers may be necessary to prevent action.[57] Gordon Winston has made a case for 'protective self-deception' as a cure for addiction: if the individual can convince himself – or pay others to convince him – that the dangers of addiction are even greater than they in fact are, he will be helped to get off the hook.[58] This, however, I find somewhat implausible from a psychological point of view. Wishful thinking (assuming that this is what Winston means by self-deception) can hardly operate through long-term interest.[59] More to the point is the suggestion that the individual can deliberately pay others to induce in him, e.g. by hypnosis, an erroneous but useful belief in the lethal dangers of addiction, for it is indeed a basic feature of deliberation that it can take account of long-term effects.

[55] Kolakowski (1961), pp. 127–8, quoted from Hirschman (1967), p. 32.
[56] Kolakowski (1978), vol. II, p. 525.
[57] Nisbett and Ross (1980), p. 271, also make this point.   [58] Winston (1980), pp. 319–20.
[59] This follows from the observation made in note 53 to Ch. I: the unconscious cannot relate to the future and sacrifice short-term pleasure for the sake of long-term satisfaction.

The idea of useful mistakes, fortunate errors and beneficial bias attracts a certain kind of thinker, those who are fascinated by the counter-intuitive, paradoxical and perverse workings of the human mind and of human societies. As I know from personal experience, this fascination may turn into an obsession, so that one begins to take as axiomatic that deliberate efforts will *never* succeed and that the goal will *only* be realized by accident, as a by-product, or through fortunate mistakes. And it is then only a very short step to the implicit or explicit belief that these perverse mechanisms for goal-attainment can be *explained* by their tendency to bring about such happy outcomes. I urge the reader to study the long quotes from Hirschman and Kolakowski given above, to see whether they do not suggest some explanatory connection. Once again, we encounter the pervasive *search for meaning* discussed in II.10 above. I now want to face the issue somewhat more systematically, by looking at the possible mechanisms by which bias could be explained by the beneficial consequences for utility or truth.

Let me begin with the issue of truth. Nisbett and Ross, citing among others Alvin Goldman, suggest that the defective cognitive mechanisms can be rationalized as being parts of an *optimal package solution*.[60] Given the importance of stability to beliefs and belief systems, and also the time constraints that may prohibit careful consideration of the evidence, the biases may look quite rational when evaluated from higher-order epistemic goals. In the language of II.10 above, this argument would be closer to the version of the theodicy elaborated by Malebranche than to the standard Leibnizian version. Cognitive errors, on this view, would be inevitable by-products of the best of all possible cognitive systems, but they could not be rationalized on the grounds that they actually make a positive contribution to truth. In fact, Nisbett and Ross also emphasize the fragility of a Leibnizian theory of error:

The assumption that errors may cancel each other out, that two inferential wrongs miraculously produce an inferential right, may seem Panglossian and facile, and we are reluctant to press the point without more specific evidence. Less facile, perhaps, is the more general and essentially statistical argument that if a reasonably large number of independent biases operate, the net error that results is bound to be less than the sum of their individual effects.[61]

---

[60] Nisbett and Ross (1980), pp. 191–2, quoting Goldman (1978). Rorty (1980a, b) suggests that self-deception and weakness of will can also be understood in this light. In her argument *habit* is the crucial feature of human life that makes for both integrity *and* such irrational phenomena as self-deception and weakness of will.
[61] Nisbett and Ross (1980), p. 268.

But although the Malebranchian version would seem more plausible on *a priori* grounds, it still remains to be shown that the actual cognitive system has the *optimal* amount of bias.

Passing now to the issue of utility, I begin by stating my

Fourth proposition: There is no reason to suppose that beliefs which serve certain interests are also to be explained by those interests.

This is not the exact converse of the third proposition, since it covers a larger variety of explanations. Beliefs may be explained causally or functionally, in terms of the interests of the believer or in terms of the interests of people other than the believer. This gives a total of four cases, of which one is difficult to envisage concretely, viz. the causal shaping of beliefs by the interests of people other than the believer. Before I discuss the other three cases, I want to restate the general idea (II.10) that the mere fact that a belief furthers some interest in itself provides no explanation whatsoever. The idea that all beneficial bias can be explained by the benefits to the believer has only to be explicitly stated to be seen as absurd. Yet, as I have been arguing, the subterranean influence of this idea as an unstated assumption can hardly be exaggerated. To demonstrate benefits is to bestow meaning – and to find meaning is to provide an explanation.

It follows fairly immediately from what has been said earlier that if a belief serves the interests of the believer, we would not expect it to have been shaped by those interests. This can happen, but the presumption is that it will not. And in any case, the instances where this coincidence is observed always rest on an ambiguity in the notion of 'interest'. Interest-induced beliefs are shaped by the drive to find momentary relief from frustration and unhappiness. This, while certainly a strong interest, is not what we have in mind when we say that the belief serves the interest of the believer, for then we rather have in mind the realization of some more permanent goal. Excessive optimism about chances of success *always* gives a warm glow of happiness, and *sometimes* provides the motivation needed to achieve at least some degree of success. But in these cases the interest being served is not the same as the interest which has explanatory power.

In other cases, however, the interest that is served can actually also provide an explanation. If certain illusions or distortions systematically serve the interests of the believer, they may become entrenched by a process of natural selection or reinforcement. In particular, if the cognitive apparatus has some defects leading to bias in one direction, then a compensating bias might be favoured by one of these mechanisms. Needless to say, this is sheer speculation, but the logical possibility should not be overlooked.

Vastly more central, however, is the idea that belief systems may be explained by the fact that they serve the interests of some person or persons other than the believer, e.g. the ruling or dominant class in a society. This is *not* the idea that all beliefs in a society serve the interests of the ruling class and can be explained by the fact that they do, but the weaker notion that when a belief system as a matter of fact serves those interests, they also have explanatory power.[62] As argued in III.2 for the analogous case of wants, the fact that the minds of the oppressed and exploited work in a way beneficial to the oppressors and exploiters does not in itself provide any explanation of those mental states. But this is not to say that these beneficial consequences for the dominant group could not have explanatory force. There are many plausible mechanisms that could bring it about that certain widely held beliefs are widely held because of the benefits they bring to some dominant group. The members of that group could try to inculcate, either directly or by the intermediary of a professional group of ideologists,[63] certain beliefs among the subjects that will prove beneficial to their domination. Or the dominant group could selectively sustain certain spontaneously arising beliefs and repress others, by a process analogous to artificial selection.[64]

I believe, however, that in general these mechanisms are less widespread than frequently argued by Marxists, e.g. by those who subscribe to the theory of 'hegemony'. It *is* a massive fact of history that the values and the beliefs of the subjects tend to support the rule of the dominant group, but I believe that in general this occurs through the spontaneous invention of an ideology by the subjects themselves, by way of dissonance reduction, or through their illusionary perception of social causality (IV.2). A striking example is the spontaneous invention of religion, already discussed in III.2 above. When Marx

[62] For this distinction, see also Elster (1979), pp. 33–4.

[63] It follows from the argument in note 42 that an intelligent ruling class should hire independent ideologists to do the propaganda, rather than try to do its own proselytizing. (I owe this point to E. O. Wright.)

[64] Dahl (1977) shows how the contest between French and Italian schools of criminology in the late nineteenth century was decided not on scientific grounds (both were essentially worthless), but because the Italian school was too deterministic to appeal to the judges and penologists whose cooperation was needed. Punishment requires a modicum of free will to make sense.

says that the social principles of Christianity 'preach the necessity of a ruling and an oppressed class, and for the latter all they have to offer is the pious wish that the former may be charitable',[65] it is hard not to believe that he wanted the argument to have some explanatory force in terms of the benefits of religion for the ruling class; and similarly for his use of the term 'opium of the people'. But opium can be taken as well as given; not all addicts are manipulated into addiction.[66] As will be clear by now, I am strongly in sympathy with Paul Veyne's view that the oppressed believe in the superiority and even the divinity of the ruler because it is good *for them*, although the fact that they so believe also is beneficial for the ruler.

To this view two objections may be raised. The first[67] is that the ruling class, being in control of the means of education, could have corrected the distorted and illusionary beliefs of the subject had it so chosen; therefore, the fact that it did not makes it at least co-responsible for the ideology. To this I have three brief replies. First, moral responsibility cannot serve as a ground for imputing causal responsibility (one cannot infer 'is' from 'ought'[68]) and it is with causation exclusively that I am concerned here. Secondly, acts of omission normally cannot serve as causes,[69] although they may serve as the basis for ascribing moral responsibility. And thirdly, the objection presupposes that the ruling class does not share the beliefs in question, e.g. that the Roman emperors did not themselves believe in their divine nature. But, following Veyne, this appears to be a misunderstanding of religious psychology. The subjects will believe only in the superiority of rulers who never stoop to prove it, because they believe in it implicitly. One can hardly believe, for instance, that many Soviet citizens are impressed by the words of praise daily bestowed on their rulers by the media.

The second objection[70] is the following, Given that the legitimation was spontaneously invented by the oppressed, can we not reasonably

---

[65] Marx (1847), p. 231.

[66] Thompson (1968), pp. 417–18.

[67] This objection was raised by G. A. Cohen and Martin Hollis in comments on an earlier draft of this chapter.

[68] Hart and Honoré (1959), p. 73. Elsewhere (*ibid.* p. 47) the authors appear to violate this principle, when they argue (i) that omissions can act as causes and (ii) that moral considerations are relevant for singling out the causally relevant omission among the infinitely many possible ones that could be cited.

[69] For a different view, see Lukes (1974), pp. 50–1, and Morris (1978), p. 322.

[70] This objection was raised by G. A. Cohen.

assert that in the absence of such an ideology (e.g. in the presence of a rebellious ideology) the rulers would have cracked down on the subjects by violent repression? And if this is granted, does it not follow that in class societies the rule of the dominant class will be stabilized *by some mechanism*, be it an endogenous and spontaneous belief in the natural superiority of the oppressors or a harshly repressive system? And from this, must we not conclude that at a high level of generality there is a functional explanation for the presence of such mechanisms? That there is *some* mechanism can be explained in terms of the stabilizing effect, even though other arguments may be needed to explain why this or that particular mechanism is realized. In other words, when asked 'Why is it there?', one could answer 'Because if it had not been there, something else with the same consequences would have been there.' And this could seem to provide an explanation in terms of these consequences. Against this I would raise an objection analogous to the one made in III.2 above concerning the counterfactual analysis of power. The fact that in the absence of the actually operating cause some other cause would have brought about the same or a similar effect does not in any way detract from the explanatory force of the actual cause.

REFERENCES

Abelson, R. P. 1963. Computer simulation of hot cognition. In S. Tomkins and S. Messick (eds.), *Computer simulation of personality*, pp. 277–98. New York: Wiley.

Acton, H. B. 1967. Dialectical materialism. In *The Encyclopedia of Philosophy*. New York: Macmillan.

Ainslie, G. 1975. Specious reward. *Psychological Bulletin* 82: 463–96.

1982. A behavioral economic approach to the defense mechanism: Freud's energy theory revisited. *Social Science Information*

1984. 'Behavioral economics 11: motivated involuntary behavior', *Social Science Information* 23, 247–74.

Ainslie, G. and Schafer, E. 1981. The application of economic concepts to the motivational conflict in alcoholism. In D. Gottheil *et al.* (eds.), *Matching patient needs and treatment methods in alcoholism and drug abuse*, pp. 215–45. Springfield, Ill.: C. C. Thomas.

Arendt, H. 1958. *The human condition*. University of Chicago Press.

1973. *On revolution*. Harmondsworth: Pelican Books.

Arrow, K. 1963. *Social choice and individual values*. New York: Wiley.

Arrow, K. and Hurwicz, L. 1972. An optimality criterion for decision-making under uncertainty. In C. F. Carter and J. L. Ford (eds.), *Uncertainty and expectation in economics*, pp. 1–11. Clifton, N. J.: Kelley.

Asch, S. 1956. Studies of independence and conformity: I. A minority of one against a unanimous majority. *Psychological Monographs* 70.

Aschenbrenner, K. M. 1977. Influence of attribute formulation on the evaluation of apartments by multi-attribute utility procedures. In H. Jungermann and G. de Zeeuw (eds.), *Decision making and change in human affairs*, pp. 81–97. Dordrecht: Reidel.

d'Aspremont, C. and Gevers, L. 1977. Equity and the informational basis of collective choice. *Review of Economic Studies* 44: 199–210.

Axelrod, R. and Hamilton, W. D. 1981. The evolution of cooperation. *Science* 211: 1390–6.

Barry, B. 1978. Comment. In S. Benn *et al.*, *Political participation*, pp. 37–48. Canberra: Australian National University Press.

1979. *Economists, sociologists and democracy*, 2nd edn. Chicago: Chicago University Press.

Bateson, G. 1956. Towards a theory of schizophrenia. In Bateson (1972), pp. 201–27.

1972. *Steps to an ecology of mind*. New York: Ballantine Books.

Baumol, W. 1965. *Welfare economics and the theory of the state*, 2nd edn. London: Bell.

Benn, S. 1978. The problematic rationality of political participation. In S. Benn *et al.*, *Political participation*, pp. 1–22. Canberra: Australian National University Press.

167

Berelsen, B. R. 1954. Democratic theory and democratic practice. Ch. 16 in B. R. Berelsen, P. F. Lazarsfeld and W. N. McPhee, *Voting*. University of Chicago Press.
Berlin, I. 1963–4. 'From hope and fear set free'. Quoted after the reprint in I. Berlin, *Concepts and categories*, pp. 173–98. Harmondsworth: Penguin, 1981.
    1969. *Two concepts of liberty*. Oxford University Press.
Bernstein, E. 1899. *Die Voraussetzungen des Sozialismus*. Many editions.
Bloom, G. F. 1940. A reconsideration of the theory of exploitation. *Quarterly Journal of Economics* 55: 413–42.
Bodemann, E. 1895. *Die Leibniz-Handschriften*. Hanover.
Borch, K. 1968. *The economics of uncertainty*. Princeton University Press.
Borkenau, F. 1934. *Die Übergang vom feudalen zum bürgerlichen Weltbild*. Paris: Felix Alcan.
Boudon, R. 1977. *Effets pervers et ordre social*. Paris: Presses Universitaires de France.
Bourdieu, P. 1979. *La Distinction*. Paris: Editions de Minuit.
Bronfenbrenner, M. 1971. *Income distribution theory*. London: Macmillan.
Buchanan, J. and Brennan, G. 1980. *The power to tax*. Cambridge University Press.
Buchanan, J. and Tullock, G. 1962. *The calculus of consent*. Ann Arbor: University of Michigan Press.
Burke, E. 1955. *Reflections on the Revolution in France*. New York: Bobbs-Merrill.
Burnyeat, M. F. 1980. Aristotle on learning to be good. In A. Rorty (ed.), *Essays on Aristotle's ethics*, pp. 69–92. Berkeley: University of California Press.
Bøe, A. 1956. *From Gothic revival to functional form*. Oslo: Universitetsforlaget.
Capra, F. 1976. *The Tao of physics*. Huntington, N. Y.: Fontana Books.
Cohen, G. A. 1978. *Karl Marx's theory of history: a defence*. Oxford University Press.
    1979. Freedom, capitalism and the proletariat. In A. Ryan (ed.), *The idea of freedom*, pp. 9–25. Oxford University Press.
Coleman, D. C. 1973. Gentlemen and players. *Economic History Review*, 2nd series 26: 92–116.
Coser, L. 1971. Social conflict and the theory of social change. In C. G. Smith (ed.), *Conflict resolution: contributions of the behavioral sciences*, pp. 58–65. Notre Dame, Ind.: University of Notre Dame Press.
Cyert, R. M. and de Groot, M. H. 1975. Adaptive utility. In R. H. Day and T. Groves (eds.), *Adaptive economic models*, pp. 223–46. New York: Academic Press.
Dahl, T. S. 1977. *Barnevern og samfunnsvern*. Oslo: Pax.
Davidson, D. 1980. *Essays on actions and events*. Oxford University Press.
Davis, K. and Moore, W. E. 1945. Some principles of stratification. *American Sociological Review* 10: 242–9.
Dennett, D. 1976. Conditions of personhood. In A. Rorty (ed.), *The identities of persons*, pp. 175–96. Berkeley: University of California Press.
Descartes, R. 1897–1910. *Oeuvres Complètes*, ed. C. Adam and P. Tannery. 11 vols. Paris: Vrin.
Dickinson, Emily 1970. *Complete poems*, ed. Thomas H. Johnson. London: Faber and Faber.
Dresser, C. 1862. *The art of decorative design*. London.
Dreyfus, H. L. and Dreyfus, S. 1978. Inadequacies in the decision analysis model of rationality. In C. A. Hooker, J. J. Leach and E. F. McClennen (eds.), *Foundations and applications of decision theory. Volume I: Theoretical foundations*, pp. 115–24. Dordrecht: Reidel.
Elster, J. 1975. *Leibniz et la formation de l'esprit capitaliste*. Paris: Aubier-Montaigne.
    1976. Some conceptual problems in political theory. In B. Barry (ed.), *Power and political theory*, pp. 245–70. Chichester: Wiley.

1978a. *Logic and society.* Chichester: Wiley.
1978b. Exploring exploitation. *Journal of Peace Research* 15: 3–17.
1978c. The labor theory of value. *Marxist Perspectives* 1: 70–101.
1979. *Ulysses and the sirens.* Cambridge University Press.
1980a. Négation active et négation active: essai de sociologie ivanienne. *Archives Européennes de Sociologie* 21: 329–49.
1980b. Reply to comments, in Symposium on Elster (1978a), *Inquiry* 23: 213–32.
1981. Snobs (review of Bourdieu 1979). *London Review of Books* 3 (20): 10–12.
1982a. *Explaining technical change.* Cambridge University Press.
1982b. Deception and self-deception in Stendhal. Unpublished lecture, Oxford University.
1982c. A paradigm for the social sciences? (Review of van Parijs 1981). *Inquiry* 25: 378–85.
1982d. Marxism, functionalism and game theory. *Theory and Society* 11: 453–82.
Engels, F. 1845. *The condition of the working class in England.* In Marx and Engels, *Collected works,* vol. IV. London: Lawrence and Wishart.
Farber, L. 1976. *Lying, despair, jealousy, envy, sex, suicide, drugs and the good life.* New York: Basic Books.
Farrell, B. A. 1981. *The status of psychoanalytic theory.* Harmondsworth: Pelican Books.
Feller, W. 1968. *An introduction to probability theory and its applications,* vol. I, 3rd edn. New York: Wiley.
Fellner, W. 1965. *Probability and profits.* Homewood, Ill.: Irwin.
Fenoaltea, S. 1975. The rise and fall of a theoretical model: the manorial system. *Journal of Economic History* 35: 386–409.
Festinger, L. 1957. *A theory of cognitive dissonance.* Stanford University Press.
Fingarette, H. 1969. *Self-deception.* London: Routledge and Kegan Paul.
Finley, M. I. 1965. Technical innovation and economic progress in the ancient world. Reprinted as Ch. 11 in Finley (1981).
1973. *Democracy: ancient and modern.* London: Chatto and Windus.
1976. The freedom of the citizen in the Greek world. Reprinted as Ch. 5 in Finley (1981).
1981. *Economy and society in ancient Greece. London:* Chatto and Windus.
Fitzhugh, G. 1857. *Cannibals all!* Reprint Cambridge, Mass.: Harvard University Press, 1960.
Foucault, M. 1975. *Surveiller et punir.* Paris: Gallimard.
Frankfurt, H. F. 1971. Freedom of will and the concept of a person. *Journal of Philosophy* 68: 5–20.
Georgescu-Roegen, N. 1954. Choice, expectations and measurability. *Quarterly Journal of Economics* 68: 503–34.
Gibbard, A. 1986. Interpersonal comparisons: preference, good and the intrinsic reward of a life. In J. Elster and A. Hylland (eds.), *Foundations of social choice theory.* Cambridge University Press, pp. 165–94.
Goldman, A. 1972. Toward a theory of social power. *Philosophical Studies* 23: 221–68.
1978. Epistemics. *Journal of Philosophy* 75: 509–24.
Goldmann, L. 1954. *Le Dieu caché.* Paris: Gallimard.
Goldstine, H. 1972. *The computer from Pascal to von Neumann.* Princeton University Press.
Goodin, R. 1986. Laundering preferences. In J. Elster and A. Hylland (eds.), *Foundations of social choice theory.* Cambridge University Press, pp. 75–102.
Gorman, W. M. 1967. Tastes, habits and choices. *International Economic Review* 8: 218–22.

Gullestad, S. and Tschudi, F. 1982. Labelling theory of mental illness: a critique illustrated by two case studies. *Psychiatry and Social Science* 2: 213–26.

Haavelmo, T. 1970. Some observations on welfare and economic growth. In W. A. Eltis, M. Scott and N. Wolfe (eds.), *Induction, growth and trade: essays in honour of Sir Roy Harrod*, pp. 65–75. Oxford University Press.

Habermas, J. 1982. Diskursethik – Notizen zu einem Begründungs-program. Mimeographed.

Hammond, P. and Mirrlees, J. 1973. Agreeable plans. In J. Mirrlees and N. H. Stern (eds.), *Models of economic growth*, pp. 283–99. London: Macmillan.

Harsanyi, J. 1977. *Rational behavior and bargaining equilibrium in games and social situations.* Cambridge University Press.

Hart, H. L. A. and Honoré, A. M. 1959. *Causation in the law.* Oxford University Press.

Heal, G. 1973. *The theory of economic planning.* Amsterdam: North Holland.

Heckscher, E. 1955. *Mercantilism*, vols. I–II. London: Allen and Unwin.

Hegel, G. W. F. 1970. *Werke in 12 Bänden.* Frankfurt: Suhrkamp.

    1977. *The Phenomenology of Spirit.* Oxford University Press.

Heimer, C. and Stinchcombe, A. 1980. Love and irrationality. *Social Science Information* 19: 697–754.

Hintikka, J. 1961. *Knowledge and belief.* Ithaca, N. Y.: Cornell University Press.

Hirsch, F. 1976. *Social limits to growth.* Cambridge, Mass.: Harvard University Press.

Hirschman, A. 1967. *Development projects observed.* Washington, D.C.: The Brookings Institution.

    1982. *Shifting involvements: private interest and public action.* Princeton University Press.

Hogarth, R. M. 1977. Methods for aggregating opinions. In H. Jungermann and G. de Zeeuw (eds.), *Decision making and change in human affairs*, pp. 231–56. Dordrecht: Reidel.

Janis, I. 1972. *Victims of group-think.* Boston: Houghton Mifflin.

Johansen, L. 1977. *Lectures on macroeconomic planning. Part 1: General aspects.* Amsterdam: North Holland.

Jones, O. 1856. *The grammar of ornament.* London; reprint New York; van Nostrand, 1972.

Jones, R. A. 1977. *Self-fulfilling prophecies.* Hillsdale, N. J.: Lawrence Erlbaum.

Kahneman, D. and Tversky, A. 1979. Prospect theory. *Econometrica* 47: 263–91.

Kant, I. 1795. *Perpetual peace.* In H. Reiss (ed.), *Kant's political writings*, pp. 93–130. Cambridge University Press, 1977.

Katona, G. 1951. *Psychological analysis of economic behavior.* New York: McGraw-Hill.

Kelly, J. 1978. *Arrow impossibility theorems.* New York: Academic Press.

Kenny, A. 1963. *Action, emotion and will.* London: Routledge and Kegan Paul.

    1965–6. Happiness. *Proceedings of the Aristotelian Society* (n.s.) 66: 93–102.

    1970. Intention and purpose in law. In R. Summers (ed.), *Essays in legal philosophy*, pp. 146–63. Oxford: Blackwell.

    1975. *Will, freedom and power.* Oxford: Blackwell.

    1976. Human abilities and dynamic modalities. In J. Manninen and R. Tuomela (eds.), *Essays on explanation and understanding*, pp. 209–32. Dordrecht: Reidel.

Knei-Paz, B. 1977. *The social and political thought of Leon Trotsky.* Oxford University Press.

Kolakowski, L. 1978. *Main Currents of Marxism*, vols. I–III. Oxford University Press.

Kolm, S.-C. 1979. La philosophie bouddhiste et les 'hommes économiques'. *Social Science Information* 18: 489–588.

    1981a. Altruismes et efficacités: le sophisme de Rousseau. *Social Science Information* 20: 293–354.

1981b. Efficacité et altruisme: les sophismes de Mandeville, Smith et Pareto. *Revue Economique* 32: 5–31.

Koopmans, T. 1960. Stationary ordinal utility and impatience. *Econometrica* 28: 287–309.

Koopmans, T., Diamond, P. and Williamson, R. 1964. Stationary utility and time perspective. *Econometrica* 32: 82–100.

Koyré, A. 1966. *Etudes galiléennes.* Paris: Hermann.

Laqueur, W. 1980. *The terrible secret.* Boston: Little, Brown.

Lehrer, K. 1978. Consensus and comparison. A theory of social rationality. In C. A. Hooker, J. J. Leach and E. F. McClennen (eds.), *Foundations and applications of decision theory. Vol. I: Theoretical foundations,* pp. 283–310. Dordrecht: Reidel.

Leibniz, G. W. 1875–90. *Die philosophische Schriften,* ed. Gerhardt, 7 vols. Reprint Hildesheim: Olms, 1965.

Levenson, J. 1968. *Confucian China and its modern fate,* vols. I–III. Berkeley: University of California Press.

Lipsey, R. G. and Lancaster, K. 1956–7. The general theory of the second best. *Review of Economic Studies* 24: 11–32.

Loevinger, J. 1976. *Ego-development.* San Francisco: Jossey-Bass.

Luce, R. D. and Raiffa, H. 1957. *Games and decisions.* New York: Wiley.

Lukes, S. 1974. *Power: a radical view.* London: Macmillan.

Lyons, D. 1965. *Forms and limits of utilitarianism.* Oxford University Press.

MacIntyre, A. 1958. *The unconscious.* London: Routledge and Kegan Paul.

Mahoney, M. J. and Thoresen, C. E. (eds.) 1974. *Self-control: power to the person.* Monterey, Calif.: Brooks/Cole.

Maital, S. and Maital, S. 1978. Is discounting the future irrational? Mimeographed.

March, J. 1978. Bounded rationality, ambiguity and the engineering of choice. *Bell Journal of Economics* 9: 587–608.

Marcuse, H. 1964. *One-dimensional man.* Boston: Beacon Press.

Marx, K. 1847. *The Communism of the Rheinischer Beobachter.* In Marx and Engels, *Collected works,* vol. VI. London: Lawrence and Wishart, 1976.

1857–8. *Grundrisse.* Reprint Harmondsworth: Pelican Books, 1973.

1867. *Capital I.* Reprint New York: International Publishers, 1967.

1879–80. Randglossen zu Wagner. In *Marx-Engels Werke,* vol. XIX. Berlin: Dietz, 1962.

1894. *Capital III.* Reprint New York: International Publishers, 1967.

Merton, R. 1957. *Social theory and social structure.* Glencoe, Ill.: Free Press.

Meyer, R. F. 1977. State-dependent time preference. In D. E. Bell, R. L. Kenney and H. Raiffa (eds.), *Conflicting objectives in decisions,* pp. 232–45. New York: Wiley.

Midgaard, K. 1980. On the significance of language and a richer concept of rationality. In L. Lewin and E. Vedung (eds.), *Politics as rational action,* pp. 83–97. Dordrecht: Reidel.

Mill, J. S. 1859. Bentham. In J. S. Mill, *Utilitarianism,* pp. 78–125. London: Fontana Books, 1962.

Millay, Edna St Vincent 1975. *Collected poems,* ed. N. Millay. New York: Harper and Row.

Mitroff, I. I. and Mason, R. O. 1981. *Creating a dialectical social science.* Dordrecht: Reidel.

Morris, J. M. 1978. Non-events. *Philosophical Studies* 34: 321–4.

Nagel, T. 1979. *Mortal questions.* Cambridge University Press.

Newton-Smith, W. 1981. *The rationality of science.* London: Routledge and Kegan Paul.

172   *References*

Nietzsche, F. 1887. *Zur Genealogie der Moral.* In *Werke in zwei Bänden,* vol. II. München: Hanser, 1967.
  1888. *Ecce homo.* In *Werke in zwei Bänden,* vol. II. München: Hanser, 1967.
Nisbett, R. and Ross, L. 1980. *Human inference: strategies and shortcomings of social judgment.* Englewood Cliffs, N. J.: Prentice-Hall.
North, D. and Thomas, R. P. 1971. *The rise of the Western world.* Cambridge University Press.
Nozick, R. 1969. Newcomb's problem and two principles of choice. In N. Rescher (ed.), *Essays in honor of Carl Hempel,* pp. 440–72. Dordrecht: Reidel.
  1974. *Anarchy, state and utopia.* Oxford: Blackwell.
Parfit. D. 1973. Later selves and moral principles. In A. Montefiore (ed.), *Philosophy and personal relations.* London: Routledge and Kegan Paul.
  1981. Prudence, morality and the prisoner's dilemma. *Proceedings of the British Academy.* Oxford University Press.
van Parijs, P. 1981. *Evolutionary explanation in the social sciences.* Totowa, N. J.: Rowman and Littlefield.
Parkin, F. 1968. *Middle class radicalism.* Manchester University Press.
Pateman, C. 1970. *Participation and democratic theory.* Cambridge University Press.
Pattanaik, P. 1978. *Strategy and group choice.* Amsterdam: North Holland.
Pears, D. 1974. Freud, Sartre and self-deception. In R. Wollheim (ed.), *Freud,* pp. 97–112. New York: Anchor Books.
Popper, K. 1957. *The poverty of historicism.* London: Routledge and Kegan Paul.
Pruyser, P. W. 1974. *Between belief and unbelief.* New York: Harper and Row.
Pugin, A. W. 1836. *Contrasts.* Reprinted New York: Humanities Press, 1969.
  1841. *True principles of Christian or pointed architecture.* London: John Weale.
Rader, T. 1972. *Theory of microeconomics.* New York: Academic Press.
Raiffa, H. 1968. *Decision analysis.* Reading, Mass.: Addison-Wesley.
Rapoport, A. and Chammah, A. 1965. *Prisoner's dilemma.* Ann Arbor: University of Michigan Press.
Rawls, J. 1971. *A theory of justice.* Cambridge, Mass.: Harvard University Press.
Rorty, A. 1980a. Self-deception, akrasia and immorality. *Social Science Information* 19: 905–22.
  1980b. *Akrasia* and conflict. *Inquiry* 23: 193–212.
Runciman, W. G. and Sen, A. 1965. Games, justice and the general will. *Mind* 74: 554–62.
Ruskin, J. 1853. The nature of Gothic. In *The stones of Venice,* vol. II of *The works of John Ruskin.* London: George Allen, 1904.
Russel, R. 1966. The effects of slavery upon nonslaveholders in the ante-bellum South. In H. D. Woodman (ed.), *Slavery and the Southern economy,* pp. 117–27. New York: Pantheon.
Ryan, A. 1978. Comment. In S. Benn *et al., Political participation,* pp. 31–6. Canberra: Australian National University Press.
Samuelson, P. 1976. Speeding-up of time with age in recognition of life as fleeting. In A. M. Tang, F. M. Westfield and J. S. Worley (eds.), *Evolution, welfare and time in economics: essays in honour of Nicholas Georgescu-Roegen,* pp. 154–68. Lexington, Mass.: Lexington Books.
Sartre, J. P. 1943. *L'être et le néant.* Paris: Gallimard.
Schafer, R. 1976. *A new language for psychoanalysis.* New Haven: Yale University Press.
Scheff, T. J. 1966. *Being mentally ill: a sociological theory.* Chicago: Aldine.

Scheler, M. 1972. *Ressentiment.* New York: Schocken Books.
Schelling, T. C. 1960. *The strategy of conflict.* Cambridge, Mass.: Harvard University Press.
  1978. Egonomics, or the art of self-management. *American Economic Review: Papers and Proceedings* 68: 290–4.
  1984. *Choice and Consequence.* Cambridge, Mass.: Harvard University Press.
Schotter, A. 1981. *The economic theory of social institutions.* Cambridge University Press.
Schumpeter, J. 1934. *The theory of economic development.* Cambridge, Mass.: Harvard University Press.
  1954. *Capitalism, socialism and democracy.* London: Allen and Unwin.
Segrè, E. 1980. *From X-rays to quarks.* San Francisco: Freeman.
Sen, A. 1967. Isolation, assurance and the social rate of discount. *Quarterly Journal of Economics* 80: 112–24.
  1970. *Collective choice and social welfare.* San Francisco: Holden-Day.
  1974. Choice, orderings and morality. In S. Körner (ed.), *Practical reason,* pp. 54–67. Oxford: Blackwell.
  1975. *Employment, technology and development.* Oxford University Press.
  1976. Liberty, unanimity and rights. *Economica* 43: 217–45.
  1979. Informational analysis of moral principles. In R. Harrison (ed.), *Rational action,* pp. 115–32. Cambridge University Press.
  1980–1. Plural utility. *Proceedings of the Aristotelian Society* (n.s.) 81: 193–215.
Sewall, R. B. 1974. *The life of Emily Dickinson.* London: Faber and Faber.
Shepard, R. N. 1964. On subjectively optimum selection among multiattribute alternatives. In M. W. Shelley and G. L. Bryan (eds.), *Human judgment and optimality,* pp. 257–80. New York: Wiley.
Skinner, B. F. 1981. Selection by consequences. *Science* 213: 501–4.
Smullyan, R. 1978. *What is the name of this book?* Englewood Cliffs, N. J.: Prentice-Hall.
  1980. *This book needs no title.* Englewood Cliffs, N. J.: Prentice-Hall.
Stendhal 1949. *Vie de Henry Brulard,* ed. Martineau. Paris: Le Divan.
  1950. *Souvenirs d'égotisme,* ed. Martineau. Paris: Le Divan.
  1952. *Lucien Leuwen.* In *Romans et Nouvelles,* ed. Pléiade, vol. i. Paris: Gallimard.
  1965. *De l'amour.* Paris: Garnier-Flammarion.
  1970. *Racine et Shakespeare.* Paris: Garnier-Flammarion.
  1981. *Oeuvres Intimes,* ed. Pléiade, vol. i. Paris: Gallimard.
Stigler, G. and Becker, G. 1977. De gustibus non est disputandum. *American Economic Review* 67: 76–90.
Stinchcombe, A. 1974. Merton's theory of social structure. In L. Coser (ed.), *The idea of social structure: papers in honor of Robert Merton,* pp. 11–33. New York: Harcourt, Brace, Jovanovich.
  1980. Is the prisoner's dilemma all of sociology? *Inquiry* 23: 187–92.
Stouffer, S. A. *et al.* 1949. *The American soldier.* Princeton University Press.
Strotz, R. H. 1955–6. Myopia and inconsistency in dynamic utility maximization. *Review of Economic Studies* 23: 165–80.
Sundt, E. 1862. Nordlandsbåden. In *Verker i Utvalg,* vol. vii. Oslo: Gyldendal, 1976.
Suzuki, D. T. 1969. *The Zen doctrine of no-mind.* London: Rider.
Taylor, C. 1976. Responsibility for self. In A. Rorty (ed.), *The identities of persons,* pp. 281–300. Berkeley: University of California Press.
  1979. What's wrong with negative liberty. In A. Ryan (ed.), *The idea of freedom,* pp. 175–94. Oxford University Press.

Taylor, M. 1976. *Anarchy and cooperation*. Chichester: Wiley.
Taylor, M. and Ward, H. 1982. Chickens, whales and lumpy goods: alternative models of public goods provision. *Political Studies* 30: 350–70.
Thaler, R. H. and Shefrin, H. M. 1981. An economic theory of self-control. *Journal of Political Economy* 89: 392–406.
Thompson, E. P. 1968. *The making of the English working class*. Harmondsworth: Pelican Books.
Tocqueville, A. de 1952. *L'ancien régime et la révolution. Edition des Oeuvres Complètes*, vol. i. Paris: Gallimard.
   1953. *L'ancien régime et la révolution. Edition des Oeuvres Complètes*, vol. ii. Paris: Gallimard.
   1962. *Ecrits et discours politiques. Edition des Oeuvres Complètes*. Paris: Gallimard.
   1969. *Democracy in America*. New York: Anchor Books.
Trivers, R. 1971. The evolution of reciprocal altruism. *Quarterly Review of Biology* 46: 35–57.
Tsou, T. 1980. Back from the brink of revolutionary–'feudal' totalitarianism: some preliminary reflections. Mimeographed.
Tversky, A. 1981. Choice, preference and welfare: some psychological observations. Paper presented to a colloquium on 'Foundations of social choice theory', Ustaoset (Norway).
   1982. Self deception and self perception: some psychological observations. Paper presented to a colloquium on 'The multiple self', Maison des Sciences de l'Homme (Paris).
Tversky, A. and Kahneman, D. 1974. Judgment under uncertainty. *Science* 185: 1124–30.
   1981. The framing of decisions and the rationality of choice. *Science* 211: 543–58.
Ullmann-Margalit, E. and Morgenbesser, S. 1977. Picking and choosing. *Social Research* 44: 757–85.
Veblen, T. 1915. *Imperial Germany and the industrial revolution*. London: Macmillan.
   1970. *The theory of the leisure class*. London: Allen and Unwin.
Veyne, P. 1976. *Le pain et le cirque*. Paris: Seuil.
Watkin, D. 1977. *Architecture and morality*. Oxford University Press.
Watzlawick, P. 1978. *The language of change*. New York: Basic Books.
Weber, M. 1920. Die protestantische Ethik und der Geist des Kapitalismus. In *Gesammelte Aufsätze zur Religionssoziologie*, vol. i. Tübingen: Mohr.
   1968. *Gesammelte Aufsätze zur Wissenschaftslehre*. Tübingen: Mohr.
Weintraub, E. 1979. *Microfoundations: the compatibility of microeconomics and macroeconomics*. Cambridge University Press.
von Weizsäcker, C. C. 1971. Notes on endogenous change of tastes. *Journal of Economic Theory* 3: 345–72.
Wetlesen, J. 1979. *The sage and the way: Spinoza's philosophy of freedom*. Assen: Van Gorcum.
Wicklund, R. A. and Brehm, J. W. 1976. *Perspectives on cognitive dissonance*. Hillsdale, N. J.: Lawrence Erlbaum.
Williams, B. A. O. 1973. Deciding to believe. In *Problems of the self*, pp. 136–51. Cambridge University Press.
   1981. *Moral luck*. Cambridge University Press.
Williams, G. C. 1966. *Adaptation and natural selection*. Princeton University Press.
Winston, G. 1980. Addiction and backsliding: a theory of compulsive consumption. *Journal of Economic Behavior and Organization* 1: 295–324.

Winter, S. 1964–5. Economic 'natural selection' and the theory of the firm. *Yale Economic Essays* 4: 225–72.

Winters, B. 1979. Willing to believe. *Journal of Philosophy* 76: 243–56.

Wollheim, R. 1971. *Freud.* Cambridge University Press.

1974. *On art and the mind.* Cambridge, Mass.: Harvard University Press.

1980. *Art and its objects,* 2nd edn. Cambridge University Press.

Zeldin, T. 1973. *France 1848–1945,* vol. i. Oxford University Press.

Zinoviev, A. 1963. *Philosophical problems of many-valued logic.* Dordrecht: Reidel.

1978. *L'avenir radieux.* Lausanne: Editions Age d'Homme.

1979. *The yawning heights.* London: The Bodley Head.

INDEX